HISTORY OF BRITISH LITERATURE

HISTORY OF BRITISH LITERATURE

P. K. Sinha
Jagdish K. Ghosh

Commonwealth

History of British Literature

Edition : 2021

ISBN 978-81-311-0328-9

Published by :
COMMONWEALTH PUBLISHERS PVT. LTD.
4831/24, Prahlad Street,
Ansari Road, Darya Ganj,
New Delhi - 110002
Ph. : 23275511, 23257835
e-mail : commonwealthbooks@gmail.com

Laser Typesetting by :
Rishu Computers
Delhi

Printed at :
Roshan Offset Printers
Delhi

Preface

British literature refers to literature associated with the United Kingdom, Isle of Man, Channel Islands, as well as to literature from England, Ireland, Scotland and Wales, prior to the formation of the UK. By far the largest part of British literature is written in the English language, but there are bodies of written works in Latin, Welsh, Scottish Gaelic, Scots, Cornish, Manx, Jerriais, Guernesiais and other languages. Northern Ireland has a literary tradition in English, Ulster Scots and Irish.

The earliest form of English literature developed after the settlement of the Saxons and other Germanic tribes in England after the withdrawal of the Romans and is known as Old English or Anglo-Saxon. Literature in the Celtic languages of the islands is the oldest surviving vernacular literature in Europe. The Welsh literary tradition stretches from the 6th century to the 21st century.

The present book comprehensively explains the historical development of British literature. It aims to provide education, entertainment and enlightenment to the readers. It is intended for advanced level students of literature, who are taking exams or modules in this field. It may also be suitable for teachers, researchers and the general reader who is interested in the history of literature.

Authors

Contents

1

Introduction to British Literature

British literature refers to literature associated with the United Kingdom, the Isle of Man and the Channel Islands as well as to literature from England, Wales and Scotland prior to the formation of the United Kingdom. By far the largest part of British literature is written in the English language, but there are bodies of written works in Latin, Welsh, Scottish Gaelic, Scots, Cornish, Manx, Jèrriais, Guernésiais and other languages. Northern Ireland has a literary tradition in English, Ulster Scots and Irish. Irish writers have also played an important part in the development of English-language literature.

Literature in the Celtic languages of the islands is the oldest surviving vernacular literature in Europe. The Welsh literary tradition stretches from the 6th century to the 21st century. The oldest Welsh literature does not belong to the territory we know as Wales today, but rather to northern England and southern Scotland. But though it is dated to be from the 6th, 7th, and 8th centuries, it has survived only in 13th- and 14th century manuscript copies.

Old English Literature

Old English period :450-1066 The earliest form of English literature developed after the settlement of the Saxons and other Germanic tribes in England after the withdrawal of the Romans and is known as Old English or Anglo-Saxon. Epic poem Beowulf is the most famous work in Old English. A hero of the Geats, Beowulf battles three antagonists:

> Grendel, Grendel's mother; and a Dragon. The only surviving manuscript is the Nowell Codex. The precise date of the manuscript is debated, but most estimates place it close to the year 1000.(The oldest surviving text in English is Cædmon's *Hymn*)

A popular poem of the time was "The Dream of the Rood." It was inscribed upon the Ruthwell Cross.

Another poem was "Judith (poem)." It was a retelling of the story found in the Latin Bible's Book of Judith of the beheader of the Assyrian general Holofernes.

Chronicles contained a range of historical and literary accounts; one example is the *Anglo-Saxon Chronicle.*

Late Medieval Literature

Following the Norman Conquest, the development of Anglo-Norman literature in the Anglo-Norman realm introduced literary trends from Continental Europe such as the *chanson de geste.*

In the later medieval period a new form of English now known as Middle English evolved. This is the earliest form which is comprehensible to modern readers and listeners, albeit not easily The most significant Middle English author was the poet Geoffrey Chaucer who was active in the late 14th century. His main works were *The Canterbury Tales* and *Troilus and Criseyde.*

The multilingual audience for literature in the 14th century can be illustrated by the example of John

Gower, who wrote in Latin, Middle English and Anglo-Norman.

Religious literature, such as hagiographies enjoyed popularity.

Women writers such as Marie de France and Julian of Norwich were also active.

- Sir Gawain and the Green Knight (Most likely the Pearl Poet)
- Le Morte d'Arthur (Sir Thomas Malory)

For a comparatively small country, Ireland has made a large contribution to world literature in all its branches. The Irish literature that is best known outside the country is in English, but the Irish language also has the most significant body of written literature, both ancient and recent, in any Celtic language, in addition to a strong oral tradition of legends and poetry.

In Medieval Welsh literature the period before 1100 is known as the period of *Y Cynfeirdd* ("The earliest poets") or *Yr Hengerdd* ("The old poetry"). It roughly dates from the birth of the Welsh language until the arrival of the Normans in Wales towards the end of the 11th century.

Geoffrey of Monmouth was one of the major figures in the development of British history and the popularity for the tales of King Arthur. He is best known for his chronicle *Historia Regum Britanniae* (History of the Kings of Britain) spread Celtic motifs to a wider audience, including accounts of Arthur's father Uther Pendragon, the wizard Merlin, the sword Excalibur.

The Jersey poet Wace is considered the founder of Jersey literature and contributed to the development of the Arthurian legend in British literature. His *Brut* showed the interest of Norman patrons in the mythologising of the new English territories of the Anglo-Norman realm. His *Roman de Rou* placed the Dukes of Normandy within an epic context.

William Langland's Piers Plowman is considered by many critics to be one of the early great works of English literature along with Chaucer's *Canterbury Tales* and *Sir Gawain and the Green Knight* during the Middle Ages. Its also the first allusion to a literary tradition of Robin Hood.

Since at least the 14th century, poetry in English has been written in Ireland and by Irish writers abroad. The earliest poem in English by a Welsh poet dates from about 1470.

Among the earliest Lowland Scots literature is Barbour's *Brus* (14th century). Whyntoun's Kronykil and Blind Harry's *Wallace* date from the (15th century). From the 13th century much literature based around the royal court in Edinburgh and the University of St Andrews was produced by writers such as Henrysoun, Dunbar, Douglas and Lyndsay.

In the Cornish language *Passhyon agan Arloedh* ("The Passion of our Lord"), a poem of 259 eight-line verses written in 1375, is one of the earliest surviving works of Cornish literature. The most important work of literature surviving from the Middle Cornish period is *An Ordinale Kernewek* ("The Cornish Ordinalia"), a 9000-line religious drama composed around the year 1400. The longest single surviving work of Cornish literature is *Bywnans Meriasek* (The Life of Meriasek), a play dated 1504, but probably copied from an earlier manuscript. Sir Thomas More coined the word "utopia", a name he gave to the ideal, imaginary island nation whose political system he described in *Utopia*, published in 1516.

- Mabinogion
- Ulster Cycle
- Early English Jewish literature

Early Modern English Literature

Shakespeare's career straddled the change of Tudor and Stuart dynasties and encompassed English history and the emerging imperial idea of the 17th century

The sonnet form and other Italian literary influences arrived in English literature. The sonnet was introduced into English by Thomas Wyatt in the early 16th century.

In the later 16th century English poetry was characterised by elaboration of language and extensive allusion to classical myths. The most important poets of this era include Edmund Spenser and Sir Philip Sidney.

The most important literary achievements of the English Renaissance were in drama. William Shakespeare, widely regarded as the greatest writer in the English language, wrote over 35 plays in several genres, including tragedy, comedy, and history. Other leading playwrights of the time included Ben Jonson, and Christopher Marlowe.

At the Reformation the translation of liturgy and Bible into vernacular languages provided new literary models. The Anglican *Book of Common Prayer* and the *Authorized King James Version* of the Bible have been hugely influential. King James Bible as one of the biggest translation projects in the history of English up to this time, was started in 1604 and completed in 1611.

It represents the culmination of a tradition of Bible translation into English that began with the work of William Tyndale. It became the standard Bible of the Church of England, and some consider it one of the greatest literary works of all time. Sir Francis Bacon termed phrase *"Knowledge is Power"*, his works are deemed so influential they're included in the Western canon.

Major poets of the 17th century included John Donne and other metaphysical poets, and John Milton with religious epic *Paradise Lost*. Another seminal work of Milton was *Areopagitica*, among history's most influential and impassioned philosophical defences of the principle of a right to freedom of speech, which was written in opposition to licensing and censorship and is regarded as one of the most eloquent defenses of press freedom ever written.

1660 to 1800

Diarists John Evelyn and Samuel Pepys depicted everyday London life and the cultural scene of the times, eyewitness accounts of great events, such as the Great Plague of London, the Great Fire of London. The publication of *The Pilgrim's Progress* in 1678 established John Bunyan as a notable writer of English literature. The early 18th century is known as the Augustan Age of English literature. The poetry of the time was highly formal, as exemplified by the works of Alexander Pope.

Although the documented history of Irish theatre began at least as early as 1601, the earliest Irish dramatists of note were William Congreve, one of the most interesting writers of Restoration comedies, and Oliver Goldsmith and Richard Brinsley Sheridan, who were two of the most successful playwrights on the London stage in the 18th century.

The English novel developed during the 18th century, partly in response to an expansion of the middle-class reading public. One of the major early works in this genre was the seminal castaway novel *Robinson Crusoe* by Daniel Defoe. The 18th century novel tended to be loosely structured and semi-comic. Major novelists of the middle and later part of the century included Henry Fielding, Laurence Sterne, and Tobias Smollett, who was a great influence on Charles Dickens.

Although the epics of Celtic Ireland were written in prose and not verse, most people would probably consider that Irish fiction proper begins in the 18th century with the works of Jonathan Swift (especially *Gulliver's Travels*) and Oliver Goldsmith (especially *The Vicar of Wakefield*).

— First novel in English

— Cavalier poet

Non English-language Literatures

As the Norman nobles of Scotland assimilated to indigenous culture they commissioned Scots versions of popular continental romances, for example: *Launcelot o the Laik* and *The Buik o Alexander*. In the early 16th century, Gavin Douglas produced a Scots translation of the Aeneid. Chaucerian, classical and French literary language continued to influence Scots literature up until the Reformation. The Complaynt of Scotland shows the interplay of language and ideas between the kingdoms of Scotland and England in the years leading up to the Union of the Crowns.

The earliest datable text in Manx (preserved in 18th century manuscripts), a poetic history of the Isle of Man from the introduction of Christianity, dates to the 16th century at the latest.

The first book to be printed in Welsh was published in 1546. From the Reformation until the 19th century most literature in the Welsh language was religious in character.

The earliest surviving examples of Cornish prose are *Pregothow Treger* (The Tregear Homilies), a set of 66 sermons translated from English by John Tregear around 1555–1557.

The Book of Common Prayer and Bible were translated into Manx in the 17th and 18th centuries. A tradition of *carvals*, religious songs or carols, developed. Religious literature was common, but secular writing much rarer.

In Scotland, after the 17th century, anglicisation increased, though Lowland Scots was still spoken by the vast majority of the population. At the time, many of the oral ballads from the borders and the North East were written down. Writers of the period include Robert Sempill (c.1595–1665), Lady Wardlaw and Lady Grizel Baillie.

The first printed work in Manx dates from 1707: a translation of a Prayer Book catechism in English by Bishop Thomas Wilson.

In the Scots-speaking areas of Ulster there was traditionally a considerable demand for the work of Scottish poets, often in locally printed editions. Alexander Montgomerie's *The Cherrie and the Slae* in

1700, shortly over a decade later an edition of poems by Sir David Lindsay, nine printings of Allan Ramsay's *The Gentle shepherd* between 1743 and 1793, and an edition of Robert Burns' poetry in 1787, the same year as the Edinburgh edition, followed by reprints in 1789, 1793 and 1800. Among other Scottish poets published in Ulster were James Hogg and Robert Tannahill.

In the 18th century, Scottish writers such as Ramsay, Robert Fergusson, Robert Burns and Sir Walter Scott continued to use Lowland Scots. Scott introduced vernacular dialogue to his novels. The Habbie stanza was developed as a poetic form.

The first printed Jèrriais literature appears in the first newspapers following the introduction of the printing press at the end of the 18th century. The earliest identified dated example of printed poetry in Jèrriais is a fragment by Matchi L'Gé (Matthew Le Geyt 1777 – 1849) dated 1795.

Some 60 to 70 volumes of Ulster *rhyming weaver* poetry were published between 1750 and 1850, the peak being in the decades 1810 to 1840. These weaver poets, such as James Orr, looked to Scotland for their cultural and literary models and were not simple imitators but clearly inheritors of the same literary tradition following the same poetic and orthographic practices; it is not always immediately possible to distinguish traditional Scots writing from Scotland and Ulster.

The importance of translation in spreading the influence of English literature to other cultures of the islands can be exemplified by the abridged Manx version of *Paradise Lost* by John Milton published in 1796 by Thomas Christian. The influence also went the other way as Romanticism discovered inspiration in the literatures and legends of the Celtic countries of the islands. The Ossian hoax typifies the growth of this interest.

Increased literacy in rural and outlying areas and wider access to publishing through, for example, local newspapers encouraged regional literary development as the 19th century progressed. Some writers in lesser-used languages and dialects of the islands gained a literary following outside their native regions, for example William Barnes in Dorset, George Métivier (1790–1881) in Guernsey and Robert Pipon Marett in Jersey. George Métivier published *Rimes Guernesiaises,* a collection of poems in Guernésiais and French in 1831. The poems had first appeared in newspapers from 1813 onward. The first printed anthology of Jèrriais poetry, *Rimes Jersiaises,* was published in 1865.

Scots was used in the narrative by Ulster novelists such as W. G. Lyttle (1844–1896). Scots also regularly appeared in Ulster newspaper columns. Scottish authors as Robert Louis Stevenson, William Alexander, George MacDonald and J. M. Barrie also wrote in Lowland Scots or used it in dialogue. The first major novelist in the Welsh language was Daniel Owen, author of works such as *Rhys Lewis* (1885) and *Enoc Huws* (1891). Edward Faragher (1831–1908) has been considered the last important native writer of Manx. He wrote poetry, reminiscences of his life as a fisherman, and translations of selected Aesop's Fables.

19th Century English Literature

Romanticism

Major political and social changes at the end of the eighteenth century, particularly the French Revolution, prompted a new breed of writing known as

Romanticism. William Wordsworth and Samuel Taylor Coleridge began the trend for bringing emotionalism and introspection to English literature, with a new concentration on the individual and the common man. The reaction to urbanism and industrialisation prompted poets to explore nature, for example the Lake Poets. The third major Lake poet Robert Southey, his verse endures lasting popularity, but perhaps his most enduring contribution to literary history is the immortal children's classic, *The Story of the Three Bears,* the original *Goldilocks* story.

Around the same period, the iconoclastic printer William Blake, largely disconnected from the major streams of elite literature of the time, was constructing his own highly idiosyncratic poetic creations, while the Scottish nationalist poet Robert Burns was collecting and adapting the folk songs of Scotland into a body of national poetry for his homeland.

The major "second generation" Romantic poets included George Gordon Byron, 6th Baron Byron. They flouted social convention and often used poetry as a political voice. Amongst Lord Byron's best-known works are the brief poems *She Walks in Beauty, When We Two Parted,* and *So, we'll go no more a roving,* in addition to narrative poems *Childe Harold's Pilgrimage* and *Don Juan.* Another key poet of Romantic movement John Keats, his letters, which expound on his aesthetic theory of negative capability, are among the most celebrated by any writer. Percy Shelley famous for his association with John Keats and Lord Byron, was the third major romantic poet of the second generation. Critically regarded among the finest lyric poets in the English language, Shelley is most famous for such classic anthology verse works as

Ozymandias, and long visionary poems which included *Prometheus Unbound*

Novel

At the same time, Jane Austen was writing highly polished novels about the life of the landed gentry, seen from a woman's point of view, and wryly focused on practical social issues, especially marriage and money, notably with *Sense and Sensibility, Pride and Prejudice, Mansfield Park* and *Emma*

Walter Scott's novel-writing career was launched in 1814 with *Waverley,* often called the first historical novel, and was followed by *Ivanhoe.* His popularity in England and further abroad did much to form the modern stereotype of Scottish culture. Other novels by Scott which contributed to the image of him as a patriot include *Rob Roy.* He was the highest earning and most popular author up to that time.

Mary Shelley, best known for her Gothic novel *Frankenstein* in 1818, Frankenstein's chilling tale also suggests modern organ transplants, tissue regeneration, reminding us of the moral issues raised by today's medicine.

From the mid-1820s to mid-1840s, fashicnable novels depicting the lives of the upper class dominated the literature market.

Charles Dickens emerged on the literary scene in the 1830s, confirming the trend for serial publication. Dickens wrote vividly about London life and struggles of the poor, *Oliver Twist,* but in a good-humoured fashion, accessible to readers of all classes. The immortal *A Christmas Carol* he called his "little Christmas book". *Great Expectations* is quest for maturity. Dickens early works are masterpieces of comedy such as *The Pickwick Papers*. Later his works became darker, without losing his genius for caricature.

It was in the Victorian era (1837–1901) that the novel became the leading form of literature in English. Most writers were now more concerned to meet the tastes of a large middle-class reading public than to please aristocratic patrons. The best known works of the era include the emotionally powerful works of the Brontë sisters; Charlotte's *Jane Eyre,* Emily's *Wuthering Heights* and Anne's *Agnes Grey* were released in 1847 after their long search to secure publishers: the satire *Vanity Fair* by William Makepeace Thackeray and Anthony Trollope's insightful portrayals of the lives of the landowning and professional classes of Victorian England. The novels of George Eliot, notably *Middlemarch,* are frequently held in the highest regard for their combination of high Victorian literary detail combined with an intellectual breadth that removes them from the narrow confines they often depict. An alternative to mainstream works, the Penny Dreadful publications were aimed at working class adolescents, where the infamous Sweeney Todd was introduced.

An interest in rural matters and the changing social and economic situation of the countryside may be seen in the novels of Thomas Hardy and others. Wilkie Collins novel *The Moonstone,* is generally considered the first detective novel in the English language.

Literature for children was published during the Victorian period, some of which has become globally well-known, such as work of Lewis Carroll with *Alice's Adventures in Wonderland.* Anna Sewell wrote the classic animal novel *Black Beauty*. At the end of the Victorian Era, Beatrix Potter best known for her children's books, featuring animal characters, notably *The Tale of Peter Rabbit*

Bram Stoker, the author of *Dracula*, featuring as its primary antagonist the vampire Count Dracula. *Dracula* has been attributed to many literary genres including vampire literature, horror fiction, the gothic novel and invasion literature.

H. G. Wells, whom alongside Jules Verne is referred to as "The Father of Science Fiction", invented a number of themes now classic in science fiction. *The War of the Worlds*, describing an invasion of late Victorian England by Martians using tripod fighting machines, equipped with advanced weaponry. It is a seminal depiction of an alien invasion of Earth. His novel *The Time Machine* is generally credited with the popularization of the concept of time travel using a vehicle that allows an operator to travel purposefully and selectively. The term "*time machine*" coined by Wells, is now universally used to refer to such a vehicle.

Henry Rider Haggard wrote the genesis of the Lost World literary genre *King Solomon's Mines*. An important forerunner of modernist literature, Joseph Conrad with novella *Heart of Darkness*, is widely regarded as a significant work of English literature and part of the Western canon.

Victorian Poets

Leading poetic figures of Victorian era included Alfred Tennyson, 1st Baron Tennyson, Robert Browning (and his wife, Elizabeth Barrett Browning), and Matthew Arnold, whilst multi-disciplinary talents such as John

Ruskin and Dante Gabriel Rossetti were also famous for their poetry. The poetry of this period was heavily influenced by the Romantics, but also went off in its own directions. Particularly notable was the development of the dramatic monologue, a form used by many poets in this period, but perfected by Browning, most of his poems were in the form of dramatic monologues.

Towards the end of the century, English poets began to take an interest in French symbolism and Victorian poetry entered a decadent *fin-de-siècle* phase. Two groups of poets emerged, the *Yellow Book* poets who adhered to the tenets of Aestheticism, including Algernon Charles Swinburne, Oscar Wilde and Arthur Symons and the Rhymer's Club group that included Ernest Dowson, Lionel Johnson and William Butler Yeats. Poetry of A. E. Housman consisted of wistful evocation of doomed youth in the English countryside, grew in popularity early 20th century.

Irish Literature

In the 19th century, the Irish playwright Dion Boucicault was an extremely popular writer of comedies. However, it was in the last decade of the century that the Irish theatre finally came of age with the emergence of George Bernard Shaw and Oscar Wilde. All of these writers lived mainly in England and wrote in English, with the exception of some works in French by Wilde.

The Celtic Revival, was begun by William Butler Yeats, Augusta, Lady Gregory, John Millington Synge, Seán O'Casey, James Joyce and others. The Revival stimulated new appreciation of traditional Irish literature. The movement also encouraged the creation of works written in the spirit of Irish culture, as distinct from British culture.

Anglo-Welsh literature

Anglo-Welsh literature is a term used to describe works written in the English language by Welsh writers, notably Dylan Thomas, especially if they either have subject matter relating to Wales or (as in the case of Anglo-Welsh poetry in particular) are influenced by the Welsh language in terms of patterns of usage or syntax. It has been recognized as a distinctive entity only since the 20th century. The need for a separate identity for this kind of writing arose because of the parallel development of modern Welsh literature, ie. literature in the Welsh language.

Scottish literature

Scottish literature in the 19th century, following the example of Walter Scott, tended to produce novels that did not reflect the realities of life in that period.

Robert Louis Stevenson's short novel *Strange Case of Dr Jekyll and Mr Hyde* (1886) depicts the dual personality of a kind and intelligent physician who turns into a psychopathic monster after imbibing a drug intended to separate good from evil in a personality. His *Kidnapped* is a fast-paced historical novel set in the aftermath of the '45 Jacobite Rising, and *Treasure Island* is the classic pirate adventure.

The Kailyard school of Scottish writers presented an idealised version of society and brought elements of fantasy and folklore back into fashion. J. M. Barrie author of *Peter Pan* is one example of this mix of modernity and nostalgia.

English Literature since 1900

Sir Arthur Conan Doyle was born in Scotland of Irish parents, but his Sherlock Holmes stories have typified a fog-filled London for readers worldwide The major lyric poet of the first decades of the 20th century was Thomas Hardy, who concentrated on poetry after the harsh response to his last novel, *Jude the Obscure.*

The most widely popular writer of the early years of the 20th century was arguably Rudyard Kipling, a highly versatile writer of novels, short stories and poems, notably *The Jungle Book,* often based on his experiences in British India. Kipling's inspirational poem *"If"* is a national favourite. Kenneth Grahame wrote children's classic *The Wind in the Willows.* John Buchan wrote the adventure novel *The Thirty-Nine Steps.* The Great Maytham Hall Garden in Kent inspired Frances Hodgson Burnett novel *The Secret Garden.*

From around 1910, the Modernist Movement began to influence English literature. Whereas their Victorian predecessors had usually been happy to cater to mainstream middle-class taste, 20th century writers often felt alienated from it, and responded by writing more intellectually challenging works or by pushing the boundaries of acceptable content.

Major poets of this period in Britain included American-born T. S. Eliot, Ezra Pound, and Irishman William Butler Yeats. Free verse and other stylistic innovations came to the forefront in this era.

The experiences of the First World War were reflected in the work of war poets such as Wilfred Owen, Rupert Brooke, Isaac Rosenberg, Edmund Blunden and Siegfried Sassoon. Following the Arab

Revolt, T. E. Lawrence *"Lawrence of Arabia"* autobiographical account in *Seven Pillars of Wisdom*.

Important novelists between the two World Wars include Irish writer James Joyce, alongside D. H. Lawrence, C. S. Forester, Virginia Woolf, Enid Blyton, E. M. Forster, P. G. Wodehouse.

Joyce's increasingly complex works included *Ulysses*, an interpretation of the Odyssey set in Dublin, and culminated in the famously obscure *Finnegans Wake*. Lawrence wrote with understanding about the social life of the lower and middle classes, and the personal life of those who could not adapt to the social norms of his time. He attempted to explore human emotions more deeply than his contemporaries and challenged the boundaries of the acceptable treatment of sexual issues in works such as *Lady Chatterley's Lover*. Virginia Woolf was an influential feminist, and a major stylistic innovator associated with the stream-of-consciousness technique. Her novels included *To the Lighthouse, Mrs Dalloway*, and *The Waves*. Robert Graves is most renowned for *I Claudius*. E.M. Forster works include *A Passage to India*.

Daphne Du Maurier wrote the highly acclaimed *Rebecca*. Intellectual Aldous Huxley's futuristic novel *Brave New World* anticipates developments in reproductive technology and sleep-learning that combine to change society. Malcolm Lowry is best known for *Under the Volcano*. Classics of children's literature consisted of A A Milne collection of books about fictional bear *Winnie-the-Pooh*, author Mary Norton with tiny people *The Borrowers*, the T H White Arthurian tale *The Sword in the Stone*, while Hugh Lofting created the character *Doctor Dolittle* Novelists who wrote in a more traditional style, such as John

Galsworthy and Arnold Bennett continued to receive great acclaim in the interwar period. At the same time the Georgian poets maintained a more conservative approach to poetry.

One of the most significant English writers of this period was George Orwell. An acclaimed essayist and novelist, Orwell's works are considered among the most important social and political commentaries of the 20th century. Dealing with issues such as poverty in *The Road to Wigan Pier* and *Down and Out in Paris and London,* totalitarianism in *Nineteen Eighty-Four* and colonialism in *Burmese Days*. Orwell's works were often semi-autobiographical and in the case of *Homage to Catalonia,* wholly autobiographical.

Major fantasy novelists C. S. Lewis (*The Chronicles of Narnia*) and J. R. R. Tolkien (*The Lord of the Rings*), were leading figures in the English faculty at Oxford University and in the informal Oxford literary group known as the "Inklings".

Ian Fleming created the character James Bond, chronicling his adventures in twelve novels and two short story collections such as *Casino Royale, Dr. No,* and *Goldfinger,* Notable children's works consisted of Dodie Smith novel *The Hundred and One Dalmatians* Agatha Christie was an English crime writer of novels, short stories and plays, best remembered for her 80 detective novels and her successful West End theatre plays. Her works, particularly featuring detectives *Hercule Poirot* or *Miss Jane Marple,* have given her the title the 'Queen of Crime' and made her one of the most important and innovative writers in the development of the genre, with some of her most famous works being *Murder on the Orient Express, Death on the Nile.* The leading poets of the middle and later

20th century included the traditionalist John Betjeman, Philip Larkin, Ted Hughes and the Northern Irish Catholic Seamus Heaney, who lived in the Republic of Ireland for much of his later life.

Notable War novels Alistair MacLean classic's *Where Eagles Dare, The Guns of Navarone,* Jack Higgins' *The Eagle Has Landed,* and Louis de Bernières' *Captain Corelli's Mandolin.*

Critically acclaimed British books of the latter 20th century include John Fowles with *The French Lieutenant's Woman,* Patrick O'Brian's *Master and Commander,* Richard Adams symbolic *Watership Down,* Giles Foden's *Last King of Scotland,* Nick Hornby with *High Fidelity,* Alex Garland's *The Beach,* Helen Fielding's *Bridget Jones's Diary,* and Ken Follet's novel *The Pillars of the Earth*

Major British novelists of the middle and later 20th century included Evelyn Waugh, William Golding, Graham Greene, Anthony Burgess, Henry Green, Anthony Powell, Kingsley Amis, V.S.Naipaul, JG Ballard, Frederick Forsyth, Roald Dahl, Arthur C Clarke, Anthony Horowitz, Iris Murdoch, Brian Aldiss, John Wyndham, Clive Barker and Douglas Adams. Turn of the 21st century, major writers include Ian McEwan, Philip Pullman, Salman Rushdie, Neil Gaiman, Alan Moore, Terry Pratchett and JK Rowling.

In drama, the drawing room plays of the post war period were challenged in the 1950s by the Angry Young Men, exemplified by as John Osborne's iconic play *Look Back in Anger.* Also in the 1950s, the bleak absurdist play *Waiting for Godot,* by the Irish playwright Samuel Beckett profoundly affected British drama. The Theatre of the Absurd influenced playwrights of the later decades of the 20th century, including Harold Pinter, whose works are often characterized by menace or claustrophobia, and Tom Stoppard. Stoppard's works are however also notable for their high-spirited wit and the great range of intellectual issues which he tackles in different plays.

Non-English Literature Since 1900

In the late 19th and early 20th century, Welsh literature began to reflect the way the Welsh language was increasingly becoming a political symbol. Two important literary nationalists were Saunders Lewis and Kate Roberts.

In the early 20th century in Scotland, a renaissance in the use of Lowland Scots occurred, its most vocal figure being Hugh MacDiarmid. Other contemporaries were Douglas Young, Sidney Goodsir Smith, Robert Garioch and Robert McLellan. However, the revival was largely limited to verse and other literature.

The end of the First World War saw a decline in the quantity of poetry published in Jèrriais and Guernésiais in favour of short-story-like newspaper columns in prose, some being collected in book or booklet form – this being a common genre in the Norman mainland. For example, a collection of Thomas Henry Mahy's *Dires et Pensées du Courtil Poussin,* was published in 1922. The imported eisteddfod tradition in the Channel Islands encouraged recitation and performance, a tradition that continues today. The German military occupation of the Channel Islands 1940–1945 encouraged increased use of the vernacular languages among those who remained, but the German censorship permitted little original writing to be published. Within the restrictions, *Les Chroniques de Jersey,* the only surviving French language newspaper in the Islands, republished considerable quantities of older Jèrriais literature for purposes of morale and the assertion of identity. The post-Liberation social changes meant, however, that vernacular l iterature has never regained the situation it had enjoyed previously.

Christopher Whyte (Crisdean MhicIlleBhain) is a Scottish Gaelic poet, who won in 2002 a Saltire Society Research Book of the Year award for his edition of Sorley Maclean's *Dàin do Eimhir*

Sorley MacLean's work in Scottish Gaelic in the 1930s gave new value to modern literature in that language.

Highly anglicised Lowland Scots is often used in contemporary Scottish fiction, for example, the Edinburgh dialect of Lowland Scots in *Trainspotting* by Irvine Welsh. Edwin Morgan is the current Makar (Scottish national poet) and also produces translations of world literature.

Translations are an important feature of the literatures of the regional languages of the islands, for example: Alice in Wonderland has been translated into Manx as *Contoyryssyn Ealish ayns Cheer ny Yindyssyn* by Brian Stowell (published in 1990) and into Cornish as *Alys in Pow an Anethow* by Nicholas Williams (published in 2009), and the Rubaiyat of Omar Khayyam was translated into Jèrriais, from the English version by Edward FitzGerald, during the German Occupation by Frank Le Maistre, and into Scots by Rab Wilson (published in 2004). Alexander Hutchison has translated the poetry of Catullus into Scots, and in the 1980s Liz Lochhead produced a Scots translation of Tartuffe by Molière.

With the revival of Cornish there have been newer works written in the language. The bard Pol Hodge is an example of a poet writing in Cornish. Among the few novels published in Cornish are Melville Bennetto's *An Gurun Wosek a Geltya* (The Bloody Crown of the Celtic Countries) in 1984; subsequently Michael Palmer published *Jory* (1989) and *Dyroans* (1998).

A collection of short stories *P'tites Lures Guernésiaises* (in Guernésiais with parallel English translation) by various writers was published in 2006.

Original literature continues to be promoted by organisations and institutions such as the Eisteddfod or the Mod. In Welsh poetry, Alan Llwyd came to prominence when he achieved the rare feat of winning both the Crown and the Chair at the 1973 National Eisteddfod and then repeated the feat in 1976. He also wrote the script for the Oscar-nominated Welsh-language film *Hedd Wyn* (1992) about the life of poet Hedd Wyn, who was killed in World War I.

2

Origin of Celtic Languages and Literature

The Celtic languages are descended from Proto-Celtic, or "Common Celtic", a branch of the greater Indo-European language family. The term "Celtic" was used to describe this language group by Edward Lhuyd in 1707, having much earlier been used by Greek and Roman writers to describe tribes in central Gaul. During the 1st millennium BC, they were spoken across Europe, from the Bay of Biscay and the North Sea, up the Rhine and down the Danube to the Black Sea and the Upper Balkan Peninsula, and into Asia Minor (Galatia).

Today, Celtic languages are limited to a few areas on the western fringe of Europe, notably Ireland, the peninsula of Brittany in France, and areas of the United Kingdom including Wales, Scotland and Cornwall. Celtic languages are also spoken on the Isle of Man, Cape Breton Island and in Patagonia. The spread to Cape Breton and Patagonia occurred in modern times. In all these areas the Celtic languages are now only spoken by minorities although there are continuing efforts at revival. Although Celtic languages were spoken in Australia before federation in 1901, these have died out.

Divisions

Proto-Celtic apparently divided into four sub-families:

1) Gaulish and its close relatives Lepontic, Noric, and Galatian. These languages were once spoken in a wide arc from France to Turkey and from Belgium to northern Italy. They are now all extinct.

2) Celtiberian, anciently spoken in the Iberian peninsula, in the areas of modern Northern Portugal, and Galicia, Asturias, Cantabria, Aragón, and León in Spain. Lusitanian, from Southern Portugal, may also have been a Celtic language. These are now also extinct.

3) Goidelic, including Irish, Scottish Gaelic, and Manx. At one time there were Irish on the coast of southwest England and on the coast of north and south Wales.

4) Brythonic (also called British or Brittonic), including Welsh, Breton, Cornish, Cumbric, and possibly also Pictish though this may be a sister language rather than a daughter of British (Common Brythonic). Before the arrival of Scotti on the Isle of Man in the 9th century there may have been a Brythonic language in the Isle of Man. Kenneth Jackson used the term "Brittonic" for the form of the British language after the changes in the 6th century.

Scholarly handling of the Celtic languages has been rather argumentative owing to lack of much primary source data. Some scholars distinguish Continental Celtic and Insular Celtic, arguing that the differences between the Goidelic and Brythonic languages arose after these split off from the Continental Celtic languages. Other scholars distinguish between P-Celtic and Q-Celtic, putting most the Gaulish and Brythonic languages in the former group and the Goidelic and Celtiberian languages in the latter. The P-Celtic languages (also called Gallo-Brittonic) are sometimes seen as a central innovating area as opposed to the more conservative peripheral Q-Celtic languages.

The Breton language is Brythonic, not Gaulish, though there may be some input from the latter. When the Anglo-Saxons moved into Great Britain, several waves of the native Britons or "Welsh" (from a Germanic word for "foreigners") crossed the English Channel and landed in Brittany. They brought their Brythonic language with them, which evolved into Breton – which is still partially intelligible with Modern Welsh and Cornish.

In the P/Q classification scheme the first language to split off from Proto-Celtic was Gaelic. It has characteristics that some scholars see as archaic but others see as also being in the Brythonic languages. With the Insular/Continental classification scheme the split of the former into Gaelic and Brythonic is seen as being late.

The distinction of Celtic into these four sub-families most likely occurred about 900 BC according to Gray and Atkinson but, because of estimation uncertainty, it could be any time between 1200 and 800 BC. However, they only considered Gaelic and Brythonic. The controversial paper by Forster and Toth included Gaulish and put the break-up much earlier at 3200 BC ± 1500 years. They support the Insular Celtic hypothesis. The early Celts were commonly associated with the archaeological Urnfield culture, the Hallstatt culture, and the La Tène culture, though the earlier assumption of association between language and culture is now considered to be less strong.

Classifications

There are two main competing schemata of categorization. The older scheme, argued for by Schmidt (1988) among others, links Gaulish with Brythonic in a P-Celtic node, originally leaving just Goidelic as Q-Celtic. The difference between P and Q languages is the treatment of Proto-Celtic **kʷ*, which became **p* in the P-Celtic languages but **k* in Goidelic. An example is the Proto-Celtic verb root **kʷrin-* "to buy", which became *pryn-* in Welsh but *cren-* in Old Irish. However, a classification based on a single feature is seen as risky by its critics, particularly as the sound change occurs in other language groups (Oscan and Greek).

The other scheme, defended for example by McCone (1996), links Goidelic and Brythonic together as an Insular Celtic branch, while Gaulish and Celtiberian are referred to as Continental Celtic. According to this theory, the "P-Celtic" sound change of [k◎] to [p] occurred independently or areally. The proponents of the Insular Celtic hypothesis point to other shared innovations among Insular Celtic languages, including inflected prepositions, VSO word order, and the lenition of intervocalic [m] to [◎], a nasalized voiced bilabial fricative (an extremely rare sound). There is, however, no assumption that the Continental Celtic languages descend from a common "Proto-Continental Celtic" ancestor. Rather, the Insular/Continental schemata usually considers Celtiberian the first branch to split from Proto-Celtic, and the remaining group would later have split into Gaulish and Insular Celtic.

There are legitimate scholarly arguments in favour of both the Insular Celtic hypothesis and the P-Celtic/

Q-Celtic hypothesis. Proponents of each schema dispute the accuracy and usefulness of the other's categories. However, since the 1970s the division into Insular and Continental Celtic has become the more widely held view (Cowgill 1975; McCone 1991, 1992; Schrijver 1995).

When referring only to the modern Celtic languages, since no Continental Celtic language has living descendants, "Q-Celtic" is equivalent to "Goidelic" and "P-Celtic" is equivalent to "Brythonic".

Within the Indo-European family, the Celtic languages have sometimes been placed with the Italic languages in a common Italo-Celtic subfamily, a hypothesis that is now largely discarded, in favour of the assumption of language contact between pre-Celtic and pre-Italic communities.

Characteristics of Celtic Languages

Although there are many differences between the individual Celtic languages, they do show many family resemblances. While none of these characteristics is necessarily unique to the Celtic languages, there are few if any other languages which possess them all. They include:

1) Consonant mutations (Insular Celtic only)
2) Inflected prepositions (Insular Celtic only)
3) Two grammatical genders (modern Insular Celtic only; Old Irish and the Continental languages had three genders)
4) A vigesimal number system (counting by twenties)
5) Verb-subject-object (VSO) word order (probably Insular Celtic only)

6) An interplay between the subjunctive, future, imperfect, and habitual, to the point that some tenses and moods have ousted others

7) An impersonal or autonomous verb form serving as a passive or intransitive

   a) Welsh *dysgaf* "I teach" vs. *dysgir* "is taught, one teaches", Irish "déanaim" "I do/make" vs. "déantar" "is done".

8) No infinitives, replaced by a quasi-nominal verb form called the verbal noun or verbnoun

9) Frequent use of vowel mutation as a morphological device, e.g. formation of plurals, verbal stems, etc.

10) Use of preverbal particles to signal either subordination or illocutionary force of the following clause

    a) mutation-distinguished subordinators/ relativizers

    b) particles for negation, interrogation, and occasionally for affirmative declarations

11) Infixed pronouns positioned between particles and verbs

12) Lack of simple verb for the imperfective "have" process, with possession conveyed by a composite structure, usually BE + preposition

13) Use of periphrastic phrases to express verbal tense, voice, or aspectual distinctions

14) Distinction by function of the two versions of BE verbs traditionally labelled substantive (or existential) and copula

15) Bifurcated demonstrative structure

16) Suffixed pronominal supplements, called confirming or supplementary pronouns
17) Use of singulars and/or special forms of counted nouns, and use of a singulative suffix to make singular forms from plurals, where older singulars have disappeared.

Celtic Literature

Celtic literature may be literature about Celts, or elements of Irish literature, British literature or Celtic-influenced literature from elsewhere. Although often written in English, Celtic literature may be composed in Celtic languages: Irish, Welsh, Cornish, Manx, Scottish Gaelic and Breton or their older forms; literature in Scots and Ulster Scots may also be included within the concept.

The Gaelic Revival reintroduced Celtic themes into modern literature. The concept of Celticity encouraged cross-fertilisation between Celtic cultures. There have been modern texts based around Celtic literature. Bernard Cornwell writes about the Arthurian legends in his series The Warlord Chronicles. Other writers of Celtic literature in English include Dylan Thomas and Sian James.

Celtic Revival covers a variety of movements and trends, mostly in the 19th and 20th centuries, which drew on Celtic art and traditions. Although the revival was complex and multifaceted, occurring across many fields and in various countries in North-West Europe, its best known incarnation is probably the Irish Literary Revival also called the Celtic Twilight. Here, Irish writers including William Butler Yeats, Lady Gregory, "AE" Russell, Edward Martyn and Edward Plunkett (AKA Lord Dunsany) stimulated a new appreciation of traditional Irish literature and Irish poetry in the late 19th and early 20th century.

In many, but not all, facets the revival came to represent a reaction against modernism. This is particularly true in Ireland, where the relationship between the archaic and the modern was antagonistic, where history was fractured, and where, according to Terry Eagleton, "as a whole [the nation] had not leapt at a bound from tradition to modernity" It was also a corollary, and part of, the general movement of medievalism; it came to be recognised that England too had (or co-opted) a Celtic heritage (via its connections with Wales and the pre-Germanic Britons), with King Arthur and other themes.

3

Latin Literature in Britain

A great deal of interest is invested in the literature of Britain in Germanic or Celtic languages, but explicit references to literature in Latin are scattered and rare. Literary production in Latin from Britain is very rich, yet it is hard to find a good description of the whole picture. This page starts as a work in progress area to cover that need.

Latin literature, the body of written works in the Latin language, remains an enduring legacy of the culture of ancient Rome. The Romans produced many works of poetry, comedy, tragedy, satire, history, and rhetoric, drawing heavily on the traditions of other cultures and particularly on the more matured literary tradition of Greece. Long after the Western Roman Empire had fallen, the Latin language continued to play a central role in western European civilization.

Latin literature is conventionally divided into distinct periods. Few works remain of Early and Old Latin; among these few surviving works, however, are the plays of Plautus and Terence, which have remained very popular in all eras down to the present, while many other Latin works, including many by the most prominent authors of the Classical period, have disappeared, sometimes being re-discovered after centuries, sometimes not. Such lost works sometimes survive as fragments in other works which have survived, but others are known from references in such works as Pliny the Elder's Naturalis Historia or the De Architectura of Vitruvius.

Classical Latin

The period of Classical Latin, when Latin literature is widely considered to have reached its peak, is divided into the Golden Age, which covers approximately the period from the start of the 1st century BC up to the mid-1st century AD, and the Silver Age, which extends into the 2nd century AD. Literature written after the mid-2nd century has often been disparaged and ignored; in the Renaissance, for example, when many Classical authors were re-discovered and their style consciously imitated. Above all, Cicero was imitated, and his style praised as the pinnacle of Latin style. Medieval Latin was often dismissed as inferior; but in fact, many great works of Latin literature were produced throughout Late Antiquity and the Middle Ages, although they are no longer as widely known as those written in the Classical period. Three works survived to inspire architects and engineers in the Renaissance, the Naturalis Historia of Pliny the Elder, the books by Frontinus on the aqueducts of Rome and the De Architectura of Vitruvius.

Medieval World

For most of the Medieval era, Latin was the dominant written language in use in western Europe. After the Roman Empire split into its Western and Eastern halves, Greek, which had been widely used all over the Empire, faded from use in the West, all the more so as the political and religious distance steadily grew between the Catholic West and the Orthodox, Greek East. The vernacular languages in the West, the languages of modern-day western Europe, developed for centuries as spoken languages only: most people did not write, and it seems that it very seldom occurred to those who wrote to write in any language other than Latin, even when they spoke French or Italian or English or another vernacular in their daily life. Very gradually, in the late Middle Ages and the early Renaissance, it became more and more common to write in the Western vernaculars.

It was probably only after the invention of printing, which made books and pamphlets cheap enough that a mass public could afford them, and which made possible modern phenomena such as the newspaper, that a large number of people in the West could read and write who were not fluent in Latin. Still, many people continued to write in Latin, although they were mostly from the upper classes and/ or professional academics. As late as the 17th century, there was still a large audience for Latin poetry and drama; it was not unusual, for example, that Milton wrote many poems in Latin, or that Francis Bacon or Baruch Spinoza wrote mostly in Latin. The use of Latin as a lingua franca continued in smaller European lands until the 20th century.

Although the number of works of non-fiction and drama, history and philosophy written in Latin has continued to dwindle, the Latin language is still not dead. Well into the twentieth century, some knowledge of Latin was required for admission into many universities, and theses and dissertations written for graduate degrees were often required to be written in Latin. Treatises in chemistry and biology and other natural sciences were often written in Latin as late as the early 20th century. Up to the present day, the editors of Latin and Greek texts in such series as the Oxford Classical Texts, the Bibliotheca scriptorum Graecorum et Romanorum Teubneriana and some others still write the introductions to their editions in polished and vital Latin. Among these Latin scholars of the 20th and 21st centuries are R.A.B. Mynors, R.J. Tarrant, L.D. Reynolds and John Brisco.

Early Latin Literature

Tragedy

1) Lucius Livius Andronicus (c. 280/260 BC–c. 200 BC)
2) Gnaeus Naevius
3) Quintus Ennius (239 - c. 169 BC)
4) Marcus Pacuvius (ca. 220-130 BC)
5) Lucius Accius (170 - c. 86 BC)

Comedy

1) Livius Andronicus
2) Gnaeus Naevius(ca. 264 – 201 BC)
3) Titus Maccius Plautus (c. 254–184 BC)
4) Publius Terentius Afer (195/185–159 BC)

Satires

1) Gaius Lucilius (c.160s - 103/2 BC)

Prose

1) Cato - agricultural writer

Golden Age of Latin Literature

Poetry

1) Lucius Pomponius - Dramatist, a writer of the Atellanae fabulae
2) Catullus - lyric poet and elegist
3) Horace - lyric poet and satirist
4) Lucretius - philosopher
5) Ovid - elegist, didactic poet and mythological poet
6) Propertius - elegist
7) Tibullus - elegist
8) Virgil - epic, didactic and pastoral poet
9) Quintus Novius - Dramatist, a writer of the Atellanae fabulae
10) Lucius Pomponius Secundus - Tragedian

Prose

1) Cicero - orator, philosopher and correspondent
2) Marcus Terentius Varro - agricultural writer and linguist
3) Publilius Syrus - writer of maxims
4) Vitruvius - architect

History

1) Livy
2) Saliust
3) Julius Caesar

Biography

1) Cornelius Nepos
2) Augustus - autobiographer

Silver Age of Latin Literature

Poetry

1) Gaius Valerius Flaccus - epic poet
2) Lucan - epic poet
3) Marcus Manilius - astronomical poet
4) Silius Italicus - epic poet
5) Statius - lyric and epic poet
6) Juvenal - satirist
7) Martial - epigrammatist
8) Persius - satirist
9) Phaedrus - fabulist

Prose

1) Aulus Gellius - essayist
2) Columella - agricultural writer
3) Petronius - novellist
4) Pliny the Elder - scientist
5) Pliny the Younger - correspondent
6) Quintilian - rhetorician
7) Sextus Julius Frontinus - engineer
8) Valerius Maximus - author of a collection of anecdotes
9) Seneca the Elder - orator

History

1) Florus
2) Marcus Velleius Paterculus
3) Tacitus

Biography

1) Suetonius
2) Quintus Curtius Rufus

Multiple Genres

Second Century

Poets

1) Hosidius Geta - Playwright

Prose

1) Apuleius - novellist and philosopher
2) Lucian - essayist, satirist
3) Marcus Aurelius - philosopher
4) Fronto - grammarian
5) Aulus Gellius - essayist
6) Tacitus - historian
7) Claudius Ptolemy - astronomer

Latin Literature in the Late Antique period

Christians

1) Augustine of Hippo - theologian, autobiographer and correspondent
2) Ausonius - elegist

3) Jerome - theologian and correspondent
4) Marcus Minucius Felix - theologian
5) Prudentius - Christian poet
6) Sidonius Apollinaris - panegyricist and correspondent
7) Tertullian - theologian

Medieval Latin Literature

Theology and Philosophy

1) Pierre Abelard
2) Aetheria
3) Albertus Magnus
4) Thomas Aquinas: *Pange Lingua*: *Summa Theologica*
5) Roger Bacon
6) Duns Scotus
7) Gildas
8) Gregory of Tours
9) Siger of Brabant
10) Tommaso da Celano: *Dies Iræ*
11) Venantius Fortunatus
12) Walter of Châtillon
13) William of Occam
14) Anicius Manlius Severinus Boethius - *Consolation of Philosophy*

Drama and poetry

1) The Archpoet
2) *Carmina Burana*

3) Goliards
4) Peter of Blois
5) Hildegard of Bingen
6) Hrotsvitha

History

1) Albert of Aix
2) Bede
3) Einhard
4) Fulcher of Chartres
5) Matthew Paris
6) Orderic Vitalis
7) Otto of Freising
8) William of Malmesbury
9) William of Tyre

Pseudo-History

1) Geoffrey of Monmouth

Encyclopedia

1) Isidore of Seville: *Etymologiæ*

Multiple Genres

1) Alcuin

Renaissance Latin

1) Dante Alighieri
2) Giovanni Boccaccio
3) Erasmus
4) Jean Buridan

5) Thomas More: *Utopia*
6) Petrarch
7) William of Ockham

Neo-Latin

1) Francis Bacon
2) Jacob Bidermann
3) Thomas Hobbes
4) John Milton
5) Baruch Spinoza
6) Maciej Kazimierz Sarbiewski
7) Elizabeth Jane Weston

Recent Latin

1) Arrius Nurus
2) Geneviève Immè
3) Alanus Divutius
4) Anna Elissa Radke
5) Ianus Novak
6) Tuomo Pekkanen

Anglo-Latin literature Upto 1847

From the 7th to the mid-19th cents, thousands of English writers produced Latin writings in great quantity, both in prose and in verse, addressed to a Latin-reading public in continental Europe and in England. Bede, Aldhelm, and Alcuin are prominent authors in the period before the Norman Conquest. From the 12th cent. onwards many Anglo-Latin writers achieved European renown. Geoffrey of Monmouth's

Historia Regum Britanniae was a principal source which disseminated the Arthurian legends, and is extant in almost 300 manuscripts. Chroniclers such as William of Malmesbury and Henry of Huntingdon were historians also renowned for their literary qualities. Virtually every literary genre is found, including hymns, letters, saints' lives, and poetry of all kinds in both quantitative and stressed metres. Epic is represented by Joseph of Exeter's De Bello Troiano, satire against the religious orders by Nigel Wireker's Speculum Stultorum, lyric and occasional poetry by Peter of Blois. Gervase of Tilbury and the Anglo-Welshman Walter Map shared a taste for folklore narratives, for stories, and for wonders. Among works of literary criticism are Geoffrey de Vinsauf's Poetria Nova and John of Garland's Parisiana Poetria.

A great deal of Latin continued to be written in the 13th and 14th cents, culminating in John Gower's 10,000-line Vox Clamantis, of which the first book is on the Peasants' Revolt. The 15th cent. represents a low point for the Latinate tradition, but it revives in the 16th cent. under the impact of humanism and the regeneration of the universities. Thomas More wrote Latin epigrams and other poems, as well as the classic Utopia.

Roger Ascham produced the most elegant Latin letter-book to appear from 16th-cent. England. The Latin poetic tradition in particular was regenerated. Thomas Campion's love elegies, first published in 1595, exceed in sensuous frankness his English poems, and many major English poets of the 16th and 17th cents such as Milton, Herbert, Crashaw, Marvell, and Cowley also wrote much Latin poetry. The much-admired and reprinted Parthenicon (Writings of a

Maid)of Elizabeth Jane Weston was the first substantial volume of collected poetry by a female British writer to appear under her own name.

In the 18th cent. Dr Johnson, Addison, and T. Gray all wrote Latin verses. After 1750 the Latin tradition declines into literary trifling, except for the productions of Walter Savage Landor, the last significant English poet to write in Latin. The publication of his extensive Poemata et Inscriptiones may be said to bring the Anglo-Latin tradition to a close.

4

History of Anglo-Norman Literature

Anglo-Norman literature is literature composed in the Anglo-Norman language developed during the period 1066–1204 when the Duchy of Normandy and England were united in the Anglo-Norman realm

The Norman language came over to England with William the Conqueror. Following the Norman conquest, the Norman language became the language of England's nobility. During the whole of the 12th century Anglo-Norman (the variety of Norman used in England) shared with Latin the distinction of being the literary language of England, and it was in use at the court until the 14th century. It was not until the reign of Henry VII that English became the native tongue of the kings of England. After the loss of the French provinces, schools for the teaching of French were established in England, among the most celebrated of which we may quote that of Marlborough. The language had undergone certain changes which distinguished it from the Old Norman spoken in Normandy; but, except for some graphical characteristics, from which certain rules of pronunciation are to be inferred, the changes to which the language was subjected were the individual modifications of the various authors, so that, while we may still speak of Anglo-Norman writers, an Anglo-Norman language, properly so called, gradually ceased to exist.

It was not till 1363 that the chancellor opened the parliamentary session with an English speech, and not until the reign of Henry VII that Statute law ceased to be written in Anglo-Norman. And although the Hundred Years' War led to a decline in the study of French and the disappearance of Anglo-Norman literature, the French language continued, through some vicissitudes, to be the classical language of the courts of justice until the 17th century. French, alongside Latin, remained the language of government until the mid-1480s. It is still an official language in the Channel Islands, though English has become dominant since 1901.

Wace and Benoît de Sainte-More compiled their histories at his bidding, and it was in his reign that Marie de France composed her poems. An event with which he was closely connected, viz. the murder of Thomas Becket, gave rise to a whole series of writings, some of which are purely Anglo-Norman. In his time appeared the works of Beroul and Thomas of Britain respectively, as well as some of the most celebrated of the Anglo-Norman *romans d'aventure*. It is important to keep this fact in mind when studying the different works which Anglo-Norman literature has left us. We will examine these works briefly, grouping them into narrative, didactic, hagiographic, lyric, satiric and dramatic literature.

Epic and Romance

The French epic came over to England at an early date.

It is believed that the *Chanson de Roland* was sung at the battle of Hastings, and some Anglo-Norman manuscripts of chansons de geste have survived to this day. The *Pelerinage de Charlemagne* (Eduard Koschwitz, *Altfranzösische Bibliothek*, 1883) was, for instance, only preserved in an Anglo-Norman manuscript of the British Museum (now lost), although the author was certainly a Parisian. The oldest manuscript of the *Chanson de Roland* that we possess is also a manuscript written in England, and amongst the others of less importance we may mention *La Chançun de Willame*, the MS. of which has (June 1903) been published in facsimile at Chiswick.

Although the diffusion of epic poetry in England did not actually inspire any new *chansons de geste*, it developed the taste for this class of literature, and the epic style in which the tales of the *Romance of Horn*, of *Bovon de Hampton*, of *Guy of Warwick* (still unpublished), of *Waldef* (still unpublished), and of *Fulk Fitz Warine* are treated, is certainly partly due to this circumstance. Although the last of these works has come down to us only in a prose version, it contains unmistakable signs of a previous poetic form, and what we possess is really only a rendering into prose similar to the transformations undergone by many of the *chansons de geste*.

The interinfluence of French and English literature can be studied in the Breton romances and the *romans d'aventure* even better than in the epic poetry of the period. The *Lay of Orpheus* is known to us only through an English imitation, *Sir Orfeo*; the *Lai du cor* was composed by Robert Biket, an Anglo-Norman poet of the 12th century (Wulff, Lund, 1888). The *The Lais of Marie de France* were written in England, and the greater number of the romances composing the *matière de Bretagne* seem to have passed from England to France through the medium of Anglo-Norman.

The legends of Merlin and Arthur, collected in the *Historia Regum Britanniae* by Geoffrey of Monmouth, passed into French literature, bearing the character which the bishop of St Asaph had stamped upon them. Chrétien de Troyes's *Perceval* is doubtless based on an Anglo-Norman poem. Robert de Boron took the subject of his Merlin from Geoffrey of Monmouth.

Finally, the most celebrated love-legend of the Middle Ages, and one of the most beautiful inventions of world-literature, the story of Tristan and Iseult, tempted two authors, Béroul and Thomas, the first of whom is probably, and the second certainly, Anglo-Norman. One *Folie Tristan* was composed in England in the last years of the 12th century.

Less fascinating than the story of Tristan and Iseult, but nevertheless of considerable interest, are the two *romans d'aventure* of Hugh of Rutland, *Ipomedon* and *Protesilaus* (still unpublished) written about 1185. The first relates the adventures of a knight who married the young duchess of Calabria, niece of King Meleager of Sicily, but was loved by Medea, the king's wife.

The second poem is the sequel to *Ipomedon,* and deals with the wars and subsequent reconciliation between Ipomedon's sons, Daunus, the elder, lord of Apulia, and Protesilaus, the younger, lord of Calabria. Protesilaus defeats Daunus, who had expelled him from Calabria. He saves his brother's life, is reinvested with the dukedom of Calabria, and, after the death of Daunus, succeeds to Apulia. He subsequently marries

Medea, King Meleager's widow, who had helped him to seize Apulia, having transferred her affection for Ipomedon to his younger son.

To these two romances by an Anglo-Norman author, *Amadas et Idoine,* of which we only possess a continental version, is to be added. Gaston Paris has proved indeed that the original was composed in England in the 12th century.

The Anglo-Norman poem on the *Life of Richard Coeur de Lion* is lost, and an English version only has been preserved. About 1250 Eustace of Kent introduced into England the *roman d'Alexandre* in his *Roman de toute chevalerie,* many passages of which have been imitated in one of the oldest English poems on Alexander, namely, *King Alisaunder.*

Fableaux, Fables and Religious Tales

In spite of the incontestable popularity enjoyed by this class of literature, we have only some half-dozen *fableaux* written in England, viz.

1) Le chevalier a la corbeille,
2) Le chevalier qui faisait parler les muets,
3) Le chevalier, sa dame et un clerc,
4) Les trois dames,
5) La gageure,
6) Le pretre d'Alison,
7) La bourgeoise d'Orleans.

As to fables, one of the most popular collections in the Middle Ages was that written by Marie de France, which she claimed to have translated from King Alfred. In the *Contes moralisés,* written by Nicole Bozon shortly before 1320, a few fables bear a strong resemblance to those of Marie de France.

The religious tales deal mostly with the Mary Legends, and have been handed down to us in three collections:

1. The Adgar's collection. Most of these were translated from William of Malmesbury by Adgar in the 12th century ("Adgar's Marien-Legenden," *Altfr. Biblioth.* ix.; J. A. Herbert, *Rom.* xxxii. 394).
2. The collection of Everard of Gateley, a monk of St. Edmund at Bury, who wrote *c.* 1250 three Mary Legends.
3. An anonymous collection of sixty Mary Legends composed *c.* 1250, some of which have been published in Hermann Suchier's *Bibliotheca Normannica*; in the *Altf. Bibl.*

Another set of religious and moralizing tales is to be found in Chardri's *Set dormans* and *Josaphat, c.* 1216.

History

Of far greater importance, however, are the works which constitute Anglo-Norman historiography. The first Anglo-Norman historiographer is Geoffrey Gaimar, who wrote his *Estorie des Angles* (between 1147 and 1151) for Dame Constance, wife of Ralph FitzGilbert. This history comprised a first part (now lost), which was merely a translation of Geoffrey of Monmouth's *Historia Regum Britanniae,* preceded by a history of the Trojan War, and a second part which carries us as far as the death of William Rufus. For this second part he has consulted historical documents, but he stops at the year 1087, just when he has reached the period about which he might have been able to give us some first-hand information.

The *History of the Dukes of Normandy* by Benoît de Sainte-More is based on the work of Wace. It was composed at the request of Henry II. about 1170, and takes us as far as the year 1135. The 43,000 lines which it contains are of but little interest to the historian; they are too evidently the work of a *romancier courtois,* who takes pleasure in recounting love-adventures such as those he has described in his romance of Troy. Other works, however, give us more trustworthy information, for example, the anonymous poem on Henry II.'s *Conquest of Ireland* in 1172, which, together with the *Expugnatio hibernica* of Giraud de Barri, constitutes our chief authority on this subject. The *Conquest of Ireland* was republished in 1892 by Goddard Henry Orpen, under the title of *The Song of Dermot and the Earl* . Similarly, Jourdain Fantosme, who was in the north of England in 1174, wrote an account of the wars between Henry II., his sons, William the Lion of Scotland and Louis VII., in 1173 and 1174.

Not one of these histories, however, is to be compared in value with *The History of William the Marshal, Count of Striguil and Pembroke,* regent of England from 1216–1219, which was found and subsequently edited by Paul Meyer . This masterpiece of historiography was composed in 1225 or 1226 by a professional poet of talent at the request of William, son of the marshal. It was compiled from the notes of the marshal's squire, John d'Early, who shared all the vicissitudes of his master's life and was one of the executors of his will. This work is of great value for the history of the period 1186–1219, as the information furnished by John d'Early is either personal or obtained at first hand. In the part which deals with the period before 1186, it is true, there are various mistakes, due to the author's ignorance of contemporary history, but these slight blemishes are amply atoned for by the literary value of the work. The style is concise, the anecdotes are well told, the descriptions short and picturesque; the whole constitutes one of the most living pictures of medieval society.

Very pale by the side of this work appear the *Chronique* of Peter of Langtoft, written between 1311 and 1320, and mainly of interest for the period 1294-1307; the *Chronique* of Nicholas Trevet, dedicated to Princess Mary, daughter of Edward I.; the *Scala Chronica* compiled by Thomas Gray of Heaton, which carries us to the year 1362-1363; the *Black Prince,* a poem by the poet Chandos Herald, composed about 1386, and relating the life of the Black Prince from 1346-1376; and, lastly, the different versions of the *Brutes,* the form and historical importance of which have been indicated by Paul Meyer and by F.W.D. Brie.

Finally we may mention, as ancient history, the translation of Eutropius and Dares, by Geoffrey of Waterford, who gave also the *Secret des Secrets,* a translation from a work wrongly attributed to Aristotle, which belongs to the next division.

Didactic Literature

Didactic literature is the most considerable, if not the most interesting, branch of Anglo-Norman literature: it comprises a large number of works written chiefly with the object of giving both religious and profane instruction to Anglo-Norman lords and ladies. The following list gives the most important productions arranged in chronological order:

1) Philippe de Thaun, *Comput;*
2) *Bestiaire;*
3) *Lois de Guillaume le Conquérant;*
4) *Oxford Psalter;*
5) *Cambridge Psalter;*
6) *London Psalter;*
7) *Disticha Catonis;*
8) *Le Roman de fortune,* a summary of Boethius' *De consolatione philosophiae* (*Consolation of Philosophy*), by Simon de Fresne;
9) *Quatre livres des rois,* translated into French in the 12th century, and imitated in England soon after;
10) *Donnei des Amanz,,* the conversation of two lovers, overheard and carefully noted by the poet, of a purely didactic character, in which are included three interesting pieces, the first being an episode of the story of Tristram, the second a fable, *L'homme et le serpent,* the third a tale, *L'homme et l'oiseau,* which is the basis of the celebrated *Lai de l'oiselet;*
11) *Livre des Sibiles;*
12) *Enseignements Trebor;*
13) *Lapidaire de Cambridge;*
14) Frere Angier de Ste. Frideswide, *Dialogues;*
15) *Li dialoge Grégoire le pape;*
16) *Petite philosophie;*
17) *Histoire de Marie et de Jésus;*
18) *Poème sur l'Ancien Testament;*
19) *Le Corset* and *Le Miroir,* by Robert de Gretham;

20) *Lumière as Lais;*
21) two Anglo-Norman versions of *Quatre soeurs* (Justice, Truth, Peace, Mercy);
22) another *Comput* by Raüf de Lenham, 1256;
23) *Le chastel d'amors;*
24) *Poème sur l'amour de Dieu et sur la haine du péché;*
25) *Le mariage des neuf filles du diable;*
26) *Ditie d' Urbain;*
27) *Dialogue de l'évêque Saint Julien et son disciple;*
28) *Poème sur l'antichrist et le jugement dernier;*
29) Wilham de Waddington produced at the end of the 13th century his *Manuel des péchés,* which was adapted in England by Robert of Brunne in his *Handlying Sinne.*

In the 14th century we find:

1) Nicole Bozon's *Contes moralisés;*
2) *Traité de naturesse;*
3) *Sermons* in verse;
4) *Proverbes de bon enseignement.*

We have also a few handbooks on the teaching of French. Gautier de Biblesworth wrote such a treatise *à Madame Dyonise de Mountechensi pur aprise de langage; Orthographia gallica; La manière de language,* written in 1396; *Un petit livre pour enseigner les enfants de leur entreparler comun françois,* c. 1399. The important *Mirour de l'omme,* by John Gower, contains about 30,000 lines written in very good French at the end of the 14th century.

Hagiography

Among the numerous lives of saints written in Anglo-

Norman the most important ones are the following, the list of which is given in chronological order:

1) *Voyage de Saint Brandan* (or *Brandain*), written in 1121, by an ecclesiastic for Queen Aelis of Louvain;
2) life of St. Catherine by Clemence of Barking ;
3) life of St Giles, c. 1170, by Guillaume de Berneville;
4) life of St. Nicholas, life of Our Lady, by Wace; Uhlemann, *Gram. Krit. Studien zu Wace's Conception und Nicolas*, 1878;
5) life of St. George by Simon de Fresne;
6) *Expurgatoire de Ste. Patrice,* by Marie de France;
7) *La vie de St. Edmund le Rei,* by Denis Pyramus, end of 12th century;
8) Henri d'Arci's life of St. Thais, poem on the Antichrist, *Visio S. Pauli*;
9) life of St. Gregory the Great by Frère Angier, 30 April 1214;
10) life of St. Modwenna, between 1225 and 1250;
11) Fragments of a life of St Thomas Becket, c. 1230 ; and another life of the same by Benoit of St. Alban, 13th century;
12) a life of Edward the Confessor, written before 1245, by an anonymous monk of Westminster; life of St. Auban, c. 1250.
13) *The Vision of Tnudgal,* an Anglo-Norman fragment, is preserved in MS. 312, Trinity College, Dublin; the MS. is of the 14th century; the author seems to belong to the 13th.

In this category we may add the life of Hugh of Lincoln, 13th century. Other lives of saints were recognized to be Anglo-Norman by Paul Meyer when examining the MSS. of the Welbeck library.

Lyric Poetry

The only extant songs of any importance are the seventy-one *Ballads* of Gower. The remaining songs are mostly of a religious character. Most of them have been discovered and published by Paul Meyer. Although so few have come down to us such songs must have been numerous at one time, owing to the constant intercourse between English, French and Provençals of all classes. An interesting passage in *Piers Plowman* furnishes us with a proof of the extent to which these songs penetrated into England. We read of:

> "... dykers and deluers that doth here dedes ille,
>
> And dryuen forth the longe day with 'Deu, vous saue,
>
> Dame Emme!'"

One of the finest productions of Anglo-Norman lyric poetry written in the end of the 13th century, is the *Plainte d'amour,* and we may mention, merely as literary curiosities, various works of a lyrical character written in two languages, Latin and French, or English and French, or even in three languages, Latin, English and French. In *Early English Lyrics* we have a poem in which a lover sends to his mistress a love-greeting composed in three languages, and his learned friend replies in the same style.

Satire

The popularity enjoyed by the *Roman de Renart* and the Anglo-Norman version of the *Riote du Monde* in England is proof enough that the French spirit of satire was keenly appreciated. The clergy and the **fair sex** presented the most attractive target for the shots of the satirists. However, an Englishman raised his voice in favour of the ladies in a poem entitled *La Bonté des dames,* and Nicole Bozon, after having represented "Pride" as a feminine being whom he supposes to be the daughter of Lucifer, and after having fiercely attacked the women of his day in the *Char d'Orgueil,* also composed a *Bounté des femmes* in which he covers them with praise, commending their courtesy, their humility, their openness and the care with which they bring up their children. A few pieces of political satire show us French and English exchanging amenities on their mutual shortcomings. The *Roman des Français,* by André de Coutances, was written on the continent, and cannot be quoted as Anglo-Norman although it was composed before 1204, it is a very spirited reply to French authors who had attacked the English.

Drama

This must have had a considerable influence on the development of the sacred drama in England, but none of the French plays acted in England in the 12th and 13th centuries has been preserved. *Adam,* which is generally considered to be an Anglo-Norman mystery of the 12th century, was probably written in France at the beginning of the 13th century, and the so-called Anglo-Norman *Resurrection* belongs also to continental French. It is necessary to state that the earliest English moralities seem to have been imitations of the French ones.

5

English Renaissance Theatre

English Renaissance theatre, also called early modern English theatre, refers to the theatre of England, largely based in London, which occurred between the Reformation and the closure of the theatres in 1642. It includes the drama of William Shakespeare, Christopher Marlowe and many other world-famous playwrights.

English Renaissance theatre is sometimes called "Elizabethan theatre." The term "Elizabethan theatre", however, covers only the plays written and performed publicly in England during the reign of Queen Elizabeth (1558–1603). As such, "Elizabethan theatre" is distinguished from Jacobean theatre (associated with the reign of King James I, 1603–1625), and Caroline theatre. "English Renaissance theatre" or "early modern theatre" refers to all three sub-classifications taken together.

Background

Renaissance theatre derived from several medieval theatre traditions, such as the mystery plays that formed a part of religious festivals in England and other parts of Europe during the Middle Ages. The mystery plays were complex retellings of legends based on biblical themes, originally performed in churches but later becoming more linked to the secular celebrations that grew up around religious festivals. Other sources include the morality plays and the "University drama" that attempted to recreate Greek tragedy. The Italian tradition of *Commedia dell'arte* as well as the elaborate masques frequently presented at court also contributed to the shaping of public theatre.

Companies of players attached to households of leading noblemen and performing seasonally in various locations existed before the reign of Elizabeth I. These became the foundation for the professional players that performed on the Elizabethan stage. The tours of these players gradually replaced the performances of the mystery and morality plays by local players, and a 1572 law eliminated the remaining companies lacking formal patronage by labelling them vagabonds. At court as well, the performance of masques by courtiers and other amateurs, apparently common in the early years of Elizabeth, was replaced by the professional companies with noble patrons, who grew in number and quality during her reign.

The City of London authorities were generally hostile to public performances, but its hostility was overmatched by the Queen's taste for plays and the Privy Council's support. Theatres sprang up in suburbs, especially in the liberty of Southwark, accessible across the Thames to city dwellers, but beyond the authority's control. The companies maintained the pretence that their public performances were mere rehearsals for the frequent performances before the Queen, but while the latter did grant prestige, the former were the real source of the income professional players required.

Along with the economics of the profession, the character of the drama changed toward the end of the period. Under Elizabeth, the drama was a unified expression as far as social class was concerned: the Court watched the same plays the commoners saw in the public playhouses. With the development of the private theatres, drama became more oriented toward the tastes and values of an upper-class audience. By the later part of the reign of Charles I, few new plays were being written for the public theatres, which sustained themselves on the accumulated works of the previous decades.

Theatres

The establishment of large and profitable public theatres was an essential enabling factor in the success of English Renaissance drama—once they were in operation, drama could become a fixed and permanent rather than a transitory phenomenon. The crucial initiating development was the construction of The Theatre by James Burbage and John Brayne in Shoreditch in 1576. The Theatre was rapidly followed by the nearby Curtain Theatre (1577), the Rose (1587), the Swan (1595), the Globe (1599), the Fortune (1600), and the Red Bull (1604).

Archaeological excavations on the foundations of the Rose and the Globe in the late twentieth century showed that all the London theatres had individual differences; yet their common function necessitated a similar general plan. The public theatres were three stories high, and built around an open space at the centre. Usually polygonal in plan to give an overall rounded effect (though the Red Bull and the first Fortune were square), the three levels of inward-facing galleries overlooked the open center, into which jutted the stage—essentially a platform surrounded on three sides by the audience, only the rear being restricted for the entrances and exits of the actors and seating for the musicians. The upper level behind the stage could be used as a balcony, as in *Romeo and Juliet* or *Antony and Cleopatra*, or as a position from which an actor could harangue a crowd, as in *Julius Caesar*.

Usually built of timber, lath and plaster and with thatched roofs, the early theatres were vulnerable to fire, and were replaced (when necessary) with stronger structures. When the Globe burned down in June 1613, it was rebuilt with a tile roof; when the Fortune burned down in December 1621, it was rebuilt in brick (and apparently was no longer square).

A different model was developed with the Blackfriars Theatre, which came into regular use on a longterm basis in 1599. The Blackfriars was small in comparison to the earlier theatres and roofed rather than open to the sky; it resembled a modern theatre in ways that its predecessors did not. Other small enclosed theatres followed, notably the Whitefriars (1608) and the Cockpit (1617). With the building of the Salisbury Court Theatre in 1629 near the site of the defunct Whitefriars, the London audience had six theatres to choose from: three surviving large open-air "public" theatres, the Globe, the Fortune, and the Red Bull, and three smaller enclosed "private" theatres, the Blackfriars, the Cockpit, and the Salisbury Court. Audiences of the 1630s benefited from a half-century of vigorous dramaturgical development; the plays of Marlowe and Shakespeare and their contemporaries were still being performed on a regular basis (mostly at the public theatres), while the newest works of the newest playwrights were abundant as well (mainly at the private theatres).

Around 1580, when both the Theatre and the Curtain were full on summer days, the total theatre capacity of London was about 5000 spectators. With the building of new theatre facilities and the formation of new companies, the capital's total theatre capacity exceeded 10,000 after 1610. In 1580, the poorest citizens could purchase admittance to the Curtain or the Theatre for a penny; in 1640, their counterparts could gain admittance to the Globe, the Cockpit, or the Red Bull—for exactly the same price.

Performances

The acting companies functioned on a repertory system; unlike modern productions that can run for months or years on end, the troupes of this era rarely acted the same play two days in a row. Thomas Middleton's *A Game at Chess* ran for nine straight performances in August 1624 before it was closed by the authorities—but this was due to the political content of the play and was a unique, unprecedented, and unrepeatable phenomenon. Consider the 1592 season of Lord Strange's Men at the Rose Theatre as far more representative: between Feb. 19 and June 23 the company played six days a week, minus Good Friday and two other days. They performed 23 different plays, some only once, and their most popular play of the season, *The First Part of Hieronimo*, 15 times. They never played the same play two days in a row, and rarely the same play twice in a week. The workload on the actors, especially the leading performers like Edward Alleyn, must have been tremendous.

One distinctive feature of the companies was that they included only males. Until the reign of Charles II, female parts were played by adolescent boy players in women's costume.

Costumes

Since Elizabethan theatre did not make use of lavish scenery, instead leaving the stage largely bare with a few key props, the main visual appeal on stage was in the costumes. Costumes were often bright in color and visually entrancing. Costumes were expensive, however, so usually players wore contemporary clothing regardless of the time period of the play. Occasionally, a lead character would wear a conventionalized version of more historically accurate garb, but secondary characters would nonetheless remain in contemporary clothing.

Playwrights

The growing population of London, the growing wealth of its people, and their fondness for spectacle produced a dramatic literature of remarkable variety, quality, and extent. Although most of the plays written for the Elizabethan stage have been lost, over 600 remain.

The men (no women were professional dramatists in this era) who wrote these plays were primarily self-made men from modest backgrounds. Some of them were educated at either Oxford or Cambridge, but many were not. Although William Shakespeare and Ben Jonson were actors, the majority do not seem to have been performers, and no major author who came on to the scene after 1600 is known to have supplemented his income by acting.

Not all of the playwrights fit modern images of poets or intellectuals. Christopher Marlowe was killed in an apparent tavern brawl, while Ben Jonson killed an actor in a duel. Several probably were soldiers.

Playwrights were normally paid in increments during the writing process, and if their play was accepted, they would also receive the proceeds from one day's performance. However, they had no ownership of the plays they wrote. Once a play was sold to a company, the company owned it, and the playwright had no control over casting, performance, revision or publication.

The profession of dramatist was challenging and far from lucrative. Entries in Philip Henslowe's Diary show that in the years around 1600 Henslowe paid as little as £6 or £7 per play. This was probably at the low end of the range, though even the best writers could not demand too much more. A playwright, working alone, could generally produce two plays a year at most; in the 1630s Richard Brome signed a contract with the Salisbury Court Theatre to supply three plays a year, but found himself unable to meet the workload. Shakespeare produced fewer than 40 solo plays in a career that spanned more than two decades; he was financially successful because he was an actor and, most importantly, a shareholder in the company for which he acted and in the theatres they used. Ben Jonson achieved success as a purveyor of Court masques, and was talented at playing the patronage game that was an important part of the social and economic life of the era. Those who were playwrights pure and simple fared far less well; the biographies of early figures like George Peele and Robert Greene, and later ones like Brome and Philip Massinger, are marked by financial uncertainty, struggle, and poverty.

Playwrights dealt with the natural limitation on their productivity by combining into teams of two, three, four, and even five to generate play texts; the majority of plays written in this era were collaborations, and the solo artists who generally eschewed collaborative efforts, like Jonson and Shakespeare, were the exceptions to the rule. Dividing the work, of course, meant dividing the income; but the arrangement seems to have functioned well enough to have made it worthwhile. Of the 70-plus known works in the canon of Thomas Dekker, roughly 50 are collaborations; in a single year, 1598, Dekker worked on 16 collaborations for impresario Philip Henslowe, and earned £30, or a little under 12 shillings per week—roughly twice as much as the average artisan's income of 1s. per day.

At the end of his career, Thomas Heywood would famously claim to have had "an entire hand, or at least a main finger" in the authorship of some 220 plays. A solo artist usually needed months to write a play (though Jonson is said to have done *Volpone* in five weeks); Henslowe's Diary indicates that a team of four or five writers could produce a play in as little as two weeks. Admittedly, though, the Diary also shows that teams of Henslowe's house dramatists—Anthony Munday, Robert Wilson, Richard Hathwaye, Henry Chettle, and the others, even including a young John Webster—could start a project, and accept advances on it, yet fail to produce anything stageworthy.

Genres

Genres of the period included the history play, which depicted English or European history. Shakespeare's plays about the lives of kings, such as *Richard III* and

Henry V, belong to this category, as do Christopher Marlowe's *Edward II* and George Peele's *Famous Chronicle of King Edward the First.* There were also a number of history plays that dealt with more recent events, like *A Larum for London*, which dramatizes the sack of Antwerp in 1576.

Tragedy was a popular genre. Marlowe's tragedies were exceptionally popular, such as *Dr. Faustus* and *The Jew of Malta.* The audiences particularly liked revenge dramas, such as Thomas Kyd's *The Spanish Tragedy.*

Comedies were common, too. A sub-genre developed in this period was the city comedy, which deals satirically with life in London after the fashion of Roman New Comedy. Examples are Thomas Dekker's *The Shoemaker's Holiday* and Thomas Middleton's *A Chaste Maid in Cheapside.*

Though marginalised, the older genres like pastoral (*The Faithful Shepherdess*, 1608), and even the morality play could exert influences. After about 1610, the new hybrid sub-genre of the tragicomedy enjoyed an efflorescence, as did the masque throughout the reigns of the first two Stuart kings, James I and Charles I.

Printed Texts

Only a minority of the plays of English Renaissance theatre were ever printed; of Heywood's 220 plays noted above, only about 20 were published in book form. A little over 600 plays were published in the period as a whole, most commonly in individual quarto editions. Through much of the modern era, it was thought that play texts were popular items among Renaissance readers that provided healthy profits for the stationers who printed and sold them. By the turn of the 21st century, the climate of scholarly opinion shifted somewhat on this belief: some contemporary researchers argue that publishing plays was a risky and marginal business — though this conclusion has been disputed by others. Some of the most successful publishers of the English Renaissance, like William Ponsonby or Edward Blount, rarely published plays.

End of English Renaissance Theatre

The rising Puritan movement was hostile toward theater, as they felt that "entertainment" was sinful. Politically, playwrights and actors were clients of the monarchy and aristocracy, and most supported the Royalist cause. The Puritan faction, long powerful in London, gained control of the city early in the English Civil War, and on September 2, 1642 ordered the closure of the London theatres. The theatres remained closed for most of the next eighteen years, re-opening after the Restoration of the monarchy in 1660. The re-opened theatres performed many of the plays of the previous era, though often in adapted forms; new genres of Restoration comedy and spectacle soon evolved, giving English theatre of the later seventeenth century its distinctive character.

6

Literary Works of William Tyndale

William Tyndale (494 – 1536) was a 16th-century Protestant reformer and scholar who, influenced by the work of Desiderius Erasmus and Martin Luther, translated considerable parts of the Bible into the Early Modern English of his day. While a number of partial and complete Old English translations had been made from the seventh century onward, and Middle English translations particularly during the 14th century, Tyndale's was the first English translation to draw directly from Hebrew and Greek texts, and the first to take advantage of the new medium of print, which allowed for its wide distribution. In 1535, Tyndale was arrested, jailed in the castle of Vilvoorde outside Brussels for over a year, tried for heresy and burned at the stake. He was strangled before his body was burnt.

Much of Tyndale's work eventually found its way into the King James Version (or "Authorised Version") of the Bible, published in 1611, which, as the work of 54 independent scholars revising the existing English versions, drew significantly on Tyndale's translations. The King James Version New Testament is 83.7 per cent Tyndale's work, with the KJV Old Testament 75.7 per cent Tyndale's.

Whereas John Wycliffe had earlier produced an English translation of the Bible from Latin, Tyndale was the first to translate from the original Greek language. This was only made possible after Erasmus made the Greek New Testament available in Europe

Biography

Tyndale was born around 1490, possibly in one of the villages near Dursley, Gloucestershire. Within his immediate family, the Tyndales were also known at that period as Hychyns (Hitchins), and it was as William Hychyns that Tyndale was educated at Magdalen College School, Oxford. Tyndale's family had migrated to Gloucestershire within living memory of his birth, quite probably as a result of the Wars of the Roses, and it is known that the family derived from Northumberland but had more recently resided in East Anglia. Tyndale's uncle, Edward, was receiver to the lands of Lord Berkeley and it is this fact that provides evidence of the family's origin. Edward Tyndale is recorded in two genealogies as having been the brother of Sir William Tyndale, KB, of Deane, Northumberland, and Hockwald, Norfolk, who was knighted at the marriage of Arthur, Prince of Wales to Katherine of Aragon. Tyndale's family was therefore derived from Baron Adam de Tyndale, a tenant-in-chief of Henry I (and whose family history is related in Tyndall).

Tyndale was admitted to the Degree of Bachelor of Arts at Oxford University in 1512, the same year he became a subdeacon. He was made Master of Arts in July 1515 and was esteemed to be a man of virtuous disposition with life unspotted. The MA degree allowed him to start studying theology, but the official course did not include the study of scripture.

He was a gifted linguist (fluent in French, Greek, Hebrew, German, Italian, Latin, and Spanish in addition to his native English) and subsequently went to Cambridge (possibly studying under Erasmus, whose 1503 *Enchiridion Militis Christiani* — "Handbook of the Christian Knight" — he translated into English). It is also possible according to Monyahan that he met Thomas Bilney and John Frith at Cambridge.

Tyndale became chaplain in the house of Sir John Walsh at Little Sodbury in about 1521, and tutor to his children. His opinions involved him in controversy with his fellow clergymen, and around 1522, he was summoned before the Chancellor of the Diocese of Worcester John Bell though no formal charges were laid.

Soon afterwards, he determined to translate the Bible into English and was convinced that the way to God was through His word and that scripture should be available even to common people. Foxe describes an argument with a "learned" but "blasphemous" clergyman, who had asserted to Tyndale that, "We had better be without God's laws than the Pope's." In a swelling of emotion, Tyndale made his response: "I defy the Pope, and all his laws; and if God spares my life, I will cause the boy that drives the plow to know more of the Scriptures than the Pope himself!"

Tyndale left for London in 1523 to seek permission to translate the Bible into English and to request other help from Bishop Cuthbert Tunstall, a well-known classicist whom Erasmus had praised after working with him on a Greek New Testament. However, the bishop did not regard Tyndale's scholarly credentials highly, was suspicious of his theology and, like many highly-placed churchmen, was uncomfortable with the idea of the Bible in the vernacular. The Church at this time did not deem that a new English translation of Scripture would be helpful. Tunstall told Tyndale he had no room for him in his household. Tyndale preached and studied "at his book" in London for some time, relying on the help of a cloth merchant, Humphrey Monmouth. He then left England under a pseudonym and landed at Hamburg in 1524 with the work he had done so far on his translation of the New Testament. He completed his translation in 1525, with assistance from Observant friar William Roy.

In 1525, publication of his work by Peter Quentell in Cologne was interrupted by anti-Lutheran influence, and it was not until 1526 that a full edition of the New Testament was produced by the printer Peter Schoeffer in Worms, an imperial free city then in the process of adopting Lutheranism. More copies were soon being printed in Antwerp. The book was smuggled into England and Scotland, and was condemned in October 1526 by Tunstall, who issued warnings to booksellers and had copies burned in public. Marius notes that the "spectacle of the scriptures being put to the torch" "provoked controversy even amongst the faithful"

Following the publication of Tyndale's New Testament, Cardinal Wolsey condemned Tyndale as a heretic and Tyndale was first mentioned in open court as a heretic in January 1529.

Tyndale went into hiding, possibly for a time in Hamburg, and carried on working. He revised his New Testament and began translating the Old Testament and writing various treatises. In 1530, he wrote *The Practyse of Prelates,* opposing Henry VIII's divorce on the grounds that it was unscriptural and was a plot by Cardinal Wolsey to get Henry entangled in the papal courts. This resulted in the king's wrath being directed at him: he asked the emperor Charles V to have Tyndale apprehended and returned to England. In 1532 Thomas More published a six volume *Confutation of Tyndale's Answer* in response to Tyndale's *An Answer unto Sir Thomas More's Dialogue* in which he alleged Tyndale was a traitor and a heretic. Moynahan writes that More "despised, feared and loathed Tyndale; he, and his English Testament, were the obsessions of More's life. His hatred was not slaked by the savaging he had given Tyndale in his Dialogue, nor by the half a million words he had poured into the Confutation, this was mere flood of ink, where More was satisfied only by blood and the flames of the 'shorte fyre." Monynahan makes the case that More was a powerful factor in the betrayal and death of Tyndale.

Eventually, Tyndale was betrayed to the authorities. He was seized in Antwerp in 1535, betrayed by Henry Phillips, and held in the castle of Vilvoorde near Brussels.

He was tried on a charge of heresy in 1536 and condemned to death, despite Thomas Cromwell's intercession on his behalf. He "was strangled to death while tied at the stake, and then his dead body was burned". Foxe gives 6 October as the date of commemoration (left-hand date column), but gives no date of death (right-hand date column). The traditional date of commemoration is 6 October, but records of Tyndale's imprisonment suggest the date might have been some weeks earlier.

Tyndale's final words, spoken "at the stake with a fervent zeal, and a loud voice", were reported as

"Lord! Open the King of England's eyes." Within four years, four English translations of the Bible, all based on Tyndale's work, were published in England, and one of them was the official English Bible.

Printed Works

Most well known for his translation of the Bible, Tyndale was an active writer and translator. Not only did Tyndale's works focus on the way in which religion should be carried out, but were also greatly keyed towards the political arena.

> "They have ordained that no man shall look on the Scripture, until he be noselled in heathen learning eight or nine years and armed with false principles, with which he is an clean shut out of the understanding of the Scripture."

A critical John Bell claimed that Tyndale was arguing "we were better off to be without God's laws than the pope's". Tyndale replied that the fact that he defied the pope and all his laws did not mean he rejected the authority of the scriptures:

Legacy

In translating the Bible, Tyndale introduced new words into the English language, and many were subsequently used in the King James Bible:

1) *Jehovah.*
2) *Passover,*
3) *Atonement,* which goes beyond mere "reconciliation" to mean "to unite" or "to cover", which springs from the Hebrew kippur, the Old Testament version of kippur being the covering of doorposts with blood, or "Day of Atonement".

4) *Scapegoat.*

He also coined such familiar phrases as:

1) lead us not into temptation but deliver us from evil
2) knock and it shall be opened undo you
3) twinkling of an eye
4) a moment in time
5) fashion not yourselves to the world
6) seek and you shall find
7) ask and it shall be given you
8) judge not that you not be judged
9) the word of God which liveth and lasteth forever
10) let there be light
11) the powers that be
12) my brother's keeper
13) the salt of the earth
14) a law unto themselves
15) filthy lucre
16) it came to pass
17) gave up the ghost
18) the signs of the times
19) the spirit is willing
20) live and move and have our being
21) fight the good fight

Some of the new words and phrases introduced by Tyndale did not sit well with the hierarchy of the Roman Catholic Church, using words like 'Overseer' rather than 'Bishop' and 'Elder' rather than 'Priest', and (very controversially), 'congregation' rather than 'Church' and 'love' rather than 'charity'. Tyndale contended (citing Erasmus) that the Greek New Testament did not support the traditional Roman Catholic readings.

Contention from Roman Catholics came not only from from real or perceived errors in translation but a fear of the erosion of their social power if Christians could read the bible in their own language "the Pope's dogma is bloody" Tyndale wrote in his *Obedience of a Christian Man*. Tyndale translated "Church" as "congregation" and translated "priest" as "elder." Moynahan explains Tyndale's reasons for this: "This was a direct threat to the Church's ancient-but so Tyndale here made clear, non-scriptural- claim to be the body of Christ on earth. To change these words was to strip the Church hierarchy of its pretensions to be Christ's terrestrial representative, and to award this honour to individual worshippers who made up each congregation." Thomas More commented that searching for errors in the Tyndale Bible was similar to searching for water in the sea, and charged Tyndale's translation of *Obedience of a Christian Man* with having about a thousand falsely translated errors. More was obsessed with persecuting evangelical bible-reading Christians so his claims in this regard are likely to be biased Bishcp Cuthbert Tunstall of London declared that there were upwards of 2,000 errors in Tyndale's Bible. Tunstall in 1523 had denied Tyndale the permission required under the Constitutions of Oxford (1409), that were still in force, to translate the Bible into English.

In response to allegations of inaccuracies in his translation in the New Testament, Tyndale in the

Prologue of his 1525 tranlsation wrote that he never intentionally altered or misrepresented any of the Bible in his translation, but that he has sought to "interpret the sense of the scripture and the meaning of the spirit".

While translating, Tyndale followed Erasmus' (1522) Greek edition of the New Testament. In his Preface to his 1534 New Testament he not only goes into some detail about the Greek tenses but also points out that there is often a Hebrew idiom underlying the Greek. The Tyndale Society adduces much further evidence to show that his translations were made directly from the original Hebrew and Greek sources he had at his disposal. For example, the Prolegomena in Mombert's *William Tyndale's Five Books of Moses* show that Tyndale's Pentateuch is a translation of the Hebrew original.His translation also drew on Latin Vulgate and Luther's 1521 September Testament.

Of the first (1526) edition of Tyndale's New Testament, only three copies survive. The only complete copy is part of the Bible Collection of Württembergische Landesbibliothek, Stuttgart. The copy of the British Library is almost complete, lacking only the title page and list of contents. Another rarity of Tyndale's is the Pentateuch of which only nine remain.

Impact on the English Bible

The men who translated the Revised Standard Version in the 1940s noted that Tyndale's translation inspired the great translations to follow, including the Great Bible of 1539, the Geneva Bible of 1560, the Bishops' Bible of 1568, the Douay-Rheims Bible of 1582–1609, and the King James Version of 1611, of which the RSV translators noted: "It [the KJV] kept felicitous phrases and apt expressions, from whatever source, which had stood the test of public usage. It owed most, especially in the New Testament, to Tyndale". Many scholars today believe that such is the case. Moynahan writes: "A complete analysis of the Authorised Version, known down the generations as "the AV" or "the King James" was made in 1998. It shows that Tyndale's words account for 84% of the New Testament and for 75.8% of the Old Testament books that he translated. Joan Bridgman makes the comment in the *Contemporary Review* that, "He [Tyndale] is the mainly unrecognised translator of the most influential book in the world. Although the Authorised King James Version is ostensibly the production of a learned committee of churchmen, it is mostly cribbed from Tyndale with some reworking of his translation."

Many of the great English versions since then have drawn inspiration from Tyndale, such as the Revised Standard Version, the New American Standard Bible, and the English Standard Version. Even the paraphrases like the Living Bible have been inspired by the same desire to make the Bible understandable to Tyndale's proverbial ploughboy.

Memorials

There is a memorial to Tyndale in Vilvoorde, where he was executed. It was erected in 1913 by Friends of the Trinitarian Bible Society of London and the Belgian Bible Society. There is also a small William Tyndale Museum in the town, attached to the Protestant church.

A bronze statue by Sir Joseph Boehm commemorating the life and work of Tyndale was erected in Victoria Embankment Gardens on the Thames Embankment, London in 1884. It shows his right hand on an open Bible, which is itself resting on an early printing press.

The Tyndale Monument, was erected in 1866 on a hill above his supposed birthplace, North Nibley.

A number of colleges, schools and study centres have been named in his honour, including Tyndale House (Cambridge), Tyndale University College and Seminary (Toronto), the Tyndale-Carey Graduate School affiliated to the Bible College of New Zealand, William Tyndale College (Farmington Hills, Michigan), and Tyndale Theological Seminary (Shreveport, Louisiana, and Fort Worth, Texas), as well as the independent Tyndale Theological Seminary in Badhoevedorp, near Amsterdam, The Netherlands.

Liturgical Commemoration

By tradition Tyndale's death is commemorated on October 6. There are commemorations on this date in the church calendars of members of the Anglican Communion, initially as one of the "days of optional devotion" in the American Book of Common Prayer, and a "black-letter day" in the Church of England's Alternative Service Book.

7

Writings of John Milton

John Milton (1608-1674) was an English poet, author, polemicist and civil servant for the Commonwealth of England. He is best known for his epic poem *Paradise Lost*.

He was a scholarly man of letters, a polemical writer, and an official serving under Oliver Cromwell. Milton is believed to have been a Calvinist and the question of predestination and freedom was crucial to his intellectual orientation. He wrote at a time of religious and political flux in England, and his poetry and prose reflect deep convictions, often reacting to contemporary circumstances such as his treatise condemning censorship, *Areopagitica*. As well as English, he wrote in Latin and Italian, and had an international reputation during his lifetime.

After his death, Milton's personal reputation oscillated, a state of affairs that continued through the centuries. At an early stage he became the subject of partisan biographies, such as that of John Toland from the nonconformist perspective, and a hostile account by Anthony à Wood. Samuel Johnson described him as "an acrimonious and surly republican"; but William Hayley's 1796 biography called him the "greatest

English author". He remains generally regarded "as one of the preeminent writers in the English language and as a thinker of world importance."

Biography

One can situate both Milton's poetry and his politics historically. The phases of his life parallel major historical divisions of Stuart Britain. Under the increasingly personal rule of Charles I and its breakdown in constitutional confusion and war, Milton studied, travelled, wrote poetry mostly for private circulation, and launched a career as pamphleteer and publicist. A more detailed treatment can be found at John Milton's early life. Under the Commonwealth of England, from being thought dangerously radical and even heretical, the shift in accepted attitudes in government placed him in public office, and he acted as an official spokesman in certain of his publications. The Restoration of 1660 deprived Milton, now completely blind, of his public platform, but this period saw him complete most of his major works of poetry. Milton had a great impact on the Romantic movement in England, as shown in fellow poet William Wordsworth's sonnet London, 1802. Wordsworth calls upon him to rise from the dead and aid in returning England to its former glory.

Milton's views developed from his very extensive reading, as well as travel and experience, from his student days of the 1620s to the English Revolution. By the time of his death in 1674, Milton was impoverished and on the margins of English intellectual life, yet unrepentant for his political choices, and of Europe-wide fame.

Early life

John Milton's father, also named John Milton (1562-1647), moved to London around 1583 after being disinherited by his devout Catholic father, Richard Milton, for embracing Protestantism. In London, the senior John Milton married Sarah Jeffrey (1572-1637), the poet's mother, and found lasting financial success as a scrivener. He lived and worked out of a house on Bread Street, where the Mermaid Tavern was located in Cheapside. The elder Milton was noted for his skill as a musical composer, and this talent left Milton with a lifetime appreciation for music and friendship with musicians like Henry Lawes.

After Milton was born, on 9 December 1608 his father's prosperity provided his eldest son with a private tutor, Thomas Young, and then a place at St Paul's School in London. There he began the study of Latin and Greek, and the classical languages left an imprint on his poetry in English. His first datable compositions are two psalms done at age 15 at Long Bennington. One contemporary source is the *Brief Lives* of John Aubrey, an uneven compilation including first-hand reports. In the work, Aubrey quotes Christopher, Milton's younger brother: "When he was young, he studied very hard and sat up very late, commonly till twelve or one o'clock at night".

Milton matriculated at Christ's College, Cambridge, in 1625 and graduated with a B.A. in 1629, ranking fourth of 24 honours graduates that year in the University of Cambridge. Preparing to become an Anglican priest, he stayed on to obtain his Master of Arts degree on 3 July 1632.

Milton was probably rusticated for quarrelling in his first year with his tutor, William Chappell. He was certainly at home in the Lent Term 1626; there he wrote his *Elegia Prima,* a first Latin elegy, to Charles Diodati, a friend from St Paul's. Based on remarks of John Aubrey, Chappell "whipt" Milton. This story is now disputed. Certainly Milton disliked Chappell. Christopher Hill cautiously notes that Milton was "apparently" rusticated, and that the differences between Chappell and Milton may have been either religious or personal, as far as we can know. Another factor, possibly, was the plague, by which Cambridge was badly affected in 1625. Later in 1626 Milton's tutor was Nathaniel Tovey.

At Cambridge Milton was on good terms with Edward King, for whom he later wrote *Lycidas.* He also befriended Anglo-American dissident and theologian, Roger Williams. Milton tutored Williams in Hebrew in exchange for lessons in Dutch. Otherwise at Cambridge he developed a reputation for poetic skill and general erudition, but experienced alienation from his peers and university life as a whole. Watching his fellow students attempting comedy upon the college stage, he later observed 'they thought themselves gallant men, and I thought them fools'. Milton, due to his hair, which he wore long, and his general delicacy of manner, was known as the "Lady of Christ's".

The university curriculum was dour, and he worked towards formal debates on topics, conducted in Latin. Yet his corpus is not devoid of humour, notably his sixth prolusion and his epitaphs on the death of Thomas Hobson. While at Cambridge he wrote a number of his well-known shorter English poems, among them *On the Morning of Christ's Nativity,* his *Epitaph on the admirable Dramatick Poet, W. Shakespeare,* his first poem to appear in print, *L'Allegro* and *Il Penseroso.*

Study, Poetry and Travel

Upon receiving his M.A. in 1632, Milton retired to Hammersmith, his father's new home since the previous year. He also lived at Horton, Berkshire, from 1635 and undertook six years of self-directed private study. Christopher Hill points out that this was not retreat into a rural or pastoral idyll at all: Hammersmith was then a "suburban village" falling into the orbit of London, and even Horton was becoming deforested, and suffered from the plague. He read both ancient and modern works of theology, philosophy, history, politics, literature and science, in preparation for a prospective poetical career. Milton's intellectual development can be charted via entries in his commonplace book (like a scrapbook), now in the British Library. As a result of such intensive study, Milton is considered to be among the most learned of all English poets; in addition to his years of private study, Milton had command of Latin, Greek, Hebrew, French, Spanish, and Italian from his school and undergraduate days; he also added Old English to his linguistic repertoire in the 1650s while researching his *History of Britain,* and probably acquired proficiency in Dutch soon after.

Milton continued to write poetry during this period of study: his *Arcades* and *Comus* were both commissioned for masques composed for noble patrons, connections of the Egerton family, and performed in 1632 amd 1634 respectively. *Comus* argues for the virtuousness of temperance and chastity.

He contributed his pastoral elegy *Lycidas* to a memorial collection for one of his Cambridge classmates. Drafts of these poems are preserved in Milton's poetry notebook, known as the Trinity

Manuscript because it is now kept at Trinity College, Cambridge.

In May 1638, Milton embarked upon a tour of France and Italy that lasted up to July or August 1639. His travels supplemented his study with new and direct experience of artistic and religious traditions, especially Roman Catholicism. He met famous theorists and intellectuals of the time, and was able to display his poetic skills. For specific details to what happened within Milton's "grand tour", there appears to be just one primary source: Milton's own *Defensio Secunda*. Although there are other records, some letters and some references in his other prose tracts, the bulk of the information about the tour comes therefore from a work that, according to Barbara Lewalski, "was not intended as autobiography but as rhetoric, designed to emphasize his sterling reputation with the learned of Europe."

He travelled a route common to other Englishmen touring Europe at the time. He first went to Calais, and then on to Paris, riding horseback. While in Paris, he brought a letter from diplomat Henry Wotton which allowed him to be introduced at the British embassy. From ambassador John Scudamore, Milton received other letters of introduction and met Hugo Grotius, a Dutch law philosopher, playwright and poet. Milton left France after this meeting and visiting various landmarks. He traveled south, from Nice to Genoa and then onto Livorno and Pisa. He reached Florence in July 1638. While there, Milton enjoyed many of the sites and structures of the city. His candor of manner and erudite neo-Latin poetry made him friends in Florentine intellectual circles, and he met a number of famous and influential people through these connections including the astronomer Galileo who was under virtual house arrest at Arcetri, as well as others. He also spent time at the Florentine academies. In particular, Milton probably visited the Florentine Academy and the Academia della Crusca along with smaller academies in the area including the Apatisti (those free from the *pathos*, hence free from emotions and passions) and the Svoghati.

He left Florence in September to continue to Rome. With the connections from Florence, Milton was able to have easy access into Rome's intellectual society. His poetic abilities impressed those like Giovanni Salzilli, who praised Milton within an epigram. In late October, Milton, despite his dislike for the Society of Jesus attended a dinner given by the English College, Rome, meeting English Catholics who were also guests, theologian Henry Holden and the poet Patrick Cary. There is little else known about this time beyond that he met David Codner, an English Benedictine with court connections, who also praised Milton's poetry, and that he attended various musical events, including oratorios, operas, and melodramas. Milton left for Naples near the end of November, where he stayed only for a month because of the Spanish control. During that time, he was introduced to Giovanni Battista Manso, patron to both Torquato Tasso and to Giovanni Battista Marino. Manso became Milton's guide through Naples. He gave Milton books, and a teasing distich based on Gregory the Great's pun on "Angle" and "angel" when describing the English. Milton responded in his *Mansus* that he was grateful for the gesture of goodwill and claims Manso as his patron.

Originally, Milton wanted to leave Naples in order to travel to Sicily, and then on to Greece, but he returned to England during the summer of 1639 because of what he claimed, in *Defensio Secunda*, were "sad tidings of civil war in England." To further complicate matters, Milton received word that his childhood friend, Diodati, had died. Milton in fact stayed another seven months on the continent, and spent time at Geneva with Diodati's uncle after he returned to Rome. In *Defensio Secunda*, Milton proclaimed he was warned against a return to Rome because of his frankness about religion, but he stayed in the city for two months and was able to experience Carnival and meet Lukas Holste, a Vatican librarian who guided Milton through its collection. He was introduced to Cardinal Francesco Barberini, who invited Milton to an opera hosted by the Cardinal. Around March, Milton traveled once again to Florence and stayed there for two months, he attended further meetings of the academies and spent time with friends. After leaving Florence, he traveled through Lucca, Bologna, and Ferrara before coming to Venice. In Venice, Milton was exposed to a model of Republicanism, but he soon found another model when he traveled to Geneva. From Switzerland, Milton traveled to Paris and then to Calais before finally arriving back in England in either July or August 1639.

Civil War, Prose Tracts and Marriage

On returning to England, where the Bishops' Wars presaged further armed conflict, Milton began to write prose tracts against episcopacy, in the service of the Puritan and Parliamentary cause. Milton's first foray into polemics was *Of Reformation touching Church Discipline in England* (1641), followed by *Of Prelatical Episcopacy*, the two defences of Smectymnuus (a group of presbyterian divines named from their initials: the

"TY" belonged to Milton's old tutor Thomas Young), and *The Reason of Church-Government Urged against Prelaty*. With frequent passages of real eloquence lighting up the rough controversial style of the period, and deploying a wide knowledge of church history, he vigorously attacked the High-church party of the Church of England and their leader, William Laud, Archbishop of Canterbury.

Though supported by his father's investments, at this time Milton became a private schoolmaster, educating his nephews and other children of the well-to-do. This experience, and discussions with educational reformer Samuel Hartlib, led him to write in 1644 his short tract, *Of Education*, urging a reform of the national universities.

In June 1643 Milton paid a visit to the manor house at Forest Hill, Oxfordshire and returned with a 16-year-old bride, Mary Powell. A month later, finding life difficult with the severe 35-year-old schoolmaster and pamphleteer, Mary returned to her family. Because of the outbreak of the Civil War, she did not return until 1645; in the meantime her desertion prompted Milton, over the next three years, to publish a series of pamphlets arguing for the legality and morality of divorce. In 1643 Milton had a brush with the authorities over these writings, in parallel with Hezekiah Woodward who had more trouble. It was the hostile response accorded the divorce tracts that spurred Milton to write *Areopagitica*, his celebrated attack on censorship.

Secretary for Foreign Tongues

With the parliamentary victory in the Civil War, Milton used his pen in defence of the republican principles represented by the Commonwealth. *The Tenure of Kings and Magistrates* (1649) defended popular government and implicitly sanctioned the regicide; Milton's political reputation got him appointed Secretary for Foreign Tongues by the Council of State in March 1649. Though Milton's main job description was to compose the English Republic's foreign correspondence in Latin, he also was called upon to produce propaganda for the regime and to serve as a censor. In October 1649 he published *Eikonoklastes*, an explicit defence of the regicide, in response to the *Eikon Basilike*, a phenomenal best-seller popularly attributed to Charles I that portrayed the King as an innocent Christian martyr. A month after Milton had tried to break this powerful image of Charles I (the literal translation of Eikonoklastes is 'the image breaker'), the exiled Charles II and his party published a defence of monarchy, *Defensio Regia Pro Carolo Primo*, written by the leading humanist Claudius Salmasius. By January of the following year, Milton was ordered to write a defence of the English people by the Council of State. Given the European audience and the English Republic's desire to establish diplomatic and cultural legitimacy, Milton worked much more slowly than usual, as he drew upon the vast array of learning marshalled by his years of study to compose a suitably withering riposte. On 24 February 1652 Milton published his Latin defence of the English People, *Defensio Pro Populo Anglicano*, also known as the *First Defence*. Milton's pure Latin prose and evident learning, exemplified in the *First Defence*, quickly made him a European reputation, and the work ran to numerous editions.

In 1654, in response to a Royalist tract, *Regii sanguinis clamor*, a work that made many personal attacks on Milton, he completed a second defence of the English nation, *Defensio secunda,* which praised Oliver Cromwell, now Lord Protector, while exhorting him to remain true to the principles of the Revolution. Alexander Morus, to whom Milton wrongly attributed the *Clamor,* published an attack on Milton, in response to which Milton published the autobiographical *Defensio pro se* in 1655. In addition to these literary defences of the Commonwealth and his character, Milton continued to translate official correspondence into Latin. The probable onset of glaucoma finally resulted in total blindness by 1654, forcing him to dictate his verse and prose to amanuenses (helpers), one of whom was the poet Andrew Marvell. One of his best-known sonnets, "On His Blindness," is presumed to date from this period.

The Restoration

Though Cromwell's death in 1658 caused the English Republic to collapse into feuding military and political factions, Milton stubbornly clung to the beliefs that had originally inspired him to write for the Commonwealth. In 1659 he published *A Treatise of Civil Power,* attacking the concept of a state-dominated church (the position known as Erastianism), as well as *Considerations touching the likeliest means to remove hirelings,* denouncing corrupt practises in church governance. As the Republic disintegrated, Milton wrote several proposals to retain a non-monarchical government against the wishes of parliament, soldiers and the people:

1) *A Letter to a Friend, Concerning the Ruptures of the Commonwealth,* written in October 1659, was a response to General Lambert's recent dissolution of the Rump Parliament

2) *Proposals of certain expedients for the preventing of a civil war now feared,* written in November 1659

3) *The Ready and Easy Way to Establishing a Free Commonwealth,* in two editions, responded to General Monck's march towards London to restore the Long Parliament (which led to the restoration of the monarchy). The work is an impassioned, bitter, and futile jeremiad damning the English people for backsliding from the cause of liberty and advocating the establishment of an authoritarian rule by an oligarchy set up by unelected parliament.

Upon the Restoration in May 1660, Milton went into hiding for his life, while a warrant was issued for his arrest and his writings burnt. He re-emerged after a general pardon was issued, but was nevertheless arrested and briefly imprisoned before influential friends, such as Marvell, now an MP, intervened. On 24 February 1663 Milton remarried, for a third and final time, a Wistaston, Cheshire-born woman Elizabeth (Betty) Minshull, then aged 24, and spent the remaining decade of his life living quietly in London, only retiring to a cottage - Milton's Cottage - in Chalfont St. Giles, his only extant home, during the Great Plague of London.

During this period Milton published several minor prose works, such as a grammar textbook, *Art of Logic,* and a *History of Britain.* His only explicitly political tracts were the 1672 *Of True Religion,* arguing for toleration (except for Catholics), and a translation of a Polish tract advocating an elective monarchy. Both these works were referred to in the Exclusion debate - the attempt to exclude the heir presumptive, James, Duke of York, from the throne of England because he was Roman Catholic - that would preoccupy politics in the 1670s and '80s and precipitate the formation of the Whig party and the Glorious Revolution.

Milton died of kidney failure on 8 November 1674 and was buried in the church of St Giles Cripplegate; according to an early biographer, his funeral was attended by "his learned and great Friends in London, not without a friendly concourse of the Vulgar."

Published Poetry

Milton's poetry was slow to see the light of day, at least under his name. His first published poem was *On Shakespear* (1630), anonymously included in the Second Folio edition of Shakespeare. In the midst of the excitement attending the possibility of establishing a new English government, Milton collected his work in *1645 Poems*. The anonymous edition of *Comus* was published in 1637, and the publication of *Lycidas* in 1638 in *Justa Edouardo King Naufrago* was signed J. M. Otherwise the 1645 collection was the only poetry of his to see print, until *Paradise Lost* appeared in 1667.

Paradise Lost—Milton's *magnum opus*

Milton's *magnum opus*, the blank-verse epic poem *Paradise Lost*, which appeared in a quarto edition in 1667, was composed by the blind Milton from 1658–1664 through dictation given to a series of aides in his employ. It reflects his personal despair at the failure of the Revolution, yet affirms an ultimate optimism in human potential. Milton encoded many references to his unyielding support for the "Good Old Cause."

Milton sold the copyright of this monumental work to his publisher for a seemingly trifling £10; this was not a particularly outlandish deal at the time.

Milton followed up *Paradise Lost* with its sequel, *Paradise Regained,* published alongside the tragedy *Samson Agonistes,* in 1671. Both these works also resonate with Milton's post-Restoration political situation. Just before his death in 1674, Milton supervised a second edition of *Paradise Lost,* accompanied by an explanation of "why the poem rhymes not" and prefatory verses by Marvell. Milton republished his *1645 Poems* in 1673, as well a collection of his letters and the Latin prolusions from his Cambridge days. A 1668 edition of *Paradise Lost,* reported to have been Milton's personal copy, is now housed in the archives of the University of Western Ontario.

Paradise Lost is an epic poem in blank verse by the 17th-century English poet John Milton. It was originally published in 1667 in ten books. A second edition followed in 1674, redivided into twelve books (in the manner of the division of Virgil's *Aeneid*) with minor revisions throughout and a note on the verification. The poem concerns the Christian story of the Fall of Man: the temptation of Adam and Eve by the fallen angel Satan and their expulsion from the Garden of Eden. Milton's purpose, stated in Book I, is to "justify the ways of God to men" and elucidate the conflict between God's eternal foresight and free will.

Milton incorporates Paganism, classical Greek references, and Christianity within the poem. It deals with diverse topics from marriage, politics (Milton was politically active during the time of the English Civil War), and monarchy, and grapples with many difficult theological issues, including fate, predestination, the Trinity, and the introduction of sin and death into the world, as well as angels, fallen angels, Satan, and the war in heaven. Milton draws on his knowledge of languages, and diverse sources – primarily Genesis, much of the New Testament, the deuterocanonical Book of Enoch, and other parts of the Old Testament.

Synopsis

The story was revised into twelve books after initial publication, following the model of the *Aeneid* of Virgil. The book lengths vary – the longest being Book IX, with 1,189 lines and the shortest, Book VII, having 640. In the second edition, each book was preceded by a summary titled "The Argument". The poem follows the epic tradition of starting *in medias res* (Latin for *in the midst of things*), the background story being told in Books V-VI.

Milton's story contains two arcs: one of Satan (Lucifer) and another of Adam and Eve. The story of Satan follows the epic convention of large-scale warfare. It begins after Satan and the other rebel angels have been defeated and cast by God into Hell, or as it is also called in the poem, Tartarus. In Pandæmonium, Satan employs his rhetorical skill to organize his followers; he is aided by his lieutenants Mammon and Beelzebub. Belial and Moloch are also present. At the end of the debate, Satan nominates himself to poison the newly-created Earth. He braves the dangers of the Abyss alone in a manner reminiscent of Odysseus or Aeneas.

The story of Adam and Eve's temptation and fall is a fundamentally different, new kind of epic: a domestic one. Adam and Eve are presented for the first time in Christian literature as having a full relationship while still without sin. They have passions and distinct personalities. Satan successfully tempts

Eve by preying on her vanity and tricking her with rhetoric, and Adam, seeing Eve has sinned, knowingly commits the same sin. He declares to Eve that since she was made from his flesh, they are bound to one another so that if she dies, he must also die. In this manner Milton portrays Adam as a heroic figure but also as a deeper sinner than Eve since he is smarter than Eve and knows that what he's doing is wrong.

After eating the fruit, Adam and Eve have lustful sex, and at first, Adam is convinced that Eve was right in thinking that eating the fruit would be beneficial. However, they soon fall asleep, having terrible nightmares, and after they awake, they experience guilt and shame for the first time. Realizing that they have committed a terrible act against God, they engage in mutual recrimination.

However, Eve's pleas to Adam reconcile them somewhat. Her encouragement enables Adam and Eve both to approach God, to "bow and sue for grace with suppliant knee," and to receive grace from God. Adam goes on a vision journey with an angel where he witnesses the errors of man and the Great Flood, and is saddened by the sin that they have released through consumption of the fruit. However, he is also shown hope — the possibility of redemption — through a vision of Jesus Christ. They are then cast out of Eden and the archangel Michael says that Adam may find "A paradise within thee, happier far." They now have a more distant relationship with God, who is omnipresent but invisible (unlike the previous, tangible, Father in the Garden of Eden).

The contents of the 12 books are:

Book I: In a long, twisting opening sentence mirroring the epic poetry of the Ancient Greeks, the poet invokes the "Heavenly Muse" (the Holy Spirit) and states his theme, the Fall of Man, and his aim, to "justify the ways of God to men." Satan, Beelzebub, and the other rebel angels are described as lying on a lake of fire, from which Satan rises up to claim Hell as his own domain and delivers a rousing speech to his followers ("Better to reign in Hell, than serve in heav'n"). The logic of Satan (Satanic Logic) is introduced by: "The mind is its own place, and in itself, can make a Heaven of Hell, a Hell of Heaven."

Book II: Satan and the rebel angels debate whether to wage another war on Heaven, and Beelzebub tells them of a new world being built which is to be the home of Man. Satan decides to visit this new world, passes through the Gates of Hell, past the sentries Sin and Death, and journeys through the realm of Chaos. Here, Satan is described as having given birth to Sin with a burst of flame from his forehead, before he began open warfare with God — as Athena was born from the head of Zeus.

Book III: God observes Satan's journey and foretells how Satan will bring about Man's Fall. God emphasises, that the Fall will come about as a result of Man's own free will, and excuses himself of responsibility. The Son of God offers himself as a ransom for Man's disobedience, an offer which God accepts, ordaining the Son's future incarnation and punishment. Satan arrives at the rim of the universe, disguises himself as an angel, and is directed to Earth by Uriel, Guardian of the Sun. William Blake, *Satan Watching the Caresses of Adam and Eve,* 1808, (from William Blake's illustrations of Paradise Lost)

Book IV: Satan journeys to the Garden of Eden, where he observes Adam and Eve discussing the forbidden Tree of Knowledge of Good and Evil. Satan, observing their innocence and beauty hesitates in his task, but concludes that "reason just,/ Honour and empire" compel him to do this deed which he "should abhor." Satan tries to tempt Eve while she sleeps, but is discovered by the angels. The angel Gabriel expels Satan from the Garden.

Book V: Eve awakes and relates her dream to Adam. God sends Raphael to warn and encourage Adam: they talk of free will and predestination; Raphael tells Adam the story of how Satan inspired his angels to revolt against God.

Book VI: Raphael goes on to describe further the war in Heaven and explains how the Son of God drove Satan and his minions down to Hell.

Book VII: Raphael explains to Adam that God then decided to create another world (the Earth); he again warns Adam not to eat the fruit of the Tree of Knowledge, for "in the day thou eat'st, thou diest;/ Death is the penalty imposed, beware,/ And govern well thy appetite, lest Sin/ Surprise thee, and her black attendant Death".

Book VIII: Adam tells the story of his creation from his own perspective, providing a counterpoint to Raphael's instruction in Book VI. Adam asks Raphael for knowledge concerning the stars and the angelic nature; Raphael warns "heaven is for thee too high/ To know what passes there; be lowly wise", and advises modesty and patience.

Book IX: Satan returns to Eden and enters into the body of a sleeping serpent. The serpent tempts Eve to eat the fruit of the Tree of Knowledge. She eats and takes some fruit for Adam. Adam, realising Eve has been tricked, decides he would rather die with Eve than live without her; he eats of the fruit. At first the two become intoxicated by the fruit; they become lustful, engaging in sexual intercourse; afterwards, in their loss of innocence Adam and Eve cover their nakedness and fall into despair: "They sat them down to weep, nor only tears/ Rained at their eyes, but high winds worse within/ Began to rise, high passions, anger, hate,/ Mistrust, suspicion, discord, and shook greatly/ Their inward state of mind."

Book X: God sends his Son to Eden to deliver judgment on Adam and Eve. Satan returns in triumph to Hell.

Book XI: The Son of God pleads with his Father on behalf of Adam and Eve. God decrees the couple must be expelled from the Garden, and the angel Michael descends to deliver God's judgment. Michael begins to unfold the future history of the world to Adam.

Book XII: Michael tells Adam of the eventual coming of the Messiah, before leading Adam and Eve from the Garden. They have lost the physical Paradise, but now have the opportunity to enjoy a "Paradise within... happier farr." The poem ends: "The World was all before them/ where to choose Their place of rest/ and Providence Their guide: They hand in hand with wandering steps and slow/ Through Eden took, Their solitaire way." Milton has connected the condition of Adam and Eve with the condition of the reader of the epic.

Characters

Satan: Satan is the first major character introduced in the poem. He is introduced to Hell after a failed rebellion to wrestle control of Heaven from God. Satan's desire to rebel against his creator stems from his unwillingness to accept the fact he is a created being, and that he is not self-sufficient, which is rooted in his extreme Pride. One of the ways he tries to justify his rebellion against God is by claiming that he and the angels are self-created, declaring the angels "self-begot, self-raised", thereby eliminating God's authority over them as their creator.

Satan is narcissistic, self-pitying, and persuasive although his logic is almost always flawed, disingenuous, misguiding, or all three. Satan's persuasive powers are first evident when he makes arguments to his angel-followers as to why they should try to overthrow God. He argues that they ought to have equal rights to God and that Heaven is an unfair monarchy, stating, "Who can in reason then or right assume/ Monarchy over such as live by right/ His equals, if in power and splendor less / In freedom equal? or can introduce/ Law and edict on us, who without law/ Err not, much less for this to be our Lord,/ And look for adoration to th' abuse/ Of those imperial titles which assert/ Our being ordained to govern, not to serve?."

Satan's persuasive powers are also evident during the scene in which he assumes the body of a snake in order to convince Eve to eat from the Tree of Knowledge of Good and Evil. First, he wins Eve's trust by giving her endless compliments. And when she is perplexed (and impressed) by a "serpent" that is able to talk, Satan tells her that he gained the ability to talk by eating from the Tree of Knowledge and argues that if she were to also eat from the Tree, she would become god-like. He convinces her that the fruit will not kill her and that God will not be upset with her if she eats from the tree. Like his argument to his followers, Satan also argues against God's omnipotence, stating "Why then was [eating from the Tree of Knowledge of Good and Evil] forbid? Why but to awe,/ Why but to keep ye low and ignorant, / [God's] worshippers; he knows that in the day/ Ye eat thereof, your eyes that seem so clear,/ Yet are but dim, shall perfectly be then/ Opened and cleared, and ye shall be as gods./ So ye shall die perhaps, by putting off/ Human, to put on gods."

Unlike the Biblical Satan, Milton's Satan feels guilt and doubt before he tricks Eve, knowing the results of his actions will curse innocents. Similarly, Satan has feelings of guilt when he first enters Paradise. But his feelings always turn to hate once he reflects on his own exile from Heaven.

The role of Satan as a driving force in the poem has been the subject of much scholarly debate. Positions range from views of William Blake who stated Milton "wrote in fetters when wrote of Angels and God, and at liberty when of Devils and Hell, [because] he was a true Poet and of the Devil's party without knowing it" to critic William H. Marshall's interpretation of the poem as a Christian morality tale.

Adam: Adam is the first human in Eden created by God. He is more intelligent than Eve and is also stronger, not only physically but morally. From the questions he asks the angel Raphael, it is clear that Adam has a deep, intellectual curiosity about his existence, God, Heaven, and the nature of the world. This is a kind of curiosity that Eve does not have.

As in the Bible, Eve is subservient to Adam, but in Milton's version of the story, Adam is rather easily manipulated by Eve's charms and good looks. Adam, in Milton's version of the character, is worshipful of

Eve, partially because of her great beauty, and at times, is subservient to her wishes. Hence, the power dynamic between Adam and Eve is more complicated than the one that is established in the Bible.

Adam also feels a noble sense of responsibility towards Eve (since she was, after all, created from his rib), and he fears for her safety, especially after hearing from the angel Raphael of Satan's infiltration of Paradise.

As opposed to the Biblical Adam, this version of Adam is given a glimpse of the future of mankind (this includes a synopsis of stories from The Old and New Testaments), by the angel Michael, before he has to leave Paradise.

Eve: Eve is the second human created, taken from one of Adam's ribs and shaped into a female form of Adam. In a positive sense (depending on your point of view), she is the model of a good subject and wife. She consents to Adam leading her away from her reflection when they first meet, trusting Adam's authority in their relationship until she is influenced by Satan.

She is extremely beautiful, and her beauty not only obsesses Adam but also herself. After she is born, she gazes at her reflection in a pool of water, transfixed by her image. Even after Adam calls out to her, she returns to her image. It is not until God tells her to go to Adam that she consents to being led from the pool.

Eve first comes into contact with satanic influence in her dreams. After this incident she starts to develop the independent streak that perplexes Adam, particularly when she insists on going off by herself to work in the garden, even though Adam warns her against it.

Once she is alone, Satan tempts her to eat from the Tree of Knowledge of Good and Evil. He approaches her in the body of a snake and manipulates her by appealing to her pride and vanity.

Likewise, she soon gets Adam to eat from the tree as well, though he does this because he doesn't want to lose Eve. This creates a complexity that is not in the Biblical version of the story. In this version, Adam reasons that Eve will probably die soon from eating the fruit, so he eats the fruit because he would rather die with her than live alone.

Later, when they don't die and Adam realizes that their actions in the garden have cursed all of mankind, he is harsh on Eve, blaming her for their transgression. At this point, Eve gets on her knees and begs Adam for forgiveness. And since Adam still loves Eve, he forgives her, sharing some of the blame with her.

The Son of God: The Son of God in Paradise Lost is Jesus Christ, though he is never named explicitly, since he has not yet entered human form. The Son is very heroic and powerful, singlehandedly defeating Satan and his followers when they violently rebel against God and driving them into Hell. Also, after the Father explains to him how Adam and Eve shall fall, and how the rest of humanity will be doomed to follow them in their cursed footsteps, the Son selflessly and heroically proclaims that he will take the punishment for humanity. The Son endows hope to the poem, because although Satan conquers humanity by successfully tempting Adam and Eve, the victory is temporary because the Son will save the human race.

God the Father: God the Father is the creator of Eden, Heaven, Hell, and of each of the main characters. He is an all-powerful and all-knowing being who cannot be overthrown by even the one-third of the angels Satan incites against him. The poem portrays God's process of creation in the way that Milton believed it was done, that God created Heaven, Earth, Hell, and all the creatures that inhabit these separate planes from part of himself, not out of nothing. Thus, according to Milton, the ultimate authority of God derives from his being the "author" of creation. Satan tries to justify his rebellion by denying this aspect of God and claiming self-creation, but he admits to himself this is not the case, and that God "deserved no such return from me, whom he created what I was."

Raphael: Raphael is an angel who is sent by God to warn Adam about Satan's infiltration of Eden and to warn him that Satan is going to try to curse Adam and Eve. Raphael initially meets with both Adam and Eve but has a private discussion about Satan with Adam only. During this discussion, Raphael tells Adam the story of Satan's rebellion and subsequent exile into Hell. After this, because of Adam's curiosity, Raphael also explains to Adam how God created the Earth and the universe.

Michael: After Adam and Eve disobey God by eating from the Tree of Knowledge, God sends the angel Michael to visit Adam and Eve. His duty is to escort Adam and Eve out of Paradise. But before this happens, Michael shows Adam visions of the future which cover an outline of the Bible, from the story of Cain and Abel in Genesis, up through the story of Jesus in the New Testament. This vision is meant to show Adam what happens to mankind and to show Adam how Jesus will redeem humanity and eventually drive out Satan, Sin, and Death from the Earth.

Composition

Milton began writing the epic in 1658 at the age of fifty, during the last years of the English Republic. Infighting among different military and political factions that doomed the Republic may show up in the Council of Hell scenes in Book II. Although he probably finished the work by 1664, Milton did not publish until 1667, because of Great Plague and the Great Fire. Milton composed the entire work while completely blind. It is presumed he had glaucoma, necessitating the use of paid amanuenses and his daughters. The poet claimed that a divine spirit inspired him during the night, leaving him with verses that he would recite in the morning.

Context

The work is influenced by the Bible, Milton's own Puritan upbringing and religious perspective (including elements of Arminianism, Phineas Fletcher, Edmund Spenser, the Roman poets Virgil and Ovid, Greek poets Theocritus and Homer, Italian poet Dante Alighieri, and the traditions of epic poetry. Later in life, Milton wrote the much shorter sequel to Paradise Lost entitled *Paradise Regained,* charting the temptation of Christ by Satan, and the return of the possibility of paradise. The reputation of the sequel never equaled its antecedent.

Themes

Marriage

Milton first presents Adam and Eve in Book IV with impartiality. The relationship between Adam and Eve is one of "mutual dependence, not a relation of domination or hierarchy." While the author does place Adam above Eve in regard to his intellectual knowledge, and in turn his relation to God, he also grants Eve the benefit of knowledge through experience. Hermine Van Nuis clarifies that although there is a sense of stringency associated with the specified roles of the male and the female, each unreservedly accepts the designated role because it is viewed as an asset. Instead of believing that these roles are forced upon them, each uses the obligatory requirement as a strength in their relationship with each other. These minor discrepancies reveal the author's view on the importance of mutuality between a husband and a wife.

When examining the relationship between Adam and Eve, critics tend to accept an either Adam-or Eve—centered view in terms of hierarchy and importance to God. David Mikics argues, by contrast; these positions "overstate the independence of the characters' stances, and therefore miss the way in which Adam and Eve are entwined with each other". Milton's true vision reflects one where the husband and wife (in this instance, Adam and Eve) depend on each other and only through each other's differences are able to thrive. While most readers believe that Adam and Eve fail because of their fall from paradise, Milton would argue that the resulting strengthening of their love for one another is true victory.

Although Milton does not directly mention divorce, critics posit theories on Milton's view of divorce based on inferences found within the poem. Other works by Milton suggest he viewed marriage as an entity separate from the church. Discussing *Paradise Lost*, Biberman entertains the idea that "marriage is a contract made by both the man and the woman". Based on this inference, Milton would believe that both man and woman would have equal access to divorce, as they do to marriage.

Idolatry

Milton's 17th century contemporaries by and large criticized Milton's ideas and considered him as a radical, mostly because of his well-known Protestant views on politics and religion. One of Milton's greatest and most controversial arguments centers on his concept of what is idolatrous; this topic is deeply embedded in *Paradise Lost.*

Milton's first criticism of idolatry focuses on the practice of constructing temples and other buildings to serve as places of worship. In Book XI of Paradise Lost, Adam tries to atone for his sins by offering to build altars to worship God. In response, the angel Michael explains Adam does not need to build physical objects to experience the presence of God. Joseph Lyle points to this example, explaining "When Milton objects to architecture, it is not a quality inherent in buildings themselves he finds offensive, but rather their tendency to act as convenient loci to which idolatry, over time, will inevitably adhere." Even if the idea is pure in nature, Milton still believes that it will unavoidably lead to idolatry simply because of the nature of humans. Instead of placing their thoughts and beliefs into God, as they should, humans tend to turn to erected objects and falsely invest their faith. While Adam attempts to build an altar to God, critics note Eve is similarly guilty of idolatry, but in a different manner. Harding believes Eve's narcissism and obsession with herself constitutes idolatry.

Specifically, Harding claims that "... under the serpent's influence, Eve's idolatry and self-deification foreshadow the errors into which her 'Sons' will stray." Much like Adam, Eve falsely places her faith into herself, the Tree of Knowledge, and to some extent, the Serpent, all of which do not compare to the ideal nature of God.

Furthermore, Milton makes his views on idolatry more explicit with the creation of Pandemonium and the exemplary allusion to Solomon's temple. In the beginning of Paradise Lost, as well as throughout the poem, there are several references to the rise and eventual fall of Solomon's temple. Critics elucidate that "Solomon's temple provides an explicit demonstration of how an artifact moves from its genesis in devotional practice to an idolatrous end." This example, out of the many presented, conveys Milton's views on the dangers of idolatry distinctly. Even if one builds a structure in the name of God, even the best of intentions can become immoral. In addition, critics have drawn parallels between both Pandemonium and Saint Peter's Basilica, and the Pantheon. The majority of these similarities revolve around a structural likeness, but as Lyle explains, they play a greater role. By linking Saint Peter's Basilica and the Pantheon to Pandemonium—an ideally false structure, the two famous buildings take on a false meaning. This comparison best represents Milton's Protestant views, as it rejects both the purely Catholic perspective and the Pagan perspective.

In addition to rejecting Catholicism, Milton revolted against the idea of a monarch ruling by divine right. He saw the practice as idolatrous. Barbara Lewalski concludes that the theme of idolatry in

Paradise Lost "... is an exaggerated version of the idolatry Milton had long associated with the Stuart ideology of divine kingship". In the opinion of Milton, any object, human or non-human, that receives special attention befitting of God, is considered idolatrous.

Response and Criticism

This epic is generally considered one of the greatest works in the English language. In the verses below the portrait in the fourth edition, John Dryden linked Milton with Homer and Virgil, suggesting Milton encompassed and surpassed both:

> "Three Poets, in three distant Ages born, Greece, Italy, and England did adorn. The First in loftiness of thought surpass'd; The Next in Majesty; in both the Last. The force of Nature cou'd no farther goe: To make a third she joynd the former two."

Since Paradise Lost is based upon scripture, its significance in the Western canon has been thought by some to have lessened due to increasing secularism. This is not the general consensus, and even academics labelled as secular realize the merits of the work. In William Blake's *The Marriage of Heaven and Hell,* the "voice of the devil" argues:

> The reason Milton wrote in fetters when he wrote of Angels & God, and at liberty when of Devils & Hell, is because he was a true Poet and of the Devil's party without knowing it.

This statement summarizes what would become the most common interpretation of the work in the twentieth century. Some critics, including C. S. Lewis, and later Stanley Fish, reject this interpretation. Rather, such critics hold that the theology of *Paradise Lost* conforms to the passages of Scripture on which it is based.

The latter half of the twentieth century saw critical understanding of Milton's epic shift to a more political and philosophical focus. Rather than the Romantic conception of the Devil as hero, it is generally accepted that Satan is presented in terms that begin classically heroic, then diminish him until he is finally reduced to a dust-eating serpent unable even to control his own body. The political angle enters into consideration in the underlying friction between Satan's conservative, hierarchical view of the universe, and the contrasting "new way" of God and the Son of God as illustrated in Book III. In other words, in contemporary criticism the main thrust of the work becomes not the perfidy or heroism of Satan, but rather the tension between classical conservative "Old Testament" hierarchs (evidenced in Satan's worldview and even in that of the archangels Raphael and Gabriel), and "New Testament" revolutionaries (embodied in the Son of God, Adam, and Eve) who represent a new system of universal organization. This new order is based not in tradition, precedence, and unthinking habit, but on sincere and conscious acceptance of faith and on station chosen by ability and responsibility. Naturally, this interpretation makes much use of Milton's other works and his biography, grounding itself in his personal history as an English revolutionary and social critic.

Samuel Johnson praised the poem lavishly, but conceded that "None ever wished it longer than it is." In Paul Stevens of University of Toronto's *Milton's Satan,* he claimed the Satan figure was one of the earliest examples of an anti-hero who does not submit to authority, but the actions are greatly based on his own arrogance and delusion. Stevens also claimed Paradise Lost was a story about Milton himself, who wrote in support of events that eventually led to English Civil War. That analysis was debuted in 2009 season of TVO's Best Lecturer series.

Iconography

The first illustrations were to the fourth edition of 1688, with one engraving prefacing each book, of which up to eight of the twelve were by Sir John Baptist Medina, one by Bernard Lens II, and perhaps up to four (including Books I and XII, perhaps the most memorable) by another hand. The most notable illustrators of *Paradise Lost* are William Blake, Gustave Doré and Henry Fuseli (1799); however, the epic's illustrators also include, among others, John Martin, Edward Burney, Richard Westall, Francis Hayman. Salvador Dalí executed a set of ten colour engravings in 1974. As of June 2009, examples from this series can be viewed at the William Bennett Gallery in Manhattan. Strikingly, two *capriccios* by Gian Battista Tiepolo were used to illustrate an Italian 18th century edition. Surreal-visionary artist Terrance Lindall's rendition was published in 1982.

Milton'sViews

An unfinished religious manifesto, *De doctrina christiana,* probably written by Milton, lays out many of his heterodox theological views, and was not discovered and published until 1823. Milton's key beliefs were idiosyncratic, not those of an identifiable group or faction, and often they go well beyond the orthodoxy of the time. Their tone, however, stemmed from the Puritan emphasis on the centrality and inviolability of conscience. He was his own man, but it is *Areopagitica,* where he was anticipated by Henry

Robinson and others, that has lasted best of his prose works.

Philosophy

By the late 1650s, Milton was a proponent of monism or animist materialism, the notion that a single material substance which is "animate, self-active, and free" composes everything in the universe: from stones and trees and bodies to minds, souls, angels, and God. Milton devised this position to avoid the mind-body dualism of Plato and Descartes as well as the mechanistic determinism of Hobbes. Milton's monism is most notably reflected in *Paradise Lost* when he has angels eat (5.433–39) and engage in sexual intercourse (8.622–29) and the *De Doctrina,* where he denies the dual natures of man and argues for a theory of Creation *ex Deo.*

Political Thought

In his political writing, Milton addressed particular themes at different periods. The years 1641–42 were dedicated to church politics and the struggle against episcopacy. After his divorce writings, *Areopagitica,* and a gap, he wrote in 1649–54 in the aftermath of the execution of Charles I, and in polemic justification of the regicide and the existing Parliamentarian regime. Then in 1659–60 he foresaw the Restoration, and wrote to head it off.

A friend and ally in the pamphlet wars was Marchamont Nedham. Austin Woolrych considers that although they were quite close, there is "little real affinity, beyond a broad republicanism", between their approaches. Blair Worden remarks that both Milton and Nedham, with others such as Andrew Marvell and

James Harrington, would have taken the problem with the Rump Parliament to be not the republic, but the fact that it was not a proper republic. Woolrych speaks of "the gulf between Milton's vision of the Commonwealth's future and the reality". In the early version of his *History of Britain*, begun in 1649, Milton was already writing off the members of the Long Parliament as incorrigible.

He praised Oliver Cromwell as the Protectorate was set up; though subsequently he had major reservations. When Cromwell seemed to be backsliding as a revolutionary, after a couple of years in power, Milton moved closer to the position of Sir Henry Vane, to whom he wrote a sonnet in 1652. The group of disaffected republicans included, besides Vane, John Bradshaw, John Hutchinson, Edmund Ludlow, Henry Marten, Robert Overton, Edward Sexby and John Streater; but not Marvell, who remained with Cromwell's party. Milton had already commended Overton, along with Edmund Whalley and Bulstrode Whitelocke, in *Defensio Secunda*. Nigel Smith writes that As Richard Cromwell fell from power, he envisaged a step towards a freer republic or "free commonwealth", writing in the hope of this outcome in early 1660. Milton had argued for an awkward position, in the *Ready and Easy Way*, because he wanted to invoke the Good Old Cause and gain the support of the republicans, but without offering a democratic solution of any kind. His proposal, backed by reference (amongst other reasons) to the oligarchical Dutch and Venetian constitutions, was for a council with perpetual membership. This attitude cut right across the grain of popular opinion of the time, which swung decisively behind the restoration of the Stuart monarchy that took place later in the year. Milton, an associate of and advocate on behalf of the regicides, was silenced on political matters as Charles II returned.

Theology

Like many Renaissance artists before him, Milton attempted to integrate Christian theology with classical modes. In his early poems, the poet narrator expresses a tension between vice and virtue, the latter invariably related to Protestantism. In *Comus* Milton may make ironic use of the Caroline court masque by elevating notions of purity and virtue over the conventions of court revelry and superstition. In his later poems, Milton's theological concerns become more explicit. In 1648 he wrote a hymn *How lovely are thy dwelling fair,* a paraphrase of Psalm 84, that explains his view on God.

Milton embraced many heterodox Christian theological views. He rejected the Trinity, in the belief that the Son was subordinate to the Father, a position known as Arianism; and his sympathy or curiosity was probably engaged by Socinianism: in August 1650 he licensed for publication by William Dugard the *Racovian Catechism,* based on a non-trinitarian creed. A source has interpreted him as broadly Protestant, if not always easy to locate in a more precise religious category.

In his 1641 treatise, *Of Reformation,* Milton expressed his dislike for Catholicism and episcopacy, presenting Rome as a modern Babylon, and bishops as Egyptian taskmasters. These analogies conform to Milton's puritanical preference for Old Testament imagery. He knew at least four commentaries on *Genesis*: those of John Calvin, Paulus Fagius, David Pareus and Andreus Rivetus.

Through the Interregnum, Milton often presents England, rescued from the trappings of a worldly monarchy, as an elect nation akin to the Old Testament Israel, and shows its leader, Oliver Cromwell, as a latter-day Moses. These views were bound up in Protestant views of the Millennium, which some sects, such as the Fifth Monarchists predicted would arrive in England. Milton, however, would later criticise the "worldly" millenarian views of these and others, and expressed orthodox ideas on the prophecy of the Four Empires.

The Restoration of the Stuart monarchy in 1660 began a new phase in Milton's work. In *Paradise Lost, Paradise Regained* and *Samson Agonistes* Milton mourns the end of the godly Commonwealth. The Garden of Eden may allegorically reflect Milton's view of England's recent Fall from Grace, while Samson's blindness and captivity – mirroring Milton's own lost sight – may be a metaphor for England's blind acceptance of Charles II as king. Illustrated by *Paradise Lost* is mortalism, the belief that the soul lies dormant after the body dies.

Despite the Restoration of the monarchy Milton did not lose his personal faith; Samson shows how the loss of national salvation did not necessarily preclude the salvation of the individual, while *Paradise Regained* expresses Milton's continuing belief in the promise of Christian salvation through Jesus Christ.

Though he may have maintained his personal faith in spite of the defeats suffered by his cause, the *Dictionary of National Biography* recounts how he had been alienated from the Church of England by Archbishop William Laud, and then moved similarly from the Dissenters by their denunciation of religious tolerance in England.

> "Milton had come to stand apart from all sects, though apparently finding the Quakers most congenial. He never went to any religious services in his later years. When a servant brought back accounts of sermons from nonconformist meetings, Milton became so sarcastic that the man at last gave up his place".

Divorce

His thinking on divorce caused him the most trouble with the authorities. An orthodox presbyterian view of the time was that Milton's views on divorce constituted a one-man heresy:

Even here, though, his originality is qualified: Thomas Gataker had already identified "mutual solace" as a principal goal in marriage. Milton abandoned his campaign to legitimize divorce after 1645, but he expressed support for polygamy in the *De doctrina christiana*, the theological treatise that provides the clearest evidence for his views.

History

History was particularly important for the political class of the period, and Lewalski considers that Milton "more than most illustrates" a remark of Thomas Hobbes on the weight placed at the time on the classical Latin historical writers Tacitus, Livy, Sallust and Cicero, and their republican attitudes. Milton himself wrote that "Worthy deeds are not often destitute of worthy relaters", in Book II of his *History of Britain*. A sense of history mattered greatly to him:

Legacy and Influence

Once *Paradise Lost* was published, Milton's stature as

epic poet was immediately recognised. He cast a formidable shadow over English poetry in the 18th and 19th centuries; he was often judged equal or superior to all other English poets, including Shakespeare. Very early on, though, he was championed by Whigs, and decried by Tories: with the regicide Edmund Ludlow he was claimed as an early Whig, while the High Tory Anglican minister Luke Milbourne (1649--1720) lumped Milton in with other "Agents of Darkness" such as John Knox, George Buchanan, Richard Baxter, Algernon Sidney and John Locke.

Early Reception of the Poetry

John Dryden, an early enthusiast, in 1677 began the trend of describing Milton as the poet of the sublime. Dryden's *The State of Innocence and the Fall of Man: an Opera* (1677) is evidence of an immediate cultural influence. In 1695, Patrick Hume became the first editor of *Paradise Lost*, providing an extensive apparatus of annotation and commentary, particularly chasing down allusions.

In 1732 the classical scholar Richard Bentley offered a corrected version of *Paradise Lost*. Bentley was considered presumptuous, and was attacked in the following year by Zachary Pearce. Christopher Ricks judges that, as critic, Bentley was both acute and wrong-headed, and "incorrigibly eccentric"; William Empson also finds Pearce to be more sympathetic to Bentley's underlying line of thought than is warranted.

There was an early, partial translation of *Paradise Lost* into German by Theodore Haak, and based on that a standard verse translation by Ernest Gottlieb von Berge. A subsequent prose translation by Johann

Jakob Bodmer was very popular; it influenced Friedrich Gottlieb Klopstock. The German-language Milton tradition returned to England in the person of the artist Henry Fuseli.

Many enlightenment thinkers of the 18th century revered and commented on Milton's poetry and non-poetical works. In addition to John Dryden, among them were Alexander Pope, Joseph Addison, Thomas Newton, and Samuel Johnson. For example in The Spectator (1711) nos 267, 273, 279, 285, 291, 297, 303, 309, 315, 321, 327, 333, 339, 345, 351, 357, 363, and 369, Joseph Addison wrote extensive notes, annotations, and interpretations of certain passages of Paradise Lost. Jonathan Richardson, senior, and Jonathan Richardson, the younger, co-wrote a book of criticism, "Explanatory Notes and Remarks on Milton's Paradise Lost" (1734). In 1749, Thomas Newton published an extensive annotated edition of Milton's poetical works with the annotations provided by himself, Dryden, Pope, Addison, the Richardsons (father/son) and others. Newton's edition of Milton was a culmination of the honor bestowed upon Milton by early Enlightenment thinkers. Newton's edition may also have been published in reaction to Richard Bentley's infamous edition, described above. Samuel Johnson wrote numerous essays on Paradise Lost, and Milton was included in his monumental "Lives of the Most Eminent English Poets with Critical Observations on their Works" (1779-1781).

Romantic Theory

Edmund Burke was a theorist of the sublime, and he regarded Milton's description of Hell as exemplary of sublimity as aesthetic concept. For Burke it was to set alongside mountain-tops, a storm at sea, and infinity. In *The Beautiful and the Sublime* he wrote "No person seems better to have understood the secret of heightening, or of setting terrible things, if I may use the expression, in their strongest light, by the force of a judicious obscurity than Milton."

The Romantic poets valued his exploration of blank verse, but for the most part rejected his religiosity. William Wordsworth began his sonnet "London, 1802" with "Milton! thou should'st be living at this hour" and modeled *The Prelude,* his own blank verse epic, on *Paradise Lost.* John Keats found the yoke of Milton's style uncongenial; he exclaimed that "Miltonic verse cannot be written but in an artful or rather artist's humour." Keats felt that *Paradise Lost* was a "beautiful and grand curiosity"; but his own unfinished attempt at epic poetry, *Hyperion,* was unsatisfactory to the author because, amongst other things, it had too many "Miltonic inversions". In *The Madwoman in the Attic,* Sandra Gilbert and Susan Gubar note that Mary Shelley's novel *Frankenstein* is, in the view of many critics, "one of the key 'Romantic' readings of *Paradise Lost.*"

Later Legacy

The Victorian age witnessed a continuation of Milton's influence, George Eliot and Thomas Hardy being particularly inspired by Milton's poetry and biography. By contrast, the early 20th century, with the efforts of T.S. Eliot and Ezra Pound, witnessed a reduction in Milton's critical stature. Harold Bloom, in *The Anxiety of Influence,* could still write that "Milton is the central problem in any theory and history of poetic influence in English [...]".

Milton's *Areopagitica* is still cited as relevant to the First Amendment to the United States Constitution. A quotation from *Areopagitica* – "A good book is the precious lifeblood of a master spirit, embalmed and treasured up on purpose to a life beyond life" – is displayed in many public libraries, including the New York Public Library.

The title of Phillip Pullman's *His Dark Materials* trilogy is derived from a quotation, "His dark materials to create more worlds", line 915 of Book II in *Paradise Lost.* Pullman was concerned to produce a version of Milton's poem accessible to teenagers, and has spoken of Milton as "our greatest public poet".

T.S. Eliot believed that "of no other poet is it so difficult to consider the poetry simply as poetry, without our theological and political dispositions... making unlawful entry".

Literary Legacy

Milton left lasting contributions in the fields of poetic form and technique. His pioneering use of blank verse, in addition to his stylistic innovations were to influence the voices of poets to come. The power that Milton's works held over the poetic imagination of his time is not fully appreciated until it is realized that during the seventeenth and eighteenth centuries, poetic blank verse was considered completely apart from dramatic blank verse, and that to the literary community there was but one known poem of the sort, which was Paradise Lost. Said Isâac Watts in 1734, "Mr. Milton is esteemed the parent and author of blank verse among us". Blank verse inevitably came to mean verse that was Miltonic, and "Miltonic Verse" seldom referred to anything beyond blank verse. With

Paradise Lost, Milton singlehandedly charted a new poetic terrain that was independent from both the drama and the heroic couplet.

Though successful blank verse requires command of numerous subtleties, the lack of rhyme was in itself such a novelty that many contemporaries failed to see beyond this single aspect of Milton's poetry. Milton considered the rhymeless quality of Paradise Lost to be an extension of his own personal liberty: "This neglect then of Rhime... is to be esteem'd an example set, the first in English, of ancient liberty recover'd to heroic Poem from the troublesom and modern bondage of Rimeing.". Milton's pursuit of freedom was largely a reaction against the conservative values entrenched within the rigid formalities of the heroic couplet. Within the dominant culture that stressed elegance and finish, he was the first to grant primacy to freedom, breadth and imaginative suggestiveness. These values were to gain increasing followers over the years, eventually developing into the romantic vision of sublime terror. The conservative reaction to Milton's poetic worldview was understandably negative; yet many begrudgingly acknowledged the poet's resemblance to classical writers (the fact that Greek and Roman poetry was also unrhymed was an argument that the conservative establishment could hardly have been insensible to). Controversy notwithstanding, blank verse soon came to be the recognized medium for religious works and for translations of the classics. Unrhymed lyrics like Collins' *Ode to Evening* were not uncommon after 1740.

A second aspect of blank verse which advance was hastened by the success of Paradise Lost was the use of unconventional rhythm: "His blank-verse paragraph, and his audacious and victorious attempt to combine blank and rhymed verse with paragraphic effect in Lycidas, lay down indestructible models and patterns of English verse-rhythm, as distinguished from the narrower and more strait-laced forms of English metre". Prior to Milton, "the sense of regular rhythm...had been knocked into the English head so securely that it was part of their nature". The "Heroick measure," according to Samuel Johnson, "is pure...when the accent rests upon every second syllable through the whole line...The repetition of this sound or percussion at equal times, is the most complete harmony of which a single verse is capable". Caesural pauses, most agreed, were best placed at the middle and the end of the line. In order to support this symmetry, lines were most often octo- or deca-syllabic, with no enjambed endings.

To this schema Milton introduced many modifications, which included hypermetrical syllables (trisyllabic feet), inversion or slighting of stresses, and the shifting of pauses to all parts of the line. Milton deemed these features to be reflective of "the transcendental union of order and freedom". The freedom that he espoused was in fact so revolutionary that even his greatest admirers remained hesitant to adopt such a departure from traditional metrical schemes: "The English...had been writing separate lines for so long that they could not rid themselves of the habit". Watts preferred his lines distinct from each other, as did Goldsmith, Pemberton, and Scott of Amwell, whose general opinion it was that Milton's frequent omission of the initial unaccented foot (which gave much of the charm to L'Allegro, Il Penseroso) was "displeasing to a nice ear". It was not until the late eighteenth century that poets (beginning with Gray) began to understand "the composition of Milton's harmony...how he loved to vary his pauses, his measures, and his feet, which gives that enchanting air of freedom and wilderness to his versification".

Neo-classical diction at the time of Milton was as restrictive as its prosody. Narrow imagery paired with uniformity of sentence structure resulted in a small set of 800 nouns circumscribing the vocabulary of 90% of heroic couplets ever written up to the eighteenth century. Tradition required that the same adjectives attach to the same nouns, followed by the same verbs. Not surprisingly, Milton's pursuit of liberty extended into his vocabulary as well. This is demonstrated by his many neologisms, many of which were sourced from Latin. Words employed by Milton were very frequently obsolete, having been dropped from popular usage so completely that their meanings were no longer understood.

In 1740 Francis Peck identified some famous examples of Milton's "old" words which, now popular, included "self-same," "hue," "minstrelsy," "murky," "carol" and "chaunt". Among Milton's naturalized Latin words were "humid," "orient," "hostil," "facil," "fervid," "jubilant," "ire," "bland," "reluctant," "palpable," "fragil" and "ornate". The "Miltonian dialect" as it was called, came to be the source of emulation for many later poets; Pope was known to have used the diction of Paradise Lost in his Homer, while the lyric poetry of Gray and Collins were frequently criticized for their use of "obsolete words out of Spenser and Milton". The language of Thomson's finest poems are self consciously modeled after the Miltonian dialect, hence exhibiting the same tone and sensibilities as Paradise Lost. Owing to Milton, English poetry from Pope to Keats exhibited a steadily-increasing attention to the connotative, the imaginative and poetic, value of words.

8

Augustan Poetry

Augustan poetry is the poetry that flourished during the reign of Caesar Augustus as Emperor of Rome, most notably including the works of Virgil, Horace, and Ovid. This poetry was more explicitly political than the poetry that had preceded it, and it was distinguished by a greater degree of satire. In English literature, Augustan poetry is a branch of Augustan literature, and refers to the poetry of the eighteenth-century, specifically the first half of the century. The term comes most originally from a term that George I had used for himself. He saw himself as an Augustus. Therefore, the British poets picked up that term as a way of referring to their own endeavors, for it fit in another respect: 18th century English poetry was political, satirical, and marked by the central philosophical problem of whether the individual or society took precedence as the subject of verse.

In the Augustan era, poets were even more conversant with each other than were novelists. Their works were written as direct counterpoint and direct expansion of one another, with each poet writing satire when in opposition. There was a great struggle over the nature and role of the pastoral in the early part of the century, primarily between Ambrose Philips and Alexander Pope and then between their followers, but such a controversy was only possible because of two simultaneous movements. The more general movement, carried forward only with struggle between poets, was the same as was present in the novel: the invention of the subjective self as a worthy topic, the emergence of a priority on *individual* psychology, against the insistence on all acts of art being *performance* and public gesture designed for the benefit of society at large.

Underneath this large banner raged multiple individual battles. The other development, one seemingly agreed upon by both sides, was a gradual expropriation and reinvention of all the Classical forms of poetry. Every genre of poetry was recast, reconsidered, and used to serve new functions. Ode, ballad, elegy, satire, parody, song, and lyric poetry would all be adapted from their older uses. Odes would cease to be encomium, ballads cease to be narratives, elegies cease to be sincere memorials, satires no longer be specific entertainments, parodies no longer be *bravura* stylistic performances, songs no longer be personal lyrics, and the lyric would become a celebration of the individual rather than a lover's complaint.

These two developments (the emphasis on the individual and the willingness to reinvent genre) can be seen as extensions of Protestantism, as Max Weber argued, for they represent a gradual increase in the implications of Martin Luther's doctrine of the priesthood of all believers and the Calvinist emphasis on individual revelation of the divine (and therefore the competence and worth of the individual). It can be seen as a growth of the power and assertiveness of the bourgeoisie and an echo of the displacement of the worker from the home in growing industrialization, as Marxists such as E.P. Thompson have argued, for people were no longer allowed to remain in their families and communities when they had to travel to a factory or mill, and therefore they grew accustomed to thinking of themselves as isolates.

It can be argued that the development of the subjective individual against the social individual was a natural reaction to trade over other methods of economic production, or as a reflection of a breakdown in social cohesion unconsciously set in motion by enclosure and the migration of the poor to the cities. There are many other plausible and coherent explanations of the causes of the rise of the *subjective self,* but whatever the prime cause, poets showed the strains of the development as a largely conservative set of voices argued for a social person and largely emergent voices argued for the individual person.

Alexander Pope, the Scribblerans, and Poetry as Social Act

The entire Augustan age's poetry was dominated by Alexander Pope. Since Pope began publishing when very young and continued to the end of his life, his poetry is a reference point in any discussion of the 1710s, 1720s, 1730s, or even 1740s. Furthermore, Pope's abilities were recognized early in his career, so contemporaries acknowledged his superiority, for the most part. Indeed, seldom has a poet been as publicly acknowledged as a leader for as long as was Pope, and, unlike the case with figures such as John Dryden or William Wordsworth, a second generation did not emerge to eclipse his position.

From a technical point of view, few poets have ever approached Alexander Pope's perfection at the iambic pentameter closed couplet ("heroic verse"), and his lines were repeated often enough to lend quite a few clichés and proverbs to modern English usage. However, if Pope had few rivals, he had many enemies. His technical perfection did not shelter him from political, philosophical, or religious opponents, and Pope himself was quarrelsome in print. His very technical superiority led Pope to injudicious improvements in his editing and translation of other authors. However, Pope and his enemies (often called "the Dunces" because of Pope's successful satirizing of them in *The Dunciad* of 1727 and 1738) fought over central matters of the proper subject matter for poetry and the proper pose of the poetic voice, and the excesses and missteps, as much as the achievements, of both sides demonstrated the stakes of the battle.

The Pope/Philips debate occurred in 1709 when Alexander Pope published his *Pastorals*. Pope's *Pastorals* were of the four seasons. When they appeared, Thomas Tickell, a member of the "Little Senate" of Addison's at Button's Coffee-shop, wrote an evaluation in *Guardian* that praised Ambrose Philips's pastorals above Pope's. Pope replied by writing in *Guardian* with a mock praise of Philips's *Patorals* that heaped scorn on them. Pope quoted Philips's worst lines, mocked his execution, and delighted in pointing out his empty lines. Philips responded by putting a staff in the floor of Button's with which to beat Pope, should he appear. In 1717, Pope explained his theory of the pastoral in the *Discourse on Pastoral Poetry*. He argued that any depictions of shepherds and their mistresses in the pastoral must not be updated shepherds, that they must be icons of the Golden Age:

"we are not to describe our shepherds as shepherds at this day really are, but as they may be conceived then to have been, when the best of men followed the employment" (Gordon). Philips's *Pastorals* were not particularly awful poems, but they did reflect his desire to "update" the pastoral.

In 1724, Philips would update poetry again by writing a series of odes dedicated to "all ages and characters, from Walpole, the steerer of the realm, to Miss Pulteney in the nursery." To do so, he shortened his line length to 3.5', or almost half a normal iambic pentameter line. Henry Carey was one of the best at satirizing these poems, and his *Namby Pamby* became a hugely successful obliteration of Philips and Philips's endeavor. What is notable about Philips against Pope, however, is not so much the particular poems and their answers as the fact that *both* poets were adapting the pastoral and the ode, both altering it. Pope's insistence upon a Golden Age pastoral no less than Philips's desire to update it meant making a political statement. While it is easy to see in Ambrose Philips an effort at modernist triumph, it is no less the case that Pope's artificially restricted pastoral was a statement of what the ideal (based on an older Feudal arrangement) should be.

The Scribbleran Club wrote poetry as well as prose, and the club included among its number John Gay, who was not only a friend and collaborator of Pope's, but also one of the major voices of the era. John Gay, like Pope, adapted the pastoral. Gay, working at Pope's suggestion, wrote a parody of the updated pastoral in *The Shepherd's Week.* He also imitated the satires of Juvenal with his *Trivia.* In 1728, his *The Beggar's Opera* was an enormous success, running for an unheard-of eighty performances. All of these works have in common a gesture of compassion. In *Trivia,* Gay writes as if commisserating with those who live in London and are menaced by falling masonry and bedpan slops, and *The Shepherd's Week* features great detail of the follies of everyday life and eccentric character. Even *The Beggar's Opera,* which is a clear satire of Robert Walpole, portrays its characters with compassion. The villains have pathetic songs in their own right and are acting out of exigency rather than boundless evil. Gay's tone is almost the opposite of Jonathan Swift's. Swift famously said that he hated mankind but loved individual humans, and Gay's poetry shows a love of mankind and a gentle mocking of overly serious or pretentious individuals.

Old style poetic parody involved imitation of the style of an author for the purposes of providing amusement, but not for the purpose of ridicule. The person imitated was not satirized. Ambrose Philips's idea was of adapting and updating the pastoral to represent a contemporary lyric (i.e. to make it a form for housing the *personal* love complaints of modern shepherds), where individual personalities would be expressed, and this desire to move from the universal, typical, and idealized shepherd to the real, actual, and individual shepherd was the heart of the debate. Prior to Ambrose Philips, John Philips, whose *The Splendid Shilling* of 1701 was an imitation of John Milton's blank verse for a discussion of the miseries of poverty, was championed by Addison's Kit-Kats. *The Splendid Shilling,* like Pope's poetry and the other poetry by the "Tory Wits," is a statement of the social man. The shilling, the poverty, and the complaint are all posited in terms of the man in London, the man in society and conviviality, and not the man as a particular individual or with idiosyncrasies. It was a poem wholly consonant with the poetry of the Scribblerians. After Ambrose Philips, though, poets would begin to speak of peculiarities and actualities, rather than ideals. It is a debate and a poetic tension that would remain all the way to Samuel Johnson's discussion of the "streaks of the tulip" in the last part of the century.

Translation and Adaptation as Statement

Gay adapted Juvenal, as Pope had already adapted Virgil's *Eclogues,* and throughout the Augustan era the "updating" of Classical poets was a commonplace. These were not translations, but rather they were imitations of Classical models, and the imitation allowed poets to veil their responsibility for the comments they made. Alexander Pope would manage to refer to the King himself in unflattering tones by "imitating" Horace in his *Epistle to Augustus.* Similarly, Samuel Johnson wrote a poem that falls into the Augustan period in his "imitation of Satire III" entitled *London.* The imitation was inherently conservative, since it argued that all that was good was to be found in the old classical education, but these imitations were used for progressive purposes, as the poets who used them were often doing so to complain of the political situation.

Readers of adaptations were assumed to know the originals. Indeed, original translation was one of the standard tests in grammar school. Pope's translation of Homer's *Iliad* and *Odyssey* was not an attempt to make the works available to an Augustan audience, but rather to make a new work occupying a middle ground between Homer and Pope. The translation had to be textually accurate, but it was intended to be a Pope translation, with felicity of phrase and neatness of rhyme from Pope. Additionally, Pope would "versify" John Donne, although his work was widely available. The changes Pope makes are the content, the commentary. Pope's edition of Shakespeare claimed to be textually perfect (although it was infamously corrupt), but his desire to adapt lead him to injudicious attempts at "smoothing" and "cleaning" Shakespeare's lines.

In satire, Pope achieved two of the greatest poetic satires of all time in the Augustan period, and both arose from the imitative and adaptive demands of parody. *The Rape of the Lock* (1712 and 1714) was a gentle mock-heroic, but it was built upon Virgil's *Aeneid*. Pope applied Virgil's heroic and epic structure to the story of a young woman (Arabella Fermor) having a lock of hair snipped by an amorous baron (Lord Petre). The *structure* of the comparison forced Pope to invent mythological forces to overlook the struggle, and so he borrowed sylphs from ludicrous (to him) alchemist Paracelsus and makes them the ghosts of vain women. He created an epic battle over a game of Ombre, leading to a fiendish appropriation of the lock of hair. Finally, a deux ex machina appears and the lock of hair experiences an apotheosis. To some degree, Pope was adapting Jonathan Swift's habit, in *A Tale of a Tub*, of pretending that metaphors were literal truths, and he was inventing a mythos to go with the everyday. The parody was in no way a comment on Virgil. Instead, it was an imitation made to serve a new purpose. The epic was transformed from a paean to national foundations to a satire on the outlandish self-importance of the country nobility. The poem was an enormous success, at least with the general public.

After that success, Pope wrote some works that were more philosophical and more political and therefore more controversial, such as the *Essay on Criticism* and *Essay on Man,* as well as a failed play. As a result, a decade after the gentle, laughing satire of *The Rape of the Lock,* Pope wrote his masterpiece of invective and specific opprobrium in *The Dunciad*. Pope had translated Homer and produced an errant edition of William Shakespeare, and the 1727 *Dunciad* was an updating and redirection of John Dryden's poison-pen battle of *MacFlecknoe.* The story is that of the goddess Dulness choosing a new avatar. She settles upon one of Pope's personal enemies, Lewis Theobald, and the poem describes the coronation and heroic games undertaken by all of the dunces of Great Britain in celebration of Theobald's ascension. When Pope's enemies responded to *The Dunciad* with attacks, Pope produced the *Dunciad Variorum,* which culled from each dunce's attack any comments unflattering to another dunce, assembled the whole into a commentary upon the original *Dunciad* and added a critical comment by Pope professing his innocence and dignity. In 1743, Pope issued a new version of *The Dunciad* ("The Dunciad B") with a fourth book added. He also changed the hero from Lewis Theobald to Colley Cibber. In the fourth book of the new *Dunciad,* Pope expressed the view that, in the battle between light and dark (enlightenment and the Dark Ages), Night and Dulness were fated to win, that all things of value were soon going to be subsumed under the curtain of unknowing.

John Gay and Alexander Pope belong on one side of a line separating the celebrants of the individual and the celebrants of the social. Pope wrote *The Rape of the Lock,* he said, to settle a disagreement between two great families, to laugh them into peace. He wrote the *Essay on Criticism* and the *Essay on Man* to emphasize, time and again, the public nature of human life and the social role of letters. Even *The Dunciad,* which seems to be a serial killing of everyone on Pope's enemies list, sets up these figures as expressions of dangerous and *antisocial* forces in letters. Theobald and Cibber are marked by vanity and pride, by having no care for morality, so long as they are famous. The hireling pens Pope attacks mercilessly in the heroic games section of the *Dunciad* are all embodiments of avarice and lies. Similarly, Gay, although he always has strong touches of personal humor and the details of personal life, writes of political society, of social dangers, and of follies that must be addressed to protect the greater whole. On the other side of this line, however, were people who agreed with the *politics* of Gay and Pope (and Swift), but not in approach.

Sentiment and Poetry of Individual

The other side of this division include, early in the Augustan Age, James Thomson and Edward Yonge. Thomson's *The Seasons* (1730) are nature poetry, but they are unlike Pope's notion of the Golden Age pastoral. Thomson's poet speaks in the first person from direct observation, and his own mood and sentiment color the descriptions of landscape. *Winter,* in particular, is melancholy and meditative. Edward Yonge's *Night Thoughts* (1742 - 1744) was immediately popular. It was, even more than *Winter,* a poem of deep solitude, melancholy, and despair. In these two poets, there is the stirrings of the lyric as the Romantics would see it: the celebration of the private individual's idiosyncratic (but paradigmatic) responses to the visions of the world. Both of these works appeared in Pope's lifetime, and both were popular, but the older, more conservative poetry maintained its hold for a while to come. On the other hand, Thomas Gray's *Elegy Written in a Country Church-Yard* set off a new craze for poetry of melancholy reflection.

Gray's *Elegy* appeared in 1750, and it immediately set new ground. First, it was written in the "country," and not in or as opposed to London. In fact, the poem makes no reference at all to the life of the city and society, and it follows no classical model. Further, it is not an elegiac in the strictest sense. Also, the poem sets up the solitary observer in a privileged position. It is only by being solitary that the poet can speak of a truth that is wholly individually realized, and the poem is a series of revelations that have been granted only to the contemplative (and superior) mind. After Gray, a group often referred to as the Churchyard Poets began imitating his pose, if not his style. These imitations followed no convenient or conventional political or religious division. Oliver Goldsmith (*The Deserted Village*), Thomas Warton, and even Thomas Percy (*The Hermit of Warkworth*), each conservative by and large and Classicist (Gray himself was a professor of Greek), took up the new poetry of solitude and loss. Additionally, Thomas Chatterton, among the younger poets, also followed. The only things these poets had in common was that they were not centered in London (except Chatterton, for a time), and each of them reflected, in one way or another, on the devastation of the countryside.

Therefore, when the Romantics emerged at the end of the 18th century, they were not assuming a radically new invention of the subjective self themselves, but merely formalizing what had gone before. Similarly, the later 18th century saw a ballad revival, with Thomas Percy's *Reliques of Ancient English Poetry*. The relics were not always very ancient, as many of the ballads dated from only the 17th century (e.g. the Bagford Ballads or The Dragon of Wantley in the Percy Folio), and so what began as an antiquarian movement soon became a folk movement. When this folk-inspired impulse combined with the solitary and individualistic impulse of the Churchyard Poets, Romanticism was nearly inevitable.

9

John Bunyan's *Pilgrim's Progress*

The Pilgrim's Progress from This World to That Which Is to Come is a Christian allegory written by John Bunyan and published in February, 1678. It is regarded as one of the most significant works of English literature, has been translated into more than 200 languages, and has never been out of print.

Composition

Bunyan began the work while in the Bedfordshire county gaol for violations of the Conventicle Act, which prohibited the holding of religious services outside the auspices of the established Church of England. Early Bunyan scholars like John Brown believed *The Pilgrim's Progress* was begun in Bunyan's second shorter imprisonment for six months in 1675, but more recent scholars like Roger Sharrock believe that it was begun during Bunyan's initial, more lengthy imprisonment from 1660-1672 right after he had written his spiritual autobiography, *Grace Abounding to the Chief of Sinners*.

The English text comprises 108,260 words and is divided into two parts, each reading as a continuous narrative with no chapter divisions.

The first part was completed in 1677 and entered into the stationers' register on December 22, 1677. It was licensed and entered in the "Term Catalogue" on February 18, 1678, which is looked upon as the date of first publication. After the first edition of the first part in 1678, an expanded edition, with additions written after Bunyan was freed, appeared in 1679. The Second Part appeared in 1684. There were eleven editions of the first part in John Bunyan's lifetime, published in successive years from 1678 to 1685 and in 1688, and there were two editions of the second part, published in 1684 and 1686.

First Part

Christian, an everyman character, is the protagonist of the allegory, which centers itself in his journey from his hometown, the "City of Destruction" ("this world"), to the "Celestial City" ("that which is to come": Heaven) atop Mt. Zion. Christian finds himself weighed down by a great burden, the knowledge of his sin, which he believed came from his reading "the book in his hand," (the Bible). This burden, which would cause him to sink into Tophet (hell), is Christian's acute, immediate concern that impels him to the crisis of what to do for deliverance. Christian meets Evangelist as he is walking out in the fields, who directs him to the "Wicket Gate" for deliverance. Since Christian cannot see the "Wicket Gate" in the distance, Evangelist directs him to go to a "shining light," which Christian thinks he sees. Christian leaves his home, his wife, and children to save himself when his attempt to persuade them to go with him fails. Two men of Destruction City, Obstinate and Pliable, follow Christian to persuade him to return and are unsuccessful. Pliable then decides to accompany

Christian on the path, until the two land in the **Slough** Of Despond—whereupon Pliable extricates himself and goes back to the City; Christian is rescued from the slough by Help, who pulls him out.

On his way to the Wicket Gate, Christian is diverted by Mr. Worldly Wiseman into seeking deliverance from his burden through the Law, supposedly with the help of a Mr. Legality and his son Civility in the village of Morality, rather than through Christ, allegorically by way of the Wicket Gate. Evangelist meets the wayward Christian where he has stopped before a life-threatening mountain, Mount Sinai, on the way to Legality's home. Evangelist shows Christian that he had sinned by turning out of his way, but he assures him that he will be welcomed at the Wicket Gate if he should turn around and go there, which Christian does.

At the Wicket Gate begins the "straight and narrow" King's Highway, and Christian is directed onto it by the gatekeeper Good Will. In the Second Part, Good-will is shown to be Jesus himself. To Christian's query about relief from his burden, Good Will directs him forward to "the place of deliverance."

Christian makes his way from there to the House of the Interpreter, where he is shown pictures and tableaux that portray or dramatize aspects of the Christian faith and life. Roger Sharrock denotes them "emblems."

From the House of the Interpreter, Christian finally reaches the "place of deliverance" (allegorically, the cross of Calvary and the open sepulchre of Christ), where the "straps" that bound Christian's burden to him break, and it rolls away into the open sepulchre. This event happens relatively early in the narrative: the immediate need of Christian at the beginning of the story being quickly remedied. After Christian is relieved of his burden, he is greeted by three shining ones, who give him the greeting of peace, new garments, and a scroll as a passport into the Celestial City — these are allegorical figures indicative of Christian Baptism.

Atop the Hill of Difficulty, Christian makes his first stop for the night at the House Beautiful, which is an allegory of the local Christian congregation. Christian spends three days here, and leaves clothed with armour (Eph. 6:11-18), which stands him in good stead in his battle against Apollyon in the Valley of Humiliation. This battle lasts "over half a day" until Christian manages to wound Apollyon with his two-edged sword (a reference to the Bible, Heb. 4:12). "And with that Apollyon spread his dragon wings and sped away."

As night falls Christian enters the Valley of the Shadow of Death. When he is in the middle of the valley amidst the gloom and terror he hears the words of the Twenty-third Psalm, spoken possibly by his friend Faithful:

> Yea, though I walk through the valley of the shadow of death, I will fear no evil: for thou art with me; thy rod and thy staff they comfort me. (Psalms 23:4.)

As he leaves this valley the sun rises on a new day. Just outside the Valley of the Shadow of Death he meets Faithful, also a former resident of the City of Destruction, who accompanies him to Vanity Fair, where both are arrested and detained because of their disdain for the wares and business of the fair. Faithful is put on trial, and executed as a martyr. Hopeful, a resident of Vanity, takes Faithful's place to be Christian's companion for the rest of the way.

Along a rough stretch of road, Christian and Hopeful leave the highway to travel on the easier By-Path Meadow, where a rainstorm forces them to spend the night. In the morning they are captured by Giant Despair, who takes them to his Doubting Castle, where they are imprisoned, beaten and starved. The giant wants them to commit suicide, but they endure the ordeal until Christian realizes that a key he has, called Promise, will open all the doors and gates of Doubting Castle. Using the key, they escape.

The Delectable Mountains form the next stage of Christian and Hopeful's journey, where the shepherds show them some of the wonders of the place also known as "Immanuel's Land".

On the way, Christian and Hopeful meet a lad named Ignorance, who has the vain hope of entering the Celestial City even though he believes in work's righteousness. A ferryman named Vain Hope ferries Ignorance across the River of Death, only for Ignorance to be turned away from the gates of Celestial City and cast into hell.

Christian and Hopeful make it through the dangerous Enchanted Ground into the Land of Beulah, where they ready themselves to cross the River of Death on foot to Mount Zion and the Celestial City. Christian has a rough time of it, but Hopeful helps him over; and they are welcomed into the Celestial City.

Second Part

The Second Part of *The Pilgrim's Progress* presents the pilgrimage of Christian's wife, Christiana; their sons; and the maiden, Mercy. They visit the same stopping places that Christian visited, with the addition of

Gaius' Inn between the Valley of the Shadow of Death and Vanity Fair; but they take a longer time in order to accommodate marriage and childbirth for the four sons and their wives. The hero of the story is Greatheart, the servant of the Interpreter, who is a pilgrim's guide to the Celestial City. He kills four giants and participates in the slaying of a monster that terrorizes the city of Vanity.

The passage of years in this second pilgrimage better allegorizes the journey of the Christian life. By using heroines, Bunyan, in the Second Part, illustrates the idea that women as well as men can be brave pilgrims.

Part II, which appeared in 1684, is much more than a mere sequel to or repetition of the earlier volume. It clarifies and reinforces and justifies the story of Part I. The beam of Bunyan's spotlight is broadened to include Christian's family and other men, women, and children; the incidents and accidents of everyday life are more numerous, the joys of the pilgrimage tend to outweigh the hardships; and to the faith and hope of Part I is added in abundant measure that greatest of virtues, charity. The two parts of The Pilgrim's Progress in reality constitute a whole, and the whole is, without doubt, the most influential religious book ever written in the English language.

This is exemplified by the frailness of the pilgrims of the Second Part in contrast to those of the First: women, children, and physically and mentally challenged individuals. When Christiana's party leaves Gaius's Inn and Mr. Feeble-mind lingers in order to be left behind he is encouraged to accompany the party by Greatheart:

> But brother... I have it in commission, to comfort the feeble-minded, and to support the weak. You must needs go along with us; we will wait for you, we will lend you our help, we will deny ourselves of some things, both opinionative and practical, for your sake; we will not enter into doubtful disputations before you, we will be made all things to you, rather than you shall be left behind.

When the pilgrims end up in the Land of Beulah, they cross over the River of Death by appointment. As a matter of importance to Christians of Bunyan's persuasion reflected in the narrative of *The Pilgrim's Progress*, the last words of the pilgrims as they cross over the river are recorded. The four sons of Christian and their families do not cross, but remain for the support of the church in that place.

First Part

1) CHRISTIAN, whose name was Graceless at some time before, the protagonist in the First Part, whose journey to the Celestial City is the plot of the story.
2) EVANGELIST, the religious man who puts Christian on the path to the Celestial City. He also shows Christian a book, which readers assume to be the Bible.
3) Obstinate, one of the two residents of the City of Destruction, who run after Christian when he first sets out, in order to bring him back.
4) Pliable, the other of the two, who goes with Christian until both of them fall into the Slough of Despond. Pliable escapes from the slough and returns home.
5) Help, Christian's rescuer from the Slough of Despond.

6) MR. WORLDLY WISEMAN, a resident of a place called Carnal Policy, who persuades Christian go out of his way to be helped by a Mr. Legality and then move to the City of Morality.

7) GOODWILL, the keeper of the Wicket Gate through which one enters the "straight and narrow way" (also referred to as "the King's Highway") to the Celestial City. In the Second Part we find that this character is none other than Jesus Christ Himself.

8) Beelzebub, literally "Lord of the Flies", is one of the devil's companion archdevils who has erected a fort near the Wicket Gate from which he and his companions can shoot arrows at those who are about to enter the Wicket Gate. He is also the Lord of Vanity Fair. Christian calls him "captain" of the fiend Apollyon.

9) THE INTERPRETER, the one who has his House along the way as a rest stop for travellers to check in to see pictures and dioramas to teach them the right way to live the Christian life. He has been identified as the Holy Spirit. He also appears in the Second Part.

10) Shining Ones, the messengers and servants of "the Lord of the Hill", God. They are obviously the holy angels.

11) Formalist, one of two travellers on the King's Highway, who do not come in by the Wicket Gate, but climb over the wall that encloses it, at least from the hill and sepulcre up to the Hill Difficulty. He and his companion Hypocrisy come from the land of Vainglory. He takes one of the two bypaths that avoid the Hill Difficulty, but is lost.

12) Hypocrisy, the companion of Formalist. He takes the other of the two bypaths and is also lost.

13) Timorous, one of two who try to persuade Christian to go back for fear of the chained lions near the House Beautiful. He is a relative of Mrs. Timorous of the Second Part. His companion is

14) Mistrust.

15) Watchful, the porter of the House Beautiful. He also appears in the Second Part and receives "a gold angel" coin from Christiana for his kindness and service to her and her companions. "Watchful" is also the name of one of the Delectable Mountains' shepherds.

16) Discretion, one of the maids of the House Beautiful, who decides to allow Christian to stay there.

17) Prudence, another of the House Beautiful maidens. She appears in the Second Part.

18) Piety, another of the House Beautiful maidens. She appears in the Second Part.

19) Charity, another of the House Beautiful maidens. She appears in the Second Part.

20) APOLLYON, literally "Destroyer"; the lord of the City of Destruction and one of the devil's companion archdevils, who tries to force Christian to return to his domain and service. His battle with Christian takes place in the Valley of Humiliation, just below the House Beautiful. He appears as a dragon-like creature with scales and bats' wings. He takes darts from his body to throw at his opponents.

21) Giants "Pope" and "Pagan", allegories of Roman Catholicism and paganism as persecutors of

Protestant Christians. "Pagan" is dead, indicating the end of pagan persecution with Antiquity, and "Pope" is alive but decrepit, indicating the then diminished power and influence of the Roman Catholic pope.

22) FAITHFUL, Christian's friend from the City of Destruction, who is also going on pilgrimage. Christian meets him just after getting through the Valley of the Shadow of Death.

23) Wanton, a temptress who tries to get Faithful to leave his journey to the Celestial City. She may be the popular resident of the City of Destruction, Madam Wanton, who hosted a house party for friends of Mrs. Timorous.

24) Adam the First, "the old man" (representing carnality) who tries to persuade Faithful to leave his journey and come live with his 3 daughters: the Lust of the flesh, the Lust of the eyes, and the Pride of life.

25) Moses, the severe, violent avenger (representing the Law, which knows no mercy) who tries to kill Faithful for his momentary weakness in wanting to go with Adam the First out of the way.

26) Talkative, a hypocrite known to Christian from the City of Destruction, who lived on Prating Row. He talks fervently of religion, but has no evident works as a result of true salvation.

27) Lord Hate-good, the judge who tries Faithful in Vanity Fair.

28) Envy, the first witness against Faithful.

29) Superstition, the second witness against Faithful.

30) Pick-Thank, the third witness against Faithful.

31) HOPEFUL, the resident of Vanity Fair, who takes Faithful's place as Christian's fellow traveller. The character HOPEFUL poses an inconsistency in that there is a necessity imposed on the pilgrims that they enter the "King's Highway" by the Wicket Gate. HOPEFUL did not; however, of him we read: "... one died to bear testimony to the truth, and another rises out of his ashes to be a companion with Christian in his pilgrimage". HOPEFUL assumes FAITHFUL'S place by God's design. Theologically and allegorically it would follow in that "faith" is trust in God as far as things present are concerned, and "hope", biblically the same as "faith", is trust in God as far as things of the future are concerned. HOPEFUL would follow FAITHFUL. The other factor is Vanity Fair's location right on the straight and narrow way. IGNORANCE, in contrast to HOPEFUL, came from the Country of Conceit, that connected to the "King's Highway" by means of a crooked lane. IGNORANCE was told by CHRISTIAN and HOPEFUL that he should have entered the highway through the Wicket Gate.

32) Mr. By-Ends, a hypocritical pilgrim who perishes in the Hill Lucre silver mine with three of his friends. A "by-end" is a pursuit that is achieved indirectly. In the case of By-Ends and his companions, it is pursuing financial gain through religion.

33) Demas, a deceiver, who beckons to pilgrims at the Hill Lucre to come and join in the supposed silver mining going on in it.

34) GIANT DESPAIR, the owner of Doubting Castle, where Christians are imprisoned and murdered. He is slain by GREAT-HEART in the Second Part.

35) Giantess Diffidence, Despair's wife. She is slain by OLD HONEST in the Second Part.

36) Knowledge, one of the shepherds of the Delectable Mountains.

37) Experience, another of the Delectable Mountains shepherds.

38) Watchful, another of the Delectable Mountains shepherds.

39) Sincere, another of the Delectable Mountains shepherds.

40) IGNORANCE, "a brisk young lad", who joins the "King's Highway" by way of the "crooked lane" that comes from his native country, called "Conceit." He follows Christian and Hopeful and on two occasions talks with them. He believes that he will be received into the Celestial City because of his doing good works in accordance with God's will. Jesus Christ is for him only an example not a Savior. Christian and Hopeful try to set him right, but they fail. He gets a ferryman, Vain-Hope, to ferry him across the River of Death rather than cross it on foot as one is supposed to do. When he gets to the gates of the Celestial City, he is asked for a "certificate" needed for entry, which he does not have. The King, then, orders that he be bound and cast into hell.

41) The Flatterer, a deceiver who leads Christian and Hopeful out of their way, when they fail to look at the roadmap given them by the Shepherds of the Delectable Mountains.

42) Atheist, a mocker of CHRISTIAN and HOPEFUL, who goes the opposite way on the "King's Highway" because he boasts that he knows that God and the Celestial City do not exist.

Second Part

1) Mr. Sagacity, a guest narrator who meets Bunyan himself in his new dream and recounts the events of the Second Part up to the arrival at the Wicket Gate.

2) CHRISTIANA, wife of CHRISTIAN, who leads her four sons and neighbour MERCY on pilgrimage.

3) MATTHEW, CHRISTIAN and CHRISTIANA's eldest son, who marries MERCY.

4) SAMUEL, second eldest son, who marries Grace, Mr. Mnason's daughter.

5) JOSEPH, third eldest son, who marries Martha, Mr. Mnason's daughter.

6) JAMES, youngest son, who marries Phoebe, Gaius's daughter.

7) MERCY, CHRISTIANA's neighbour, who goes with her on pilgrimage and marries MATTHEW.

8) Mrs. Timorous, relative of the Timorous of the First Part, who comes with MERCY to see CHRISTIANA before she sets out on pilgrimage.

9) Mrs. Bat's-Eyes, a resident of The City of Destruction and friend of Mrs. Timorous. Since she has a bat's eyes, she would be blind or nearly blind, so her characterization of Christiana as blind in her desire to go on pilgrimage is hypocritical.

10) Mrs. Inconsiderate, a resident of The City of Destruction and friend of Mrs. Timorous. She characterizes Christiana's departure "a good riddance" as an inconsiderate person would.

11) Mrs. Light-Mind, a resident of The City of Destruction and friend of Mrs. Timorous. She

changes the subject from Christiana to gossip about being at a bawdy party at Madam Wanton's home.

12) Mrs. Know-Nothing, a resident of The City of Destruction and friend of Mrs. Timorous. She wonders if Christiana will actually go on pilgrimage.

13) Ill-favoured Ones, two evil characters CHRISTIANA sees in her dream, whom she and MERCY actually encounter when they leave the Wicket Gate.

14) Innocent, a young serving maid of the INTERPRETER, who answers the door of the house when Christiana and her companions arrive; and who conducts them to the garden bath, which signifies Christian baptism.

15) MR. GREAT-HEART, the guide and body-guard sent by the INTERPRETER with CHRISTIANA and her companions from his house to their journey's end. He proves to be one of the main protagonists in the Second Part.

16) Giant Grim, who "backs the [chained] lions" near the House Beautiful, slain by GREAT-HEART. He is also known as Bloody-man.

17) Humble-Mind, one of the maidens of the House Beautiful, who makes her appearance in the Second Part.

18) Mr. Brisk, a suitor of MERCY's, who gives up courting her when he finds out that she makes clothing only to give away to the poor.

19) Mr. Skill, the physician called to the House Beautiful to cure Matthew of his illness, which is caused by eating the apples of Beelzebub.

20) Giant Maul, a giant that GREAT-HEART kills as the pilgrims leave the Valley of the Shadow of Death.

21) OLD HONEST, a pilgrim that joins them, a welcome companion to GREAT-HEART.

22) Mr. Fearing, a pilgrim whom GREAT-HEART had "conducted" to the Celestial City in an earlier pilgrimage. Noted for his timidness. He is Mr. Feeble-Mind's uncle.

23) Gaius, an innkeeper with whom the pilgrims stay for some years after they leave the Valley of the Shadow of Death. He gives his daughter Phebe to JAMES in marriage. The lodging fee for his inn is paid by the Good Samaritan.

24) Giant Slay-Good, a giant that enlists the help of evil-doers on the King's Highway to abduct, murder, and consume pilgrims.

25) Mr. Feeble-Mind, rescued from Slay-Good by Mr. Great-Heart, who joins Christiana's company of pilgrims.

26) Phoebe, Gaius's daughter, who marries JAMES.

27) Mr. Ready-to-Halt, a pilgrim who meets CHRISTIANA's train of pilgrims at Gaius's door, and becomes the companion of Mr. Feeble-mind, to whom he gives one of his crutches.

28) Mr. Mnason, a resident of the town of Vanity, who puts up the pilgrims for a time, and gives his daughters Grace and Martha in marriage to SAMUEL and JOSEPH respectively.

29) Grace, Mnason's daughter, who marries SAMUEL.

30) Martha, Mnason's daughter, who marries JOSEPH.

31) Mr. Despondency, a rescued prisoner from Doubting Castle.

32) Much-Afraid, his daughter.

33) Mr. VALIANT-FOR-TRUTH, a pilgrim they find all bloody, with his sword in his hand, after leaving the Delectable Mountains.

34) Mr. Stand-Fast, a pilgrim found while praying for deliverance from Madame Bubble.

35 Madame Bubble, a witch whose enchantments made the Enchanted Ground enchanted. She is the adulterous woman mentioned in the Biblical *Book of Proverbs*.

Places in The Pilgrim's Progress

1) City of Destruction, Christian's home, representative of the world.

2) Slough of Despond, the miry swamp on the way to the Wicket Gate; one of the hazards of the journey to the Celestial City. In the First Part, Christian falling into it, sinks further under the weight of his sins (his burden) and his sense of their guilt.

3) Mount Sinai, a frightening mountain near the Village of Morality that threatens all who would go there.

4) Wicket Gate, the entry point of the straight and narrow way to the Celestial City. Pilgrims are required to enter the way by way of the Wicket Gate.

5) House of the Interpreter, a type of spiritual museum to guide the pilgrims to the Celestial City.

6) Cross and Sepulchre, emblematic of Calvary and the tomb of Christ.

7) Hill Difficulty, both the hill and the road up is called "Difficulty"; it is flanked by two treacherous byways "Danger" and "Destruction." There are three choices: CHRISTIAN takes "Difficulty" (the right way), and Formalist and Hypocrisy take the two other ways, which prove to be fatal dead ends.

8) House Beautiful, a palace that serves as a rest stop for pilgrims to the Celestial City. It apparently sits atop the Hill Difficulty. From the House Beautiful one can see forward to the Delectable Mountains. It represents the Christian congregation, and Bunyan takes its name from a gate of the Jerusalem temple.

9) Valley of Humiliation, the valley on the other side of the Hill Difficulty, going down into which is said to be extremely slippery by the House Beautiful's damsel Prudence. It is where Christian meets Apollyon in the place known as "Forgetful Green." This valley had been a delight to the "Lord of the Hill", Jesus Christ, in his "state of humiliation."

10) Valley of the Shadow of Death, a treacherous valley with a quick sand bog on one side and a deep chasm/ditch on the other side of the King's Highway going through it.

11) Gaius's inn, a rest stop in the Second Part

12) Vanity and Vanity Fair, a city through which the King's Highway passes and the yearlong fair that is held there.

13) Plain Ease, a pleasant area traversed by the pilgrims.

14) Hill Lucre, location of a reputed silver mine that proves to be the place where By-Ends and his companions are lost.

15) The Pillar of Salt, which was Lot's wife, who was turned into a pillar of salt when Sodom and Gomorrah were destroyed. The pilgrim's note that its location near the Hill Lucre is a fitting warning to those who are tempted by Demas to go into the Lucre silver mine.

16) River of God or River of the Water of Life, a place of solace for the pilgrims. It flows through a meadow, green all year long and filled with lush fruit trees. In the Second Part the Good Shepherd is found there to whom Christiana's grandchildren are entrusted.

17) By-Path Meadow, the place leading to the grounds of Doubting Castle.

18) Doubting Castle, the home of Giant Despair and his wife; only one key could open its doors and gates, the key Promise.

19) The Delectable Mountains, known as "Immanuel's Land." Lush country from whose heights one can see many delights and curiosities. It is inhabited by sheep and their shepherds, and from Mount Clear one can see the Celestial City.

20) The Enchanted Ground, an area through which the King's Highway passes that has air that makes pilgrims want to stop to sleep. If one goes to sleep in this place, one never wakes up. The shepherds of the Delectable Mountains warn pilgrims about this.

21) The Land of Beulah, a lush garden area just this side of the River of Death.
22) The River of Death, the dreadful river that surrounds Mount Zion, deeper or shallower depending on the faith of the one traversing it.
23) The Celestial City, the "Desired Country" of pilgrims, heaven, the dwelling place of the "Lord of the Hill", God. It is situated on Mount Zion.

Cultural Influence

Because of the widespread longtime popularity of "The Pilgrim's Progress", Christian's hazards – whether originally from Bunyan or borrowed by him from the Bible – the "Slough of Despond", the "Hill Difficulty", "Valley of the Shadow of Death", "Doubting Castle", and the "Enchanted Ground", his temptations (the wares of "Vanity Fair" and the pleasantness of "By-Path Meadow"), his foes ("Apollyon" and "Giant Despair"), and the helpful stopping places he visits (the "House of the Interpreter", the "House Beautiful", the "Delectable Mountains", and the "Land of Beulah") have become commonly used phrases proverbial in English. For example, "One has one's own Slough of Despond to trudge through."

Context in Christendom

The explicit Protestant theology of *The Pilgrim's Progress* made it much more popular than its predecessors. Bunyan's gifts and plain style breathe life into the abstractions of the anthropomorphized temptations and abstractions that Christian encounters and with whom he converses on his course to Heaven. Samuel Johnson said that "this is the great merit of the book, that the most cultivated man cannot find anything to praise more highly, and the child knows nothing more amusing." Three years after its publication (1681), it was reprinted in colonial America, and was widely read in the Puritan colonies.

Because of its explicit English Protestant theology *The Pilgrim's Progress* shares the then popular English antipathy toward the Roman Catholic Church. It was published over the years of the Popish Plot (1678–1681) and ten years before the Glorious Revolution of 1688, and it shows the influence of John Foxe's *Acts and Monuments*. Bunyan presents a decrepit and harmless giant to confront Christian at the end of the Valley of the Shadow of Death that is explicitly named "Pope":

Now I saw in my Dream, that at the end of this Valley lay blood, bones, ashes, and mangled bodies of men, even of Pilgrims that had gone this way formerly: And while I was musing what should be the reason, I espied a little before me a Cave, where two Giants, *Pope* and *Pagan*, dwelt in old times, by whose Power and Tyranny the Men whose bones, blood ashes, &c. lay there, were cruelly put to death. But by this place *Christian* went without much danger, whereat I somewhat wondered; but I have learnt since, that *Pagan* has been dead many a day; and as for the other, though he be yet alive, he is by reason of age, and also of the many shrewd brushes that he met with in his younger dayes, grown so crazy and stiff in his joynts, that he can now do little more than sit in his Caves mouth, grinning at Pilgrims as they go by, and biting his nails, because he cannot come at them.

When Christian and Faithful travel through Vanity Fair, Bunyan adds the editorial comment:

> But as in other *fairs,* some one Commodity is as the chief of all the *fair,* so the Ware of *Rome* and her Merchandize is greatly promoted in *this fair*: Only our *English* Nation, with some others, have taken a dislike thereat.

In the Second Part while Christiana and her group of pilgrims lead by Greatheart stay for some time in Vanity, the city is terrorized by the seven-headed beast of Revelation 17, which is driven away by Greatheart and other stalwarts. In his endnotes W.R. Owens points out about the woman, who governs the beast: "This woman was believed by Protestants to represent Antichrist, the Church of Rome."

Foreign Language Versions

Beginning in the 1850s, illustrated versions of the *The Pilgrim's Progress* in Chinese were printed in Hong Kong, Shanghai and Fuzhou and widely distributed by Protestant missionaries. Hong Xiuquan, the quasi-Christian leader of the Taiping Rebellion, declared that the book was his favorite reading.

Musical Settings

The book was the basis of an opera by Ralph Vaughan Williams, premiered in 1951. It was also the basis of a condensed radio adaptation starring John Gielgud, including, as background music, several excerpts from Vaughan Williams's orchestral works. This radio version, originally presented in 1942, was newly recorded by Hyperion Records in 1990, in a performance conducted by Matthew Best. It again starred Gielgud, and featured Richard Pasco and Ursula Howells.

English composer Ernest Austin set the whole story as a huge narrative tone poem for solo organ, with optional 6-part choir and narrator, lasting approximately 2½ hours.

Twin brothers Keith and Kurt Landaas also composed, recorded, and performed a compelling rock opera version of the work in the early 1990s. The first act focused on Christian's journey, the second on that of Christiana, and their teenage son Matthew.

A musical based on the book was presented at the LifeHouse Theater in Redlands, California, in 2004 and 2008, with book, music and lyrics by Kenneth Wright, with additional text, music and lyrics by Wayne Scott.

References in Literature

Charles Dickens' Oliver Twist (1838) is subtitled 'The Parish Boy's Progress'.

In 1847 William Makepeace Thackeray entitled his work *Vanity Fair: A Novel without a Hero* with the Vanity Fair of *Pilgrim's Progress* in mind.

In Mark Twain's *Adventures of Huckleberry Finn,* Huckleberry Finn mentions *The Pilgrim's Progress* as he describes the works of literature in the Grangerfords' library. Twain uses this to satirize the Protestant southern aristocracy.

E.E. Cummings also makes numerous references to it in his prose work, *The Enormous Room*.

"The Celestial Railroad", a short story by Nathaniel Hawthorne, recreates Christian's journey in Hawthorne's time. Progressive thinkers have replaced the footpath by a railroad, and pilgrims may now travel under steam power. The journey is considerably faster, but somewhat more questionable...

John Buchan was an admirer of Bunyan, and *Pilgrim's Progress* features significantly in his third

Richard Hannay novel, *Mr Standfast,* which also takes its title from one of Bunyan's characters.

Alan Moore in his *League of Extraordinary Gentlemen* enlists *The Pilgrim's Progress* protagonist, Christian, as a member of the earliest version of this group, *Prospero's Men,* having become wayward on his journey during his visit in Vanity Fair, stepping down an alleyway and found himself in London in the 1670s, and unable to return to his homeland. This group disbanded in 1690 after Prospero vanished into the Blazing World; however there are some parts of the text which seem to imply that Christian resigned from Prospero's league before its disbanding and that Christian traveled to the Blazing World before Prospero himself. The apparent implication is that; within the context of the League stories; the Celestial City Christian seeks and the Blazing World may in fact be one and the same.

In Louisa May Alcott's Little Women, whose protagonist Jo reads it at the outset of the novel, and tries to follow the good example of Bunyan's Christian.

C.S. Lewis wrote a book inspired by The Pilgrim's Progress called The Pilgrim's Regress, in which a character named John follows a vision to escape from The Landlord, a less friendly version of The Owner in Pilgrim's Regress. It is an allegory of C.S. Lewis' own journey from a religious childhood to a pagan adulthood in which he rediscovers his Christian God.

Henry Williamson's The Patriot's Progress references the title of The Pilgrim's Progress and the symbolic nature of John Bunyan's work. The protagonist of the semi-autobiographical novel is John Bullock, the quintessential English soldier during World War I.

The character of Billy Pilgrim in *Slaughterhouse-5: The Children's Crusade,* by Kurt Vonnegut, is a clear homage to a similar journey to enlightenment experienced by Christian, although Billy's is a journey which leads him to an existential acceptance of life and of a fatalist human condition. Vonnegut's parallel to The Pilgrim's Progress is deliberate and evident in Billy's surname.

In *Jane Eyre,* Charlotte Bronte borrows the mythic quest-plot, but not the devout substance, of *The Pilgrim's Progress.* Brontë ends *Jane Eyre* with a half-ironic allusion to *The Pilgrim's Progress.*

A classic science fiction fan novelette, *The Enchanted Duplicator* by Walt Willis and Bob Shaw, is explicitly modeled on *The Pilgrim's Progress;* it has been repeatedly reprinted over the decades since its first appearance in 1954: in professional publications, in fanzines and as a monograph.

Enid Blyton wrote "The Land of Far Beyond" as a children's version of Pilgrim's Progress. First published in 1942 by Methuen.

The book is briefly referenced in the David Foster Wallace novel Infinite Jest, when it is compared to the Eschaton vademecum that is written by Hal Incandenza.

Lois McMasters Bujold quotes "Pilgrim's Progress" in her short story "Borders of Infinity" set in her science fiction, Vorkosigan series. In the story her protagonist, Miles Vorkosigan, enters a prison camp to attempt a breakout. He meets Suegar, a long-time prisoner of the camp, who's prize possession is a scrap of paper he tore from a book (in order to make a shim for his broken boot heel) shortly before his capture. The paper contains a short quote from "Pilgrim's

Progress" and Suegar believes he is one of the two men referenced who will lead the pilgrims up the hill to the city. He comes to believe that Miles is the other "One". Miles uses the quote as inspiration to lead the prisoners to freedom.

John Steinbeck's novel The Grapes of Wrath mentions *The Pilgrim's Progress* as one of an (anonymous) character's favorite books. Steinbeck's novel was itself an allegorical spiritual journey by Tom Joad through America during the Great Depression, and often made Christian allusions to sacrifice and redemption in a world of social injustice.

10

Restoration Comedy

Restoration comedy refers to English comedies written and performed in the Restoration period from 1660 to 1710. After public stage performances had been banned for 18 years by the Puritan regime, the re-opening of the theatres in 1660 signalled a renaissance of English drama. Restoration comedy is notorious for its sexual explicitness, a quality encouraged by Charles II (1660–1685) personally and by the rakish aristocratic ethos of his court. The socially diverse audiences included both aristocrats, their servants and hangers-on, and a substantial middle-class segment. These playgoers were attracted to the comedies by up-to-the-minute topical writing, by crowded and bustling plots, by the introduction of the first professional actresses, and by the rise of the first celebrity actors. This period saw the first professional woman playwright, Aphra Behn.

Theatre Companies

Original Patent Companies, 1660–82

Charles II was an active and interested patron of the drama. Soon after his restoration, in 1660, he granted exclusive play-staging rights, so-called Royal patents, to the King's Company and the Duke's Company, led by two middle-aged Caroline playwrights, Thomas Killigrew and William Davenant. The patentees scrambled for performance rights to the previous generation's Jacobean and Caroline plays, which were the first necessity for economic survival before any new plays existed. Their next priority was to build new, splendid patent theatres in Drury Lane and Dorset Gardens, respectively. Striving to outdo each other in magnificence, Killigrew and Davenant ended up with quite similar theatres, both designed by Christopher Wren, both optimally provided for music and dancing, and both fitted with moveable scenery and elaborate machines for thunder, lightning, and waves.

The audience of the early Restoration period was not exclusively courtly, as has sometimes been supposed, but it was quite small and could barely support two companies. There was no untapped reserve of occasional playgoers. Ten consecutive performances constituted a smash hit. This closed system forced playwrights to be extremely responsive to popular taste. Fashions in the drama would change almost week by week rather than season by season, as each company responded to the offerings of the other, and new plays were urgently sought. The King's Company and the Duke's Company vied with one another for audience favour, for popular actors, and for new plays, and in this hectic climate the new genres of heroic drama, pathetic drama, and Restoration comedy were born and flourished.

United Company, 1682–95

Both the quantity and quality of the drama suffered when in 1682 the more successful Duke's Company ate the struggling King's Company, and the amalgamated *United Company* was formed. The production of new plays dropped off sharply in the 1680s, affected by both the monopoly and the political situation. The influence and the incomes of the actors dropped, too. In the late 80s, predatory investors ("Adventurers") converged on the United Company, while management was taken over by the lawyer Christopher Rich. Rich attempted to finance a tangle of "farmed" shares and sleeping partners by slashing salaries and, dangerously, by abolishing the traditional perks of senior performers, who were stars with the clout to fight back.

War of the Theatres, 1695–1700

The company owners, wrote the young United Company employee Colley Cibber, "who had made a monopoly of the stage, and consequently presum'd they might impose what conditions they pleased upon their people, did not consider that they were all this while endeavouring to enslave a set of actors whom the public were inclined to support." Performers like the legendary Thomas Betterton, the tragedienne Elizabeth Barry, and the rising young comedienne Anne Bracegirdle had the audience on their side and, in the confidence of this, they walked out.

The actors gained a Royal "licence to perform", thus bypassing Rich's ownership of both the original Duke's and King's Company patents from 1660, and formed their own cooperative company. This unique venture was set up with detailed rules for avoiding arbitrary managerial authority, regulating the ten actors' shares, the conditions of salaried employees, and the sickness and retirement benefits of both categories. The cooperative had the good luck to open in 1695 with the première of William Congreve's famous *Love For Love* and the skill to make it a huge box-office success.

London again had two competing companies. Their dash to attract audiences briefly revitalized Restoration drama, but also set it on a fatal downhill slope to the lowest common denominator of public taste. Rich's company notoriously offered Bartholomew Fair-type attractions – high kickers, jugglers, ropedancers, performing animals – while the cooperating actors, even as they appealed to snobbery by setting themselves up as the only legitimate theatre company in London, were not above retaliating with "prologues recited by boys of five, and epilogues declaimed by ladies on horseback".

First Actresses

Restoration comedy was strongly influenced by the introduction of the first professional actresses. Before the closing of the theatres, all female roles had been played by boys, and the predominantly male audiences of the 1660s and 1670s were both curious, censorious, and delighted at the novelty of seeing real women engage in risqué repartee and take part in physical seduction scenes. Samuel Pepys refers many times in his famous diary to visiting the playhouse in order to watch or re-watch the performance of particular actresses, and to how much he enjoys these experiences.

Daringly suggestive comedy scenes involving women became especially common, although of course Restoration actresses were, just like male actors, expected to do justice to all kinds and moods of plays.

(Their role in the development of Restoration tragedy is also important, compare She-tragedy.

A new speciality introduced almost as early as the actresses was the breeches role, which called for an actress to appear in male clothes (breeches being tight-fitting knee-length pants, the standard male garment of the time), for instance in order to play a witty heroine who disguises herself as a boy to hide, or to engage in escapades disallowed to girls. A quarter of the plays produced on the London stage between 1660 and 1700 contained breeches roles. Playing these cross-dressing roles, women behaved with the freedom society allowed to men, and some feminist critics, such as Jacqueline Pearson, regard them as subversive of conventional gender roles and empowering for female members of the audience. Elizabeth Howe has objected that the male disguise, when studied in relation to playtexts, prologues, and epilogues, comes out as "little more than yet another means of displaying the actress as a sexual object" to male patrons, by showing off her body, normally hidden by a skirt, outlined by the male outfit.

Successful Restoration actresses included Charles II's mistress Nell Gwyn, the tragedienne Elizabeth Barry who was famous for her ability to "move the passions" and make whole audiences cry, the 1690s comedienne Anne Bracegirdle, and Susanna Mountfort, who had many breeches roles written especially for her in the 1680s and 90s. Letters and memoirs of the period show that both men and women in the audience greatly relished Mountfort's swaggering, roistering impersonations of young women wearing breeches and thereby enjoying the social and sexual freedom of the male Restoration rake.

Celebrity Actors

During the Restoration period, both male and female actors on the London stage became for the first time public personalities and celebrities. Documents of the period show audiences being attracted to performances by the talents of particular actors as much as by particular plays, and more than by authors (who seem to have been the least important draw, no performance being advertised by author until 1699). Although the playhouses were built for large audiences—the second Drury Lane theatre from 1674 held 2000 patrons -- they were of compact design, and an actor's charisma could be intimately projected from the thrust stage.

With two companies competing for their services from 1660 to 1682, star actors were able to negotiate star deals, comprising company shares and benefit nights as well as salaries. This advantageous situation changed when the two companies were amalgamated in 1682, but the way the actors rebelled and took command of a new company in 1695 is in itself an illustration of how far their status and power had developed since 1660.

The greatest fixed stars among Restoration actors were Elizabeth Barry ("Famous Mrs Barry" who "forc 'd Tears from the Eyes of her Auditory") and Thomas Betterton, both of them active in organising the actors' revolt in 1695 and both original patent-holders in the resulting actors' cooperative.

Betterton played every great male part there was from 1660 into the 18th century. After watching *Hamlet* in 1661, Samuel Pepys reports in his diary that the young beginner Betterton "did the prince's part beyond imagination." Betterton's expressive performances seem to have attracted playgoers as magnetically as did the novelty of seeing women on the stage. He was soon established as the leading man of the Duke's Company, and played Dorimant, the seminal irresistible Restoration rake, at the première of George Etherege's *Man of Mode* (1676). Betterton's position remained unassailable through the 1680s, both as the leading man of the United Company and as its stage manager and *de facto* day-to-day leader. He remained loyal to Rich longer than many of his coworkers, but eventually it was he who headed the actors' walkout in 1695, and who became the acting manager of the new company.

Comedies

Variety and dizzying fashion changes are typical of Restoration comedy. Even though the "Restoration drama" unit taught to college students is likely to be telescoped in a way that makes the plays all sound contemporary, scholars now have a strong sense of the rapid evolution of English drama over these forty years and of its social and political causes. The influence of theatre company competition and playhouse economics is also acknowledged.

Restoration comedy peaked twice. The genre came to spectacular maturity in the mid-1670s with an extravaganza of aristocratic comedies. Twenty lean years followed this short golden age, although the achievement of Aphra Behn in the 1680s is to be noted. In the mid-1690s a brief second Restoration comedy renaissance arose, aimed at a wider audience. The comedies of the golden 1670s and 1690s peak times are extremely different from each other. An attempt is made below to illustrate the generational taste shift by describing *The Country Wife* (1675) and *The Provoked*

Wife (1697) in some detail. These two plays differ from each other in some typical ways, just as a Hollywood movie of the 1950s differs from one of the 1970s. The plays are not, however, offered as being "typical" of their decades. Indeed, there exist no typical comedies of the 1670s or the 1690s; even within these two short peak-times, comedy types kept mutating and multiplying.

Aristocratic Comedy, 1660–80

The drama of the 1660s and 1670s was vitalised by the competition between the two patent companies created at the Restoration, as well as by the personal interest of Charles II, and the comic playwrights rose to the demand for new plays. They stole freely from the contemporary French and Spanish stage, from English Jacobean and Caroline plays, and even from Greek and Roman classical comedies, and combined the looted plotlines in adventurous ways. Resulting differences of tone in a single play were appreciated rather than frowned on, as the audience prized "variety" within as well as between plays. Early Restoration audiences had little enthusiasm for structurally simple, well-shaped comedies such as those of Molière; they demanded bustling, crowded multi-plot action and fast pace. Even a splash of high heroic drama might be thrown in to enrich the comedy mix, as in George Etherege's *Love in a Tub* (1664), which has one heroic verse "conflict between love and friendship" plot, one urbane wit comedy plot, and one burlesque pantsing plot. Such incongruities contributed to Restoration comedy being held in low esteem in the 18th, 19th and early 20th centuries, but today the early Restoration total theatre experience is again valued on the stage, as well as by postmodern academic critics.

The unsentimental or "hard" comedies of John Dryden, William Wycherley, and George Etherege reflected the atmosphere at Court, and celebrated with frankness an aristocratic macho lifestyle of unremitting sexual intrigue and conquest. The Earl of Rochester, real-life Restoration rake, courtier and poet, is flatteringly portrayed in Etherege's *The Man of Mode* (1676) as a riotous, witty, intellectual, and sexually irresistible aristocrat, a template for posterity's idea of the glamorous Restoration rake (actually never a very common character in Restoration comedy). Wycherley's *The Plain Dealer* (1676), a variation on the theme of Moliere's *Le misanthrope,* was highly regarded for its uncompromising satire and earned Wycherley the appellation "Plain Dealer" Wycherley or "Manly" Wycherley, after the play's main character Manly. The single play that does most to support the charge of obscenity levelled then and now at Restoration comedy is probably Wycherley's *The Country Wife* (1675).

William Wycherley, The Country Wife (1675)

The Country Wife has three interlinked but distinct plots, which each project sharply different moods:

1. Horner's impotence trick provides the main plot and the play's organizing principle. The upper-class town rake Horner mounts a campaign for seducing as many respectable ladies as possible, first spreading a false rumour of his own impotence, in order to be allowed where no complete man may go. The trick is a great success and Horner has sex with many married ladies of virtuous reputation, whose husbands are happy to leave him alone with them. In one famously outrageous scene, the "China scene", sexual

intercourse is assumed to take place repeatedly just off stage, where Horner and his mistresses carry on a sustained double entendre dialogue purportedly about Horner's china collection. *The Country Wife* is driven by a succession of near-discoveries of the truth about Horner's sexual prowess (and thus the truth about the respectable ladies), from which he extricates himself by quick thinking and good luck. Horner never becomes a reformed character, but keeps his secret to the end and is assumed to go on merrily reaping the fruits of his planted misinformation, past the last act and beyond.

2. The married life of Pinchwife and Margery is based on Molière's *School For Wives*. Pinchwife is a middle-aged man who has married an ignorant young country girl in the hope that she will not know to cuckold him. However, Horner teaches her, and Margery cuts a swathe through the sophistications of London marriage without even noticing them. She is enthusiastic about the virile handsomeness of town gallants, rakes, and especially theatre actors (such self-referential stage jokes were nourished by the new higher status of actors), and keeps Pinchwife in a state of continual horror with her plain-spokenness and her interest in sex. A running joke is the way Pinchwife's pathological jealousy always leads him into supplying Margery with the very type of information he wishes her not to have.

3. The courtship of Harcourt and Alithea is a comparatively uplifting love story in which the witty Harcourt wins the hand of Pinchwife's sister Alithea from the hands of the Upper-class town

snob Sparkish whom she was engaged to until she discovered he only loved her for her money and nothing else except of course himself as he is generally described as a beauty whose looks deeply affect those around him but vanity is poison.

Decline of Comedy, 1678–90

When the two companies were amalgamated in 1682 and the London stage became a monopoly, both the number and the variety of new plays being written dropped sharply. There was a swing away from comedy to serious political drama, reflecting preoccupations and divisions following on the Popish Plot (1678) and the Exclusion Crisis (1682). The few comedies produced also tended to be political in focus, the whig dramatist Thomas Shadwell sparring with the tories John Dryden and Aphra Behn. Behn's unique achievement as an early professional woman writer has been the subject of much recent study.

Comedy Renaissance, 1690–1700

During the second wave of Restoration comedy in the 1690s, the "softer" comedies of William Congreve and John Vanbrugh reflected mutating cultural perceptions and great social change. The playwrights of the 1690s set out to appeal to more socially mixed audiences with a strong middle-class element, and to female spectators, for instance by moving the war between the sexes from the arena of intrigue into that of marriage. The focus in comedy is less on young lovers outwitting the older generation, more on marital relations after the wedding bells. Thomas Southerne's dark *The Wives' Excuse* (1691) is not yet very "soft": it shows a woman miserably married to the fop Friendall, everybody's friend, whose follies and indiscretions undermine her social worth, since her honour is bound up in his. Mrs Friendall is pursued by a would-be lover, a matter-of-fact rake devoid of all the qualities that made Etherege's Dorimant charming, and she is kept from action and choice by the unattractiveness of all her options. All the humour of this "comedy" is in the subsidiary love-chase and fornication plots, none in the main plot.

In Congreve's *Love for Love* (1695) and *The Way of the World* (1700), the "wit duels" between lovers typical of 1670s comedy are underplayed. The give-and-take set pieces of couples still testing their attraction for each other have mutated into witty prenuptial debates on the eve of marriage, as in the famous "Proviso" scene in *The Way of the World* (1700). Vanbrugh's *The Provoked Wife* (1697) follows in the footsteps of Southerne's *Wives' Excuse,* with a lighter touch and more humanly recognizable characters.

John Vanbrugh, The Provoked Wife (1697)

The Provoked Wife is something of a Restoration problem play in its attention to the subordinate legal position of married women and the complexities of "divorce" and separation, issues that had been highlighted in the mid-1690s by some notorious cases before the House of Lords.

Sir John Brute in *The Provoked Wife* is tired of matrimony. He comes home drunk every night and is continually rude and insulting to his wife. She is meanwhile being tempted to embark upon an affair with the witty and faithful Constant. Divorce is not an option for either of the Brutes at this time, but forms of legal separation have recently come into existence, and would entail a separate maintenance to the wife. Such an arrangement would not allow remarriage. Still, muses Lady Brute, in one of many discussions with her niece Bellinda, "These are good times. A woman may have a gallant and a separate maintenance too."

Bellinda is at the same time being grumpily courted by Constant's friend Heartfree, who is surprised and dismayed to find himself in love with her. The bad example of the Brutes is a constant warning to Heartfree to not marry.

The Provoked Wife is a talk play, with the focus less on love scenes and more on discussions between female friends (Lady Brute and Bellinda) and male friends (Constant and Heartfree). These exchanges, full of jokes though they are, are thoughtful and have a dimension of melancholy and frustration.

After a forged-letter complication, the play ends with marriage between Heartfree and Bellinda and stalemate between the Brutes. Constant continues to pay court to Lady Brute, and she continues to shilly-shally.

End of Comedy

The tolerance for Restoration comedy even in its modified form was running out at the end of the 17th century, as public opinion turned to respectability and seriousness even faster than the playwrights did. Interconnected causes for this shift in taste were demographic change, the Glorious Revolution of 1688, William's and Mary's dislike of the theatre, and the lawsuits brought against playwrights by the Society for the Reformation of Manners. When Jeremy Collier attacked Congreve and Vanbrugh in his *Short View of the Immorality and Profaneness of the English Stage* in 1698, he was confirming a shift in audience taste that had already taken place. At the much-anticipated all-star première in 1700 of *The Way of the World,* Congreve's first comedy for five years, the audience showed only moderate enthusiasm for that subtle and almost melancholy work. The comedy of sex and wit was about to be replaced by the drama of obvious sentiment and exemplary morality.

During the 18th and 19th centuries, the sexual frankness of Restoration comedy ensured that theatre producers cannibalised it or adapted it with a heavy hand, rather than actually performed it. Today, Restoration comedy is again appreciated on the stage. The classics, Wycherley's *The Country Wife* and *The Plain-Dealer,* Etherege's *The Man of Mode,* and Congreve's *Love For Love* and *The Way of the World* have competition not only from Vanbrugh's *The Relapse* and *The Provoked Wife,* but from such dark unfunny comedies as Thomas Southerne's *The Wives Excuse.* Aphra Behn, once considered unstageable, has had a major renaissance, with *The Rover* now a repertory favourite.

Distaste for sexual impropriety long kept Restoration comedy not only off the stage but also locked in a critical poison cupboard. Victorian critics like William Hazlitt, although valuing the linguistic energy and "strength" of the canonical writers Etherege, Wycherley, and Congreve, always found it necessary to temper aesthetic praise with heavy moral condemnation. Aphra Behn received the condemnation without the praise, since outspoken sex comedy was considered particularly offensive coming from a woman author. At the turn of the 20th century, an embattled minority of academic Restoration comedy enthusiasts began to appear, for example the important editor Montague Summers, whose work ensured that the plays of Aphra Behn remained in print.

"Critics remain astonishingly defensive about the masterpieces of this period", wrote Robert D. Hume as late as 1976. It is only over the last few decades that that statement has become untrue, as Restoration comedy has been acknowledged a rewarding subject for high theory analysis and Wycherley's *The Country Wife*, long branded the most obscene play in the English language, has become something of an academic favourite. "Minor" comic writers are getting a fair share of attention, especially the post-Aphra Behn generation of women playwrights which appeared just around the turn of the 18th century: Delarivier Manley, Mary Pix, Catharine Trotter, and Susannah Centlivre. A broad study of the majority of never-reprinted Restoration comedies has been made possible by Internet access (by subscription only) to the first editions at the British Library.

11

Life and Works of Charles Dickens

Charles John Huffam Dickens, FRSA, pen-name "Boz", was the most popular English novelist of the Victorian era, and one of the most popular of all time. He created some of literature's most iconic characters, with the theme of social reform running throughout his work. The continuing popularity of his novels and short stories is such that they have never gone out of print.

Much of his work first appeared in periodicals and magazines in serialised form, a popular way of publishing fiction at the time. Other writers would complete entire novels before serial publication commenced, but Dickens often wrote his in parts, in the order they were meant to appear. The practice lent his stories a particular rhythm, punctuated by one "cliffhanger" after another, to keep the public eager for the next installment.

His work has been praised for its mastery of prose, and for its teeming gallery of unique personalities, by writers such as George Gissing and G. K. Chesterton, though the same characteristics have prompted others, such as Henry James and Virginia Woolf, to criticize him for sentimentality and implausibility

Early Years

His early years seem to have been an idyllic time, although he thought himself then a "very small and not-over-particularly-taken-care-of boy". He spent time outdoors, but also read voraciously, with a particular fondness for the picaresque novels of Tobias Smollett and Henry Fielding. He spoke, later in life, of his poignant memories of childhood, and of his near photographic memory of the people and events, which he used to bring his fiction to life. John Dickens's tenuous prosperity as a clerk in the Navy Pay Office afforded a few years of private education of the young Charles at William Giles's School, in Chatham. This period came to an abrupt end after John Dickens had spent beyond his means in entertaining and otherwise maintaining his social position, and was imprisoned in the Marshalsea debtor's prison. Shortly afterwards, the rest of his family joined him in residence at the Marshalsea (on the south bank of the Thames in London), except Charles, who boarded in Camden Town at the house of family friend Elizabeth Roylance. Sundays became a treat, when with his sister Fanny, allowed out from the Royal Academy of Music, he spent the day at the Marshalsea.

Just before his father's arrest, 12-year-old Dickens had begun working ten-hour days at Warren's Blacking Warehouse, on Hungerford Stairs, near the present Charing Cross railway station. He earned six shillings a week pasting labels on jars of shoe polish. This money paid for his lodgings with Mrs. Roylance and helped support his family. Mrs. Roylance, Dickens later wrote, was "a reduced old lady, long known to our family", and whom he eventually immortalized, "with a few alterations and embellishments", as "Mrs.

Pipchin", in *Dombey & Son*. Later, lodgings were found for him in a "back-attic...at the house of an insolvent-court agent, who lived in Lant Street in The Borough...he was a fat, good-natured, kind old gentleman, with a quiet old wife; and he had a very innocent grown-up son; these three were the inspiration for the Garland family in *The Old Curiosity Shop*. The mostly unregulated, strenuous—and often cruel—work conditions of the factory employees (especially children) made a deep impression on Dickens. His experiences served to influence later fiction and essays, and were the foundation of his interest in the reform of socio-economic and labour conditions, the rigours of which he believed were unfairly borne by the poor.

After only a few months in Marshalsea, John Dickens was informed of the death of his paternal grandmother, Elizabeth Dickens, who had left him in her will the sum of £450. On the expectation of this legacy, Dickens petitioned for, and was granted, release from prison. Under the Insolvent Debtors Act, Dickens arranged for payment of his creditors, and he and his family left Marshalsea for the home of Mrs. Roylance.

Although Dickens eventually attended the Wellington House Academy in North London, his mother did not immediately remove him from the boot-blacking factory. 'The incident must have done much to confirm Dickens's determined view that a father should rule the family, a mother find her proper sphere inside the home. "I never afterwards forgot, I never shall forget, I never can forget, that my mother was warm for my being sent back." His mother's failure (in his eyes), in requesting that Charles return to the blacking factory, was no doubt a factor in the grown man's demanding and dissatisfied attitude towards women.' Resentment stemming from his situation and the conditions under which working-class people lived became major themes of his works, and it was this unhappy period in his youth to which he alluded in his favourite, and most autobiographical, novel, *David Copperfield*: "I had no advice, no counsel, no encouragement, no consolation, no assistance, no support, of any kind, from anyone, that I can call to mind, as I hope to go to heaven!" The Wellington House Academy, as it turned out, was not a good school. 'Much of the haphazard, desultory teaching, poor discipline punctuated by the headmaster's sadistic brutality, the seedy ushers and general rundown atmosphere, are embodied in Mr. Creakle's Establishment in *David Copperfield*.'

In May 1827, Dickens began work in the law office of Ellis and Blackmore, attorneys, of Holborn Court, Gray's Inn, as a junior clerk. He remained there until November 1828. Then, having worked energetically in his spare time to acquire Gurneys system of shorthand, he left to become a freelance reporter. A distant relative, Thomas Charlton, was a freelance reporter at Doctors' Commons, and Dickens was able to share his box there in order to report the legal proceedings. Here in a court near St. Paul's he was to listen for nearly four years to rambling, involved cases. This education informed works such as *Nicholas Nickleby*, *Dombey and Son*, and especially *Bleak House*—whose vivid portrayal of the tangled machinations, laborious manoeuvrings, and strangling bureaucracy of the legal system of mid-19th-century Britain did much to enlighten the general public, and was a vehicle for dissemination of

Dickens's own views regarding, particularly, the heavy burden on the poor who were forced by circumstances to "go to law".

In 1830, Dickens met his first love, Maria Beadnell. She is thought to have been the model for the character Dora in *David Copperfield*. Maria's parents disapproved of the courtship and effectively ended the relationship by sending her to school in Paris.

Journalism and Early Novels

In 1833, Dickens was able to get his very first story, *A Dinner at Poplar Walk*, published in the London periodical, *Monthly Magazine*. The following year he rented rooms at Furnival's Inn becoming a political journalist, reporting on parliamentary debate and travelling across Britain by stagecoach to cover election campaigns for the *Morning Chronicle*. His journalism, in the form of sketches which appeared in periodicals, formed his first collection of pieces *Sketches by Boz* which was published in 1836 and led to the serialization of his first novel, *The Pickwick Papers*, in March 1836. He continued to contribute to and edit journals throughout much of his subsequent literary career. Dickens's keen perceptiveness, intimate knowledge and understanding of the people, and tale-spinning genius were quickly to gain him world renown and wealth.

In 1836, Dickens accepted the job of editor of *Bentley's Miscellany*, a position that he would hold for three years, when he fell out with the owner. At the same time, his success as a novelist continued, producing *Oliver Twist* (1837–39), *Nicholas Nickleby* (1838–39), *The Old Curiosity Shop* and, finally, *Barnaby Rudge: A Tale of the Riots of 'Eighty* as part of the *Master*

Humphrey's Clock series (1840–41)—all published in monthly instalments before being made into books. Dickens had a pet raven named Grip which, when it died in 1841, Dickens had it stuffed (it is now at the Free Library of Philadelphia).

On 2 April 1836, he married Catherine Thomson Hogarth (1816 – 1879), the daughter of George Hogarth, editor of the *Evening Chronicle*. After a brief honeymoon in Chalk, Kent, they set up home in Bloomsbury. They had ten children:

1) Charles Culliford Boz Dickens C. C. B. Dickens, later known as Charles Dickens, Jr., editor for *All the Year Round*, author of the *Dickens's Dictionary of London* (1879).
2) Mary Dickens
3) Kate Macready Dickens
4) Walter Landor Dickens
5) Francis Jeffrey Dickens
6) Alfred D'Orsay Tennyson Dickens
7) Sydney Smith Haldimand Dickens
8) Sir Henry Fielding Dickens
9) Dora Annie Dickens
10) Edward Dickens Emigrated to Australia.

On 25 March 1837, Dickens moved with his family into 48 Doughty Street, London, (on which he had a three year lease at £80 a year) where he would remain until December 1839. A new addition to the household was Dickens's younger brother Frederick. Also, Catherine's 17 year old sister Mary moved with them from Furnival's Inn to offer support to her newly married sister and brother-in-law. It was not unusual for a woman's unwed sister to live with and help a newly married couple. Dickens became very attached to Mary, and she died in his arms after a brief illness in 1837. She became a character in many of his books, and her death is fictionalized as the death of Little Nell.

First Visit to America

In 1842, Dickens made his first trip to America travelling with his wife to the United States and Canada, a journey which was successful in spite of his support for the abolition of slavery. The trip is described in the short travelogue *American Notes for General Circulation* and is also the basis of some of the episodes in *Martin Chuzzlewit*. Dickens includes in *Notes* a powerful condemnation of slavery, with "ample proof" of the "atrocities" he found. He called upon President John Tyler at the White House.

During this visit, Dickens spent time in New York City, where he gave lectures, raised support for copyright laws, and recorded many of his impressions of America. He toured the City for a month, and met such luminaries as Washington Irving and William Cullen Bryant. On 14 February 1842, a Boz Ball (named after his pseudonym) was held in his honour at the Park Theater, with 3,000 of New York's elite present. Among the neighbourhoods he visited were Five Points, Wall Street, The Bowery, and the prison known as The Tombs. At this time Georgina Hogarth, another sister of Catherine, joined the Dickens household, now living at Devonshire Terrace, Marylebone, to care for the young family they had left behind. She remained with them as housekeeper, organiser, adviser and friend until her brother-in-law's death in 1870.

Shortly thereafter, he began to show interest in Unitarian Christianity, although he remained an Anglican, at least nominally, for the rest of his life. Dickens's work continued to be popular, especially *A Christmas Carol* written in 1843, the first of his Christmas books, which was reputedly a potboiler written in a matter of weeks to meet the expenses of his wife's fifth pregnancy. After living briefly abroad in Italy (1844) and Switzerland (1846), Dickens continued his success with *Dombey and Son* (1848) and *David Copperfield* (1849–50).

Philanthropy

In May 1846, Angela Burdett Coutts, the wealthy heir to the Coutts banking fortune, approached Dickens about setting up a home for the redemption of "fallen" women. Coutts envisioned a home that would offer a different approach to other organizations that offered a harsh and punishing regimen for these women, and instead provide a disciplined but supportive environment where they could learn to read and write and become proficient in domestic household chores so as to re-integrate them into society gently. After initially resisting, Dickens eventually founded the home, named Urania Cottage, in the Lime Grove section of Shepherds Bush. He would end up becoming involved in many aspects of its day-to-day running, setting the house rules, reviewing the accounts and also interviewing prospective residents, some of whom became characters in his books. He would scour prisons and workhouses for potentially suitable candidates and relied on friends, such as the Magistrate John Hardwick to bring them to his attention. Once found, each potential candidate was given an anonymous printed invitation written by

Dickens called 'An Appeal to Fallen Women', which he signed only as 'Your friend'. If the woman accepted the invitation, Dickens would personally interview her and decide if she could be admitted to the home. In late November 1851, Dickens moved into Tavistock House where he would write *Bleak House* (1852–53), *Hard Times* (1854) and *Little Dorrit* (1857). It was here he got up the amateur theatricals which are described in Forster's Life.

Middle Years

In 1856, his income from his writing had allowed him to buy Gad's Hill Place. This large house in Higham, Kent, had a particular meaning to Dickens as he had walked past it as a child and had dreamed of living in it. The area was also the scene of some of the events of Shakespeare's *Henry IV, Part 1* and this literary connection pleased him.

In 1857, in preparation for public performances of *The Frozen Deep*, a play on which he and his protégé Wilkie Collins had collaborated, Dickens hired professional actresses to play the female parts. With one of these, Ellen Ternan, Dickens formed a bond which was to last the rest of his life. When he separated from his wife, Catherine, in 1858, divorce was almost unthinkable, particularly for someone as famous as he was, and he financially supported her long afterwards. Although they appeared to be initially happy together, Catherine did not seem to share quite the same boundless energy for life which Dickens had. Nevertheless, her job of looking after their ten children, the pressure of living with a world-famous novelist, and keeping house for him, certainly did not help. An indication of his marital dissatisfaction may be seen when, in 1855, he went to meet his first love, Maria

Beadnell. Maria was by this time married as well, but seemed to have fallen short of Dickens's romantic memory of her.

During this period, whilst pondering about giving public readings for his own profit, Dickens was approached by Great Ormond Street Hospital to help it survive its first major financial crisis through a charitable appeal. Dickens, whose philanthropy was well-known, was asked to preside by the hospital's founder Charles West, who happened to be a friend of the author's. He threw himself into the task, heart and soul (a little known fact is that Dickens reported anonymously in the weekly *The Examiner* in 1849 to help mishandled children and wrote another article to help publicise the hospital's opening in 1852). On 9 February 1858, Dickens spoke at the hospital's first annual festival dinner at Freemasons' Hall and later gave a public reading of *A Christmas Carol* at St. Martin-in-the-Fields church hall. The events raised enough money to enable the hospital to purchase the neighbouring house, No. 48 Great Ormond Street, increasing the bed capacity from 20 to 75.

That summer of 1858, after separating from his wife, Dickens would undertake his first series of public readings in London for pay which ended on 22 July. After a mere 10 days rest, however, he began a gruelling and ambitious tour, which would take him through the English provinces, Scotland and Ireland, beginning with a performance in Clifton on 2 August and closing in Brighton, more than three months later, on 13 November. Altogether he was scheduled to read eighty-seven times, on some days giving both a matinée and an evening performance.

Major works, *A Tale of Two Cities* (1859); and *Great Expectations* (1861) soon followed and would prove resounding successes with both his critics and his fans. During this time he was also the publisher and editor of, and a major contributor to, the journals *Household Words* (1850–1859) and *All the Year Round* (1858–1870). A recurring theme in Dickens's writing, both as reportage for these publications and as an inspiration for his fiction, reflected the public's interest in Arctic exploration: the heroic friendship between explorers John Franklin and John Richardson gave the idea for *A Tale of Two Cities, The Wreck of the Golden Mary* and the play *The Frozen Deep*.

In early September 1860, in a field behind Gad's Hill, Dickens made a great bonfire of nearly his entire correspondence. Only those letters on business matters were spared. Since Ellen Ternan burned all of his letters as well, the dimensions of the affair between the two were unknown until the publication of *Dickens and Daughter*, a book about Dickens's relationship with his daughter Kate, in 1939. Kate Dickens worked with author Gladys Storey on the book prior to her death in 1929, and alleged that Dickens and Ternan had a son who died in infancy, though no contemporary evidence exists. On his death, Dickens settled an annuity on Ternan which made her a financially independent woman. Claire Tomalin's book, *The Invisible Woman,* set out to prove that Ternan lived with Dickens secretly for the last 13 years of his life, and was subsequently turned into a play, *Little Nell,* by Simon Gray.

In the same period, Dickens furthered his interest in the paranormal, so much that he was one of the early members of The Ghost Club.

The Franklin Incident

After Franklin died in unexplained circumstances on an expedition to find the North West Passage it was natural for Dickens to write a piece in *Household Words* defending his hero against the discovery in 1854, some four years after the search began, of evidence that Franklin's men had, in their desperation, resorted to cannibalism. Without adducing any supporting evidence he speculates that, far from resorting to cannibalism amongst themselves, the members of the expedition may have been "set upon and slain by the Esquimaux...We believe every savage to be in his heart covetous, treacherous, and cruel." Although publishing in a subsequent issue of *Household Words* a defence of the Esquimaux, written by John Rae, one of Franklin's rescue parties, who had actually visited the scene of the supposed cannibalism, Dickens refused to alter his view.

Last Years

On 9 June 1865, while returning from Paris with Ternan, Dickens was involved in the Staplehurst rail crash in which the first seven carriages of the train plunged off a cast iron bridge that was being repaired. The only first-class carriage to remain on the track was the one in which Dickens was travelling. Dickens spent some time trying to help the wounded and the dying before rescuers arrived. Before leaving, he remembered the unfinished manuscript for *Our Mutual Friend*, and he returned to his carriage to retrieve it. Typically, Dickens later used this experience as material for his short ghost story *The Signal-Man* in which the central character has a premonition of his own death in a rail crash. He based the story around several previous rail accidents, such as the Clayton Tunnel rail crash of 1861.

Dickens managed to avoid an appearance at the inquest into the crash, as it would have become known that he was travelling that day with Ternan and her mother, which could have caused a scandal. Although physically unharmed, Dickens never really recovered from the trauma of the Staplehurst crash, and his normally prolific writing shrank to completing *Our Mutual Friend* and starting the unfinished *The Mystery of Edwin Drood* after a long interval. Much of his time was taken up with public readings from his best-loved novels. Dickens was fascinated by the theatre as an escape from the world, and theatres and theatrical people appear in *Nicholas Nickleby*. The travelling shows were extremely popular. In 1866, a series of public readings were undertaken in England and Scotland. The following year saw more readings in England and Ireland.

Second Visit to America

On 9 November 1867, Dickens sailed from Liverpool embarking on his second American reading tour, which continued into 1868. Landing at Boston on 19 November, he devoted the rest of the month to a round of dinners there with such notables as Ralph Waldo Emerson, Henry Wadsworth Longfellow and his American publisher James Thomas Fields. In early December, the readings began and Dickens spent the month shuttling between Boston and New York. Although he had started to suffer from what he called the "true American catarrh", he kept to a schedule that would have challenged a much younger man, even managing to squeeze in some sleighing in Central

Park. In New York, he gave 22 readings at Steinway Hall between 9 December 1867 and 18 April 1868, and four at Plymouth Church of the Pilgrims between 16 January and 21 January 1868. During his travels, he saw a significant change in the people and the circumstances of America. His final appearance was at a banquet the American Press held in his honour at Delmonico's on 18 April, when he promised to never denounce America again. By the end of the tour, the author could hardly manage solid food, subsisting on champagne and eggs beaten in sherry. On 23 April, he boarded his ship to return to Britain, barely escaping a Federal Tax Lien against the proceeds of his lecture tour.

Farewell Readings

Between 1868 and 1869, Dickens gave a series of "farewell readings" in England, Scotland, and Ireland, until he collapsed on 22 April 1869, at Preston in Lancashire showing symptoms of a mild stroke. After further provincial readings were cancelled, he began work on his final novel, *The Mystery of Edwin Drood*. In an opium den in Shadwell, he witnessed an elderly pusher known as "Opium Sal", who subsequently featured in his mystery novel.

When he had regained sufficient strength, Dickens arranged, with medical approval, for a final series of readings at least partially to make up to his sponsors what they had lost due of his illness. There were to be twelve performances, running between 11 January and 15 March 1870, the last taking place at 8:00 pm at St. James's Hall in London. Although in grave health by this time, he read *A Christmas Carol* and *The Trial from Pickwick*. On 2 May, he made his last public appearance at a Royal Academy Banquet in the presence of the Prince and Princess of Wales, paying a special tribute to the passing of his friend, illustrator Daniel Maclise.

Death

On 8 June 1870, Dickens suffered another stroke at his home, after a full day's work on *Edwin Drood*. The next day, on 9 June, and five years to the day after the Staplehurst crash, he died at Gad's Hill Place never having regained consciousness. Contrary to his wish to be buried at Rochester Cathedral "in an inexpensive, unostentatious, and strictly private manner", he was laid to rest in the Poets' Corner of Westminster Abbey. The inscription on his tomb reads: "CHARLES DICKENS Born 7th February 1812 Died 9th June 1870." A printed epitaph circulated at the time of the funeral reads: "To the Memory of Charles Dickens (England's most popular author) who died at his residence, Higham, near Rochester, Kent, June 9th, 1870, aged 58 years. He was a sympathiser with the poor, the suffering, and the oppressed; and by his death, one of England's greatest writers is lost to the world."

On Sunday, 19 June 1870, five days after Dickens's interment in the Abbey, Dean Arthur Penrhyn Stanley delivered a memorial elegy, lauding "the genial and loving humorist whom we now mourn", for showing by his own example "that even in dealing with the darkest scenes and the most degraded characters, genius could still be clean, and mirth could be innocent." Pointing to the fresh flowers that adorned the novelist's grave, Stanley assured those present that "the spot would thenceforth be a sacred one with both the New World and the Old, as that of the representative of literature, not of this island only, but of all who speak our English tongue."

Dickens's will stipulated that no memorial be erected to honour him. The only life-size bronze statue of Dickens, cast in 1891 by Francis Edwin Elwell, is located in Clark Park in the Spruce Hill neighbourhood of Philadelphia, Pennsylvania in the United States.

Literary Style

Dickens loved the style of 18th century gothic romance, although it had already become a target for parody. One "character" vividly drawn throughout his novels is London itself. From the coaching inns on the outskirts of the city to the lower reaches of the Thames, all aspects of the capital are described over the course of his body of work.

His writing style is florid and poetic, with a strong comic touch. His satires of British aristocratic snobbery—he calls one character the "Noble Refrigerator"—are often popular. Comparing orphans to stocks and shares, people to tug boats, or dinner-party guests to furniture are just some of Dickens's acclaimed flights of fancy. Many of his characters' names provide the reader with a hint as to the roles played in advancing the storyline, such as Mr. Murdstone in the novel David Copperfield, which is clearly a combination of "murder" and stony coldness. His literary style is also a mixture of fantasy and realism.

Characters

Dickens is famed for many things—his depiction of the hardships of the working class, his intricate plots, his sense of humour. But he is perhaps most famed for the characters he created. His novels were heralded early in his career for their ability to capture the everyday man on paper and thus create a memorable character to whom readers could relate, and envision as a real person. Beginning with Pickwick Papers in 1836, Dickens wrote numerous novels, each uniquely filled with believable personalities and vivid physical descriptions. Dickens's friend and biographer, John Forster, said that Dickens made "characters real existences, not by describing them but by letting them describe themselves."

Dickensian characters—especially their typically whimsical names—are among the most memorable in English literature. The likes of Ebenezer Scrooge, Tiny Tim, Jacob Marley, Bob Cratchit, Oliver Twist, The Artful Dodger, Fagin, Bill Sikes, Pip, Miss Havisham, Charles Darnay, David Copperfield, Mr. Micawber, Abel Magwitch, Daniel Quilp, Samuel Pickwick, Wackford Squeers, Uriah Heep and many others are so well known and can be believed to be living a life outside the novels that their stories have been continued by other authors.

The author worked closely with his illustrators supplying them with an overall summary of the work at the outset and thus ensuring that his vision of his characters and settings were exactly how he envisioned them to be. He would brief the illustrator on plans for each month's instalment so that work on the two illustrations could begin before he wrote them. Marcus Stone, illustrator of Our Mutual Friend, recalled that the author was always "ready to describe down to the minutest details the personal characteristics, and... life-history of the creations of his fancy." This close working relationship with his illustrators is important to readers of Dickens today. The illustrations give us a glimpse of the characters as Dickens described them to the illustrator and approved when the drawing was finished. Film makers still use the illustrations as a basis for characterization, costume, and set design in the dramatization of Dickens's works.

Often these characters were based on people that he knew. In a few instances Dickens based the character too closely on the original and got into trouble, as in the case of Harold Skimpole in *Bleak House,* based on Leigh Hunt, and Miss Mowcher in *David Copperfield,* based on his wife's dwarf chiropodist. These are not over-dramatized caricatures, but believable people we might see walking down the street. Indeed, the acquaintances made when reading a Dickens novel are not easily forgotten. The author, Virginia Woolf, maintained that "we remodel our psychological geography when we read Dickens" as he produces "characters who exist not in detail, not accurately or exactly, but abundantly in a cluster of wild yet extraordinarily revealing remarks."

Autobiographical Elements

All authors might be said to incorporate autobiographical elements in their fiction, but with Dickens this is very noticeable, even though he took pains to mask what he considered his shameful, lowly past. *David Copperfield* is one of the most clearly autobiographical but the scenes from *Bleak House* of interminable court cases and legal arguments are drawn from the author's brief career as a court reporter. Dickens's own father was sent to prison (where he was joined by his wife and younger children) for debt, and this became a common theme in many of his books, with the detailed depiction of life in the Marshalsea prison in *Little Dorrit* resulting from Dickens's own experiences of the institution. Little Nell in *The Old Curiosity Shop* is thought to represent Dickens's sister-in-law, William Dorrit, Nicholas Nickleby's father and Wilkins Micawber are certainly Dickens's own father, just as Mrs. Nickleby and Mrs. Micawber are similar to his mother. The snobbish nature of Pip from *Great Expectations* also has some affinity to the author himself. Childhood sweethearts in many of his books (such as Little Eml'y in *David Copperfield*) may have been based on Dickens' own childhood infatuation with Lucy Stroughill. Dickens may have drawn on his childhood experiences, but he was also ashamed of them and would not reveal that this was where he gathered his realistic accounts of squalor. Very few knew the details of his early life until six years after his death when John Forster published a biography on which Dickens had collaborated. A shameful past in Victorian times could taint reputations, just as it did for some of his characters, and this may have been Dickens's own fear.

Episodic Writing

As noted above, most of Dickens's major novels were first written in monthly or weekly instalments in journals such as *Master Humphrey's Clock* and *Household Words*, later reprinted in book form. These instalments made the stories cheap, accessible and the series of regular cliff-hangers made each new episode widely anticipated. American fans even waited at the docks in New York, shouting out to the crew of an incoming ship, "Is Little Nell dead?" Part of Dickens's great talent was to incorporate this episodic writing style but still end up with a coherent novel at the end. The monthly numbers were illustrated by, amongst others, "Phiz" (a pseudonym for Hablot Browne). Among his best-known works are *Great Expectations, David Copperfield, Oliver Twist, A Tale of Two Cities, Bleak House, Nicholas Nickleby, The Pickwick Papers,* and *A Christmas Carol.*

Dickens's technique of writing in monthly or weekly instalments (depending on the work) can be understood by analysing his relationship with his illustrators. The several artists who filled this role were privy to the contents and intentions of Dickens's instalments before the general public. Thus, by reading these correspondences between author and illustrator, the intentions behind Dickens's work can be better understood. What was hidden in his art is made plain in these letters. These also reveal how the interests of the reader and author do not coincide. A great example of that appears in the monthly novel *Oliver Twist.* At one point in this work, Dickens had Oliver become embroiled in a robbery. That particular monthly instalment concludes with young Oliver being shot. Readers expected that they would be forced to wait only a month to find out the outcome of that gunshot. In fact, Dickens did not reveal what became of young Oliver in the succeeding number. Rather, the reading public was forced to wait *two* months to discover if the boy lived.

Another important impact of Dickens's episodic writing style resulted from his exposure to the opinions of his readers. Since Dickens did not write the chapters very far ahead of their publication, he was allowed to witness the public reaction and alter the story depending on those public reactions. A fine example of this process can be seen in his weekly serial

The Old Curiosity Shop, which is a chase story. In this novel, Little Nell and her Grandfather are fleeing the villain Quilp. The progress of the novel follows the gradual success of that pursuit. As Dickens wrote and published the weekly instalments, his friend John Forster pointed out: "You know you're going to have to kill her, don't you?" Why this end was necessary can be explained by a brief analysis of the difference between the structure of a comedy versus a tragedy. In a comedy, the action covers a sequence "You think they're going to lose, you think they're going to lose, they win". In tragedy, it is: "You think they're going to win, you think they're going to win, they lose". The dramatic conclusion of the story is implicit throughout the novel. So, as Dickens wrote the novel in the form of a tragedy, the sad outcome of the novel was a foregone conclusion. If he had not caused his heroine to lose, he would not have completed his dramatic structure. Dickens admitted that his friend Forster was right and, in the end, Little Nell died.

Social Commentary

Dickens's novels were, among other things, works of social commentary. He was a fierce critic of the poverty and social stratification of Victorian society. Dickens's second novel, *Oliver Twist* (1839), shocked readers with its images of poverty and crime and was responsible for the clearing of the actual London slum, Jacob's Island, that was the basis of the story. In addition, with the character of the tragic prostitute, Nancy, Dickens "humanised" such women for the reading public; women who were regarded as "unfortunates," inherently immoral casualties of the Victorian class/economic system. *Bleak House* and *Little Dorrit* elaborated expansive critiques of the Victorian institutional apparatus: the interminable lawsuits of the Court of Chancery that destroyed people's lives in *Bleak House* and a dual attack in *Little Dorrit* on inefficient, corrupt patent offices and unregulated market speculation.

Literary Techniques

Stamp in "The Centenary Edition of The Works of Charles Dickens in 36 Volumes." Dickens is often described as using 'idealised' characters and highly sentimental scenes to contrast with his caricatures and the ugly social truths he reveals. The story of Nell Trent in *The Old Curiosity Shop* (1841) was received as incredibly moving by contemporary readers but viewed as ludicrously sentimental by Oscar Wilde. "You would need to have a heart of stone", he declared in one of his famous witticisms, "not to laugh at the death of Little Nell." (although her death actually takes place off-stage). In 1903 G.K. Chesterton said "It is not the death of Little Nell, but the life of Little Nell, that I object to."

In *Oliver Twist* Dickens provides readers with an idealised portrait of a young boy so inherently and unrealistically 'good' that his values are never subverted by either brutal orphanages or coerced involvement in a gang of young pickpockets. While later novels also centre on idealised characters (Esther Summerson in *Bleak House* and Amy Dorrit in *Little Dorrit*), this idealism serves only to highlight Dickens's goal of poignant social commentary. Many of his novels are concerned with social realism, focusing on mechanisms of social control that direct people's lives (for instance, factory networks in *Hard Times* and hypocritical exclusionary class codes in *Our Mutual Friend*).Dickens also employs incredible coincidences (e.g., Oliver Twist turns out to be the lost nephew of the upper class family that randomly rescues him from the dangers of the pickpocket group). Such coincidences are a staple of eighteenth century picaresque novels such as Henry Fielding's *Tom Jones* that Dickens enjoyed so much. But, to Dickens, these were not just plot devices but an index of the humanism that led him to believe that good wins out in the end and often in unexpected ways.

Legacy

A well-known personality, his novels proved immensely popular during his lifetime. His first full novel, *The Pickwick Papers* (1837), brought him immediate fame, and this success continued throughout his career. Although rarely departing greatly from his typical "Dickensian" method of always attempting to write a great "story" in a somewhat conventional manner (the dual narrators of *Bleak House* constitute a notable exception), he experimented with varied themes, characterisations, and genres. Some of these experiments achieved more popularity than others, and the public's taste and appreciation of his many works have varied over time. Usually keen to give his readers what they wanted, the monthly or weekly publication of his works in episodes meant that the books could change as the story proceeded at the whim of the public. Good examples of this are the American episodes in *Martin Chuzzlewit* which Dickens included in response to lower-than-normal sales of the earlier chapters.

Although his popularity has waned a little since his death, he continues to be one of the best known and most read of English authors. At least 180 motion pictures and TV adaptations based on Dickens's works help confirm his success. Many of his works were adapted for the stage during his own lifetime and as early as 1913 a silent film of *The Pickwick Papers* was made. His characters were often so memorable that they took on a life of their own outside his books. Gamp became a slang expression for an umbrella from the character Mrs. Gamp and Pickwickian, Pecksniffian, and Gradgrind all entered dictionaries due to Dickens's original portraits of such characters who were quixotic, hypocritical, or emotionlessly logical. Sam Weller, the carefree and irreverent valet of *The Pickwick Papers,* was an early superstar, perhaps better known than his author at first. It is likely that *A Christmas Carol* stands as his best-known story, with new adaptations almost every year. It is also the most-filmed of Dickens's stories, with many versions dating from the early years of cinema. This simple morality tale with both pathos and its theme of redemption, sums up (for many) the true meaning of Christmas.

Indeed, it eclipses all other Yuletide stories in not only popularity, but in adding archetypal figures (Scrooge, Tiny Tim, the Christmas ghosts) to the Western cultural consciousness. A prominent phrase from the tale, *'Merry Christmas',* was popularized following the appearance of the story. The term Scrooge became a synonym for miser, with *'Bah! Humbug!'* dismissive of the festive spirit. Novelist William Makepeace Thackeray, called the book; "a national benefit, and to every man and woman who reads it a personal kindness".

Some historians claim the book significantly redefined the "spirit" and importance of Christmas, and initiated a rebirth of seasonal merriment after

Puritan authorities in 17th century England and America suppressed pagan rituals associated with the holiday. According to historian Ronald Hutton, the current state of the observance of Christmas is largely the result of a mid-Victorian revival of the holiday spearheaded by *A Christmas Carol*. Hutton argues, Dickens sought to construct Christmas as a family-centered festival of generosity, in contrast to the community-based and church-centered observations, the observance of which had dwindled during the late eighteenth and early nineteenth centuries. Superimposing his secular vision of the holiday, Dickens influenced many aspects of Christmas that are celebrated today among Western nations, such as family gatherings, seasonal food and drink, dancing, games, and a festive generosity of spirit. *A Christmas Carol* was written by Dickens in an attempt to avoid financial disaster as a result of flagging sales of *Martin Chuzzlewit*. Years later, Dickens shared that he was "deeply affected" in writing *A Christmas Carol*. The novel rejuvenated his career as a renowned author.

At a time when Britain was the major economic and political power of the world, Dickens highlighted the life of the forgotten poor and disadvantaged at the heart of empire. Through his journalism he campaigned on specific issues—such as sanitation and the workhouse—but his fiction probably demonstrated its greatest prowess in changing public opinion in regard to class inequalities. He often depicted the exploitation and repression of the poor and condemned the public officials and institutions that not only allowed such abuses to exist, but flourished as a result. His most strident indictment of this condition is in *Hard Times*, Dickens's only novel-length treatment of the industrial working class. In this work, he uses both vitriol and satire to illustrate how this marginalised social stratum was termed "Hands" by the factory owners; that is, not really "people" but rather only appendages of the machines that they operated. His writings inspired others, in particular journalists and political figures, to address such problems of class oppression.

For example, the prison scenes in *The Pickwick Papers* are claimed to have been influential in having the Fleet Prison shut down. As Karl Marx said, Dickens, and the other novelists of Victorian England, "...issued to the world more political and social truths than have been uttered by all the professional politicians, publicists and moralists put together...". The exceptional popularity of his novels, even those with. socially oppositional themes underscored not only his almost preternatural ability to create compelling storylines and unforgettable characters, but also ensured that the Victorian public confronted issues of social justice that had commonly been ignored.

His fiction, with often vivid descriptions of life in nineteenth century England, has inaccurately and anachronistically come to symbolise on a global level Victorian society (1837 - 1901) as uniformly "Dickensian", when in fact, his novels' time span spanned from the 1770s to the 1860s. In the decade following his death in 1870, a more intense degree of socially and philosophically pessimistic perspectives invested British fiction; such themes stood in marked contrast to the religious faith that ultimately held together even the bleakest of Dickens's novels. Dickens clearly influenced later Victorian novelists such as Thomas Hardy and George Gissing; however, their works display a greater willingness to confront and challenge the Victorian institution of religion. They also portray characters caught up by social forces (primarily via lower-class conditions), but they usually steered them to tragic ends beyond their control.

Novelists continue to be influenced by his books; for instance, such disparate current writers as Anne Rice, Tom Wolfe, and John Irving evidence direct Dickensian connections. Humorist James Finn Garner even wrote a tongue-in-cheek "politically correct" version of *A Christmas Carol*, and other affectionate parodies include the Radio 4 comedy *Bleak Expectations*. Matthew Pearl's novel The Last Dickens is a thriller about how Charles Dickens would have ended Edwin Drood.

Although Dickens's life has been the subject of at least two TV miniseries and two famous one-man shows, he has never been the subject of a Hollywood "big screen" biography.

Allegations of Anti-semitism and Racism

Paul Vallely writes in *The Independent* that Dickens's Fagin in *Oliver Twist* —the Jew who runs a school in London for child pickpockets—is widely seen as one of the most grotesque Jews in English literature, and the most vivid of Dickens's 989 characters.

The mud lay thick upon the stones, and a black mist hung over the streets; the rain fell sluggishly down, and everything felt cold and clammy to the touch. It seemed just the night when it befitted such a being as the Jew to be abroad. As he glided stealthily along, creeing beneath the shelter of the walls and doorways, the hideous old man seemed like some loathsome reptile, engendered in the slime and darkness through which he moved, crawling forth by night in search of some rich offal for a meal.

The character is thought to have been based on Ikey Solomon, a 19th century Jewish criminal in London, who was interviewed by Dickens during the latter's time as a journalist. Nadia Valdman, who writes about the portrayal of Jews in literature, argues that Fagin's representation was drawn from the image of the Jew as inherently evil, that the imagery associated him with the Devil, and with beasts.

The novel refers to Fagin 257 times in the first 38 chapters as "the Jew", while the ethnicity or religion of the other characters is not mentioned. In 1854, the *Jewish Chronicle* asked why "Jews alone should be excluded from the 'sympathizing heart' of this great author and powerful friend of the oppressed." Eliza Davis, whose husband had purchased Dickens's home in 1860 when he had put it up for sale, wrote to Dickens in protest at his portrayal of Fagin, arguing that he had "encouraged a vile prejudice against the despised Hebrew", and that he had done a great wrong to the Jewish people. Dickens had described her husband at the time of the sale as a "Jewish moneylender", though also someone he came to know as an honest gentleman.

Dickens took her complaint seriously. He halted the printing of *Oliver Twist*, and changed the text for the parts of the book that had not been set, which is why Fagin is called "the Jew" 257 times in the first 38 chapters, but barely at all in the next 179 references to him. In his next novel, *Our Mutual Friend*, he created the character of Riah (meaning "friend" in Hebrew), whose goodness, Vallely writes, is almost as complete as Fagin's evil. Riah says in the novel: "Men say, 'This is a bad Greek, but there are good Greeks. This is a bad Turk, but there are good Turks.' Not so with the Jews... they take the worst of us as samples of the best..." Davis sent Dickens a copy of the Hebrew bible in gratitude.

In *The Perils of Certain English Prisoners* Dickens offers an allegory of the Indian Mutiny, where the "native Sambo", a perverted paradigm of the Indian mutineers is a "double-dyed traitor, and a most infernal villain" who takes part in a massacre of women and children, in an allusion to the Cawnpore Massacre. *Perils* greatly influenced the cultural reaction from English writers to the mutiny, by attributing guilt so as to portray the imperialist dominators as victims, and the dominated as villains. Wilkie Collins, who co-wrote *Perils,* deviates from Dickens's extremism, writing the second chapter from a less biased point of view who, quoting poet Jaya Mehta, was "parodying British racism, instead of promoting it".

Contemporary literary critic Arthur Quiller-Couch praised Dickens for eschewing any real-life depiction of the incident, for fear of inflaming his "raging mad" readership further, in favour of a romantic story "empty of racial or propagandist hatred". A modern inference is that it was his son's position in India, there on military service, at the mercy of inept imperial leaders who misunderstood conquered people, that may have influenced his reluctance to set *Perils* in India, for fear that his criticism may antagonise the son's superiors.

Reacting to reports of incidents of atrocities committed by Indians, including one involving over a hundred prisoners, most of them women and children, killed, Dickens wrote in a private letter to Baronness Burdett-Coutts on 4 October 1857:

> I wish I were the Commander in Chief in India.... I should do my utmost to exterminate the Race upon whom the stain of the late cruelties rested... to blot it out of mankind and raze it off the face of the earth."

Names: 'Dickens' and 'Boz'

Charles Dickens had, as a contemporary critic put it, a "queer name". The name Dickens was used in interjective exclamations like "What the Dickens!" as a substitute for "devil". It was recorded in the OED as originating from Shakespeare's *The Merry Wives of Windsor*. It was also used as a substitute for "deuce" as in the phrase "to play the Dickens" in the meaning "to play havoc/mischief".

'Boz' was Dickens' occasional pen-name, but was a familiar name in the Dickens household long before Charles became a famous author. It was actually taken from his youngest brother Augustus Dickens' family nickname 'Moses', given to him in honor of one of the brothers in *The Vicar of Wakefield* (one of the most widely read novels during the early 19th century). When playfully pronounced through the nose 'Moses' became 'Boses', and was later shortened to 'Boz' - pronounced through the nose with a long vowel 'o'.

12

Literary Life of Jonathan Swift

Jonathan Swift (30 November 1667 - 19 October 1745) was an Irish satirist, essayist, political pamphleteer (first for the Whigs, then for the Tories), poet and cleric who became Dean of St. Patrick's, Dublin. He is remembered for works such as *Gulliver's Travels, A Modest Proposal, A Journal to Stella, Drapier's Letters, The Battle of the Books, An Argument Against Abolishing Christianity,* and *A Tale of a Tub.* Swift is probably the foremost prose satirist in the English language, and is less well known for his poetry. Swift originally published all of his works under pseudonyms—such as Lemuel Gulliver, Isaac Bickerstaff, M.B. Drapier—or anonymously. He is also known for being a master of two styles of satire: the Horatian and Juvenalian styles.

Biography

Jonathan Swift was born at No. 7, Hoey's Court, Dublin, and was the second child and only son of Jonathan Swift (a second cousin of John Dryden) and wife Abigail Erick (or Herrick), paternal grandson of Thomas Swift and wife Elizabeth Dryden, daughter of Nicholas Dryden (brother of Sir Erasmus Dryden, 1st Baronet Dryden) and wife Mary Emyley. His father was Irish born and his mother was born in England. Swift arrived seven months after his father's untimely death. Most of the facts of Swift's early life are obscure, confused and sometimes contradictory. It is widely believed that his mother returned to England when Jonathan was still very young, then leaving him to be raised by his father's family. His uncle Godwin took primary responsibility for the young Jonathan, sending him with one of his cousins to Kilkenny College.

In 1682 he attended Dublin University (Trinity College, Dublin), receiving his B.A. in 1686. Swift was studying for his Master's degree when political troubles in Ireland surrounding the Glorious Revolution forced him to leave for England in 1688, where his mother helped him get a position as secretary and personal assistant of Sir William Temple at Moor Park, Farnham. Temple was an English diplomat who, having arranged the Triple Alliance of 1668, retired from public service to his country estate to tend his gardens and write his memoirs. Growing into confidence with his employer, Swift "was often trusted with matters of great importance." Within three years of their acquaintance, Temple had introduced his secretary to William III, and sent him to London to urge the King to consent to a bill for triennial Parliaments.

When Swift took up his residence at Moor Park, he met Esther Johnson, then 8 years old, the fatherless daughter of one of the household servants. Swift acted as her tutor and mentor, giving her the nickname "Stella" and the two maintained a close, but ambiguous relationship for the rest of Esther's life.

Swift left Temple in 1690 for Ireland because of his health, but returned to Moor Park the following year. The illness, fits of vertigo or giddiness--now known to be Ménière's disease—would continue to plague Swift throughout his life. During this second stay with Temple, Swift received his M.A. from Hertford College, Oxford in 1692. Then, apparently despairing of gaining a better position through Temple's patronage, Swift left Moor Park to become an ordained priest in the Established Church of Ireland and in 1694 he was appointed to the prebend of Kilroot in the Diocese of Connor, with his parish located at Kilroot, near Carrickfergus in County Antrim.

Swift appears to have been miserable in his new position, being isolated in a small, remote community far from the centres of power and influence. While at Kilroot, however, Swift may well have become romantically involved with Jane Waring. A letter from him survives, offering to remain if she would marry him and promising to leave and never return to Ireland if she refused. She presumably refused, because Swift left his post and returned to England and Temple's service at Moor Park in 1696, and he remained there until Temple's death. There he was employed in helping to prepare Temple's memoirs and correspondence for publication. During this time Swift wrote *The Battle of the Books*, a satire responding to critics of Temple's *Essay upon Ancient and Modern Learning* (1690). *Battle* was however not published until 1704.

On January 27 1699 Temple died. Swift stayed on briefly in England to complete the editing of Temple's memoirs, and perhaps in the hope that recognition of his work might earn him a suitable position in England. However, Swift's work made enemies of some of Temple's family and friends who objected to indiscretions included in the memoirs. His next move was to approach King William directly, based on his imagined connection through Temple and a belief that he had been promised a position. This failed so miserably that he accepted the lesser post of secretary and chaplain to the Earl of Berkeley, one of the Lords Justices of Ireland. However, when he reached Ireland he found that the secretaryship had already been given to another. But he soon obtained the living of Laracor, Agher, and Rathbeggan, and the prebend of Dunlavin in St. Patrick's Cathedral, Dublin.

At Laracor, a mile or two from Trim, County Meath, and twenty miles (32 km) from Dublin, Swift ministered to a congregation of about fifteen people, and had abundant leisure for cultivating his garden, making a canal, planting willows, and rebuilding the vicarage. As chaplain to Lord Berkeley, he spent much of his time in Dublin and traveled to London frequently over the next ten years. In 1701, Swift published, anonymously, a political pamphlet, *A Discourse on the Contests and Dissentions in Athens and Rome.*

Writing Career

In February 1702, Swift received his Doctor of Divinity degree from Trinity College, Dublin. That spring he traveled to England and returned to Ireland in October, accompanied by Esther Johnson—now twenty years old—and his friend Rebecca Dingley, another member of William Temple's household. There is a great mystery and controversy over Swift's relationship with Esther Johnson nicknamed "Stella". Many hold that they were secretly married in 1716.

The title page to Swift's 1735 *Works,* depicting the author in the Dean's chair, receiving the thanks of Ireland. The Horatian motto reads, *Exegi Monumentum Ære perennius,* "I have completed a monument more lasting than brass." The 'brass' is a pun, for Wood's half-pence (alloyed with brass) is scattered at his feet. Cherubim award Swift a poet's laurel.

During his visits to England in these years Swift published *A Tale of a Tub* and *The Battle of the Books* (1704) and began to gain a reputation as a writer. This led to close, lifelong friendships with Alexander Pope, John Gay, and John Arbuthnot, forming the core of the Martinus Scriblerus Club (founded in 1713).

Swift became increasingly active politically in these years. From 1707 to 1709 and again in 1710, Swift was in London, unsuccessfully urging upon the Whig administration of Lord Godolphin the claims of the Irish clergy to the First-Fruits and Twentieths ("Queen Anne's Bounty"), which brought in about £2500 a year, already granted to their brethren in England. He found the opposition Tory leadership more sympathetic to his cause and Swift was recruited to support their cause as editor of the Examiner when they came to power in 1710. In 1711, Swift published the political pamphlet "The Conduct of the Allies," attacking the Whig government for its inability to end the prolonged war with France. The incoming Tory government conducted secret (and illegal) negotiations with France, resulting in the Treaty of Utrecht (1713) ending the War of the Spanish Succession.

Swift was part of the inner circle of the Tory government, and often acted as mediator between

Henry St. John (Viscount Bolingbroke) the secretary of state for foreign affairs (1710–15) and Robert Harley (Earl of Oxford) lord treasurer and prime minister (1711–1714). Swift recorded his experiences and thoughts during this difficult time in a long series of letters to Esther Johnson, later collected and published as *The Journal to Stella*. The animosity between the two Tory leaders eventually led to the dismissal of Harley in 1714. With the death of Queen Anne and ascension of George I that year, the Whigs returned to power and the Tory leaders were tried for treason for conducting secret negotiations with France.

Also during these years in London, Swift became acquainted with the Vanhomrigh family and became involved with one of the daughters, Esther, yet another fatherless young woman and an ambiguous relationship to confuse Swift's biographers. Swift furnished Esther with the nickname "Vanessa" and she features as one of the main characters in his poem *Cadenus and Vanessa*. The poem and their correspondence suggests that Esther was infatuated with Swift, that he may have reciprocated her affections, only to regret it and then try to break it off. Esther followed Swift to Ireland in 1714, where there appears to have been a confrontation, possibly involving Esther Johnson. Esther Vanhomrigh died in 1723 at the age of 35. Another lady with whom he had a close but less intense relationship, was Anne Long, a toast of the Kit-Cat Club.

Maturity

Before the fall of the Tory government, Swift hoped that his services would be rewarded with a church appointment in England. However, Queen Anne appeared to have taken a dislike to Swift and thwarted these efforts. The best position his friends could secure for him was the Deanery of St. Patrick's, Dublin. With the return of the Whigs, Swift's best move was to leave England and he returned to Ireland in disappointment, a virtual exile, to live "like a rat in a hole".

Once in Ireland, however, Swift began to turn his pamphleteering skills in support of Irish causes, producing some of his most memorable works: *Proposal for Universal Use of Irish Manufacture* (1720), *Drapier's Letters* (1724), and *A Modest Proposal* (1729), earning him the status of an Irish patriot.

Also during these years, he began writing his masterpiece, *Travels into Several Remote Nations of the World, in Four Parts, by Lemuel Gulliver, first a surgeon, and then a captain of several ships,* better known as *Gulliver's Travels.* Much of the material reflects his political experiences of the preceding decade. For instance, the episode in which the giant Gulliver puts out the Lilliputian palace fire by urinating on it can be seen as a metaphor for the Tories' illegal peace treaty; having done a good thing in an unfortunate manner. In 1726 he paid a long-deferred visit to London, taking with him the manuscript of *Gulliver's Travels.* During his visit he stayed with his old friends, Alexander Pope, John Arbuthnot, and John Gay, who helped him arrange for the anonymous publication of his book. First published in November 1726, it was an immediate hit, with a total of three printings that year and another in early 1727. French, German, and Dutch translations appeared in 1727 and pirated copies were printed in Ireland.

Swift returned to England one more time in 1727 and stayed with Alexander Pope once again. The visit was cut short when he received word that Esther Johnson was dying and Swift rushed back home to be with her. On 28 January 1728, Esther Johnson died, though he prayed at her bedside, even composing prayers for her comfort. Swift could not bear to be present at the end, but on the night of her death he began to write his *The Death of Mrs. Johnson.* He was too ill to attend the funeral at St. Patrick's. Many years later, a lock of hair, assumed to be Esther Johnson's, was found in his desk, wrapped in a paper bearing the words, "Only a woman's hair."

Death became a frequent feature in Swift's life from this point. In 1731 he wrote *Verses on the Death of Dr. Swift,* his own obituary published in 1739. In 1732, his good .friend and collaborator John Gay died. In 1735, John Arbuthnot, another friend from his days in London, died. In 1738 Swift began to show signs of illness and in 1742 he appears to have suffered a stroke, losing the ability to speak and realizing his worst fears of becoming mentally disabled. ("I shall be like that tree," he once said, "I shall die at the top.") In order to protect him from unscrupulous hangers on, who had begun to prey on the great man, his closest companions had him declared of "unsound mind and memory." However, it was long believed by many that Swift was really insane at this point. In his book *Literature and Western Man,* author J.B. Priestley even cites the final chapters of *Gulliver's Travels* as proof of Swift's approaching "insanity".

In part VIII of his series, *The Story of Civilization,* Will Durant describes the final years of Swift's life as such:

> "Definite symptoms of madness appeared in 1738. In 1741 guardians were appointed to take care of his

> affairs and watch lest in his outbursts of violence he should do himself harm. In 1742 he suffered great pain from the inflammation of his left eye, which swelled to the size of an egg; five attendants had to restrain him from tearing out his eye. He went a whole year without uttering a word."

In 1744, Alexander Pope died. Then, on October 19, 1745, Swift died. After being laid out in public view for the people of Dublin to pay their last respects, he was buried in his own cathedral by Esther Johnson's side, in accordance with his wishes. The bulk of his fortune (twelve thousand pounds) was left to found a hospital for the mentally ill, originally known as St. Patrick's Hospital for Imbeciles, which opened in 1757, and which still exists as a psychiatric hospital.

Epitaph

Jonathan Swift wrote his own epitaph:

> *Hic* depositum est Corpus
> IONATHAN SWIFT S.T.D.
> Hujus Ecclesiæ Cathedralis
> Decani,
> *Ubi* sæva Indignatio
> Ulterius
> Cor lacerare nequit,
> Abi Viator
> Et imitare, si poteris,
> Strenuum pro virili
> Libertatis Vindicatorem.
> Obiit 19º Die Mensis Octobris
> A.D. 1745 Anno Ætatis 78º.

The literal translation of which is: "*Here* is laid the Body of Jonathan Swift, Doctor of Sacred Theology, Dean of this Cathedral Church, *where* fierce Indignation can no longer injure the Heart. Go forth, Voyager, and copy, if you can, this vigorous (to the best of his ability) Champion of Liberty. He died on the 19th Day of the Month of October, A.D. 1745, in the 78th Year of his Age."

William Butler Yeats poetically translated it from the Latin as:

> Swift has sailed into his rest.
> Savage indignation there
> cannot lacerate his breast.
> Imitate him if you dare,
> world-besotted traveller.
> He served human liberty.

Works

Swift was a prolific writer, notable for his satires. The most recent collection of his prose works (Herbert Davis, ed. Basil Blackwell, 1965-) comprises fourteen volumes. A recent edition of his complete poetry (Pat Rodges, ed. Penguin, 1983) is 953 pages long. One edition of his correspondence (David Woolley, ed. P. Lang, 1999) fills three volumes.

Major Prose Works

Swift's first major prose play, *A Tale of a Tub,* demonstrates many of the themes and stylistic techniques he would employ in his later work. It is at once wildly playful and funny while being pointed and harshly critical of its targets. In its main thread, the *Tale* recounts the exploits of three sons, representing the main threads of Christianity, who receive a bequest from their father of a coat each, with the added instructions to make no alterations whatsoever. However, the sons soon find that their coats have fallen out of current fashion and begin to look for loopholes in their father's will which will allow them to make the needed alterations. As each finds his own means of getting around their father's admonition, they struggle with each other for power and dominance. Inserted into this story, in alternating chapters, Swift includes a series of whimsical "digressions" on various subjects.

In 1690, Sir William Temple, Swift's patron, published *An Essay upon Ancient and Modern Learning* a defense of classical writing holding up the *Epistles of Phalaris* as an example. William Wotton responded to Temple with *Reflections upon Ancient and Modern Learning* (1694) showing that the *Epistles* were a later forgery. A response by the supporters of the Ancients was then made by Charles Boyle (later the 4th Earl of Orrery and father of Swift's first biographer). A further retort on the Modern side came from Richard Bentley, one of the pre-eminent scholars of the day, in his essay *Dissertation upon the Epistles of Phalaris* (1699). However, the final words on the topic belong to Swift in his *Battle of the Books* (1697, published 1704) in which he makes a humorous defense on behalf of Temple and the cause of the Ancients.

In 1708, a cobbler named John Partridge published a popular almanac of astrological predictions. Because Partridge falsely determined the deaths of several church officials, Swift attacked Partridge in *Predictions For The Ensuing Year* by Isaac Bickerstaff, a parody predicting that Partridge would die on March 29th. Swift followed up with a pamphlet issued on March 30th claiming that Partridge had in fact died, which was widely believed despite Partridge's statements to the contrary.

Drapier's Letters (1724) was a series of pamphlets against the monopoly granted by the English government to William Wood to provide the Irish with copper coinage. It was widely believed that Wood would need to flood Ireland with debased coinage in order make a profit. In these "letters" Swift posed as a shop-keeper—a draper—in order to criticize the plan. Swift's writing was so effective in undermining opinion in the project that a reward was offered·by the government to anyone disclosing the true identity of the author. Though hardly a secret (on returning to Dublin after one of his trips to England, Swift was greeted with a banner, "Welcome Home, Drapier") no one turned Swift in. The government eventually resorted to hiring none other than Sir Isaac Newton to certify the soundness of Wood's coinage to counter Swift's accusations. In "Verses on the Death of Dr. Swift" (1739) Swift recalled this as one of his best achievements.

Gulliver's Travels, which Swift wrote a large portion of in Woodbrook House, County Laois was first published in 1726, and is regarded as his masterpiece. As with his other writings, the *Travels* was published under a pseudonym, the fictional Lemuel Gulliver, a ship's surgeon and later a sea captain. Some of the correspondence between printer Benj. Motte and Gulliver's also-fictional cousin negotiating the book's publication has survived. Though it has often been mistakenly thought of and published in bowdlerized form as a children's book, it is a great and sophisticated satire of human nature based on Swift's experience of his times. *Gulliver's Travels* is an anatomy of human nature, a sardonic looking-glass, often criticized for its apparent misanthropy. It asks its readers to refute it, to deny that it has not adequately characterized human nature and society. Each of the four books—recounting four voyages to mostly-fictional exotic lands—has a different theme, but all are attempts to deflate human pride. Critics hail the work as a satiric reflection on the failings of Enlightenment modernism.

In 1729, he published *A Modest Proposal for Preventing the Children of Poor People in Ireland Being a Burden to Their Parents or Country, and for Making Them Beneficial* to the Public, a satire in which the narrator, with intentionally grotesque logic, recommends that Ireland's poor escape their poverty by selling their children as food to the rich: "I have been assured by a very knowing American of my acquaintance in London, that a young healthy child well nursed is at a year old a most delicious, nourishing, and wholesome food..." Following the satirical form, he introduces the reforms he is actually suggesting by deriding them:

> Therefore let no man talk to me of other expedients... taxing our absentees...using [nothing] except what is of our own growth and manufacture... rejecting... foreign luxury... introducing a vein of parsimony, prudence and temperance... learning to love our country... quitting our animosities and factions... teaching landlords to have at least one degree of mercy towards their tenants.... Therefore I repeat, let no man talk to me of these and the like expedients, 'till he hath at least some glympse of hope, that there will ever be some hearty and sincere attempt to put them into practice.

13

The Book of Common Prayer

The Book of Common Prayer is the common title of a number of prayer books of the Church of England and of other Anglican churches, used throughout the Anglican Communion. The first book, published in 1549 (Church of England 1957), in the reign of Edward VI, was a product of the English Reformation following the break with Rome. Prayer books, unlike books of prayers, contain the words of structured (or liturgical) services of worship.

The work of 1549 was the first prayer book to contain the forms of service for daily and Sunday worship in English and to do so within a single volume; it included morning prayer, evening prayer, the Litany, and Holy Communion. The book included the other occasional services in full: the orders for baptism, confirmation, marriage, 'prayers to be said with the sick' and a funeral service. It set out in full the Epistle and Gospel readings for the Sunday Communion Service. Set Old Testament and New Testament readings for daily prayer were specified in tabular format as were the set Psalms; and canticles, mostly biblical, that were provided to be sung between the readings .

The 1549 book was rapidly succeeded by a reformed revision in 1552 under the same editorial hand, that of Thomas Cranmer, Archbishop of Canterbury. It never came into use because, on the death of Edward VI, his half-sister Mary I restored Roman Catholic worship. On her death, a compromise version, largely 1552 with a few amendments from 1549, was published in 1559. Following the tumultuous events leading to and including the English Civil War, another major revision was published in 1662. That edition has remained the official prayer book of the Church of England, although in the 21st century, an alternative book called *Common Worship* has largely displaced the *Book of Common Prayer* at the main Sunday worship service of most English parish churches.

The *Book of Common Prayer* appears in many variants in churches inside and outside of the Anglican Communion in over 50 different countries and in over 150 different languages. Again in many parts of the world, more contemporary books have replaced it in regular weekly worship.

Traditional Lutheran, Methodist and Presbyterian prayer books have borrowed from the *Book of Common Prayer*, and the marriage and burial rites have found their way into those of other denominations and into the English language. Like the Authorized King James Bible and the works of Shakespeare, many words and phrases from the *Book of Common Prayer* have entered popular culture.

Full Title

The full name of the 1662 Book of Common Prayer is The Book of Common Prayer and Administration of the Sacraments and other Rites and Ceremonies of the Church according to the use of the Church of England together with the Psalter or Psalms of David pointed as they are to be sung or said in churches and the form and manner of making, ordaining, and consecrating of bishops, priests, and deacons.

History

The forms of parish worship in the late medieval church in England, which followed the Latin Roman Rite, varied according to local practice. These were termed local "use". By far the most common found in Southern England was the Use of Sarum. The rite was not consolidated into a single book. Instead, the forms of service that were to be included in the Book of Common Prayer were drawn from the Missal, Breviary for the daily office, Manual (for the occasional services; Baptism, Marriage, Burial etc), and Pontifical (for the services appropriate to a bishop—Confirmation, Ordination).

The work of producing English-language books for use in the liturgy was largely that of Thomas Cranmer, Archbishop of Canterbury at first under the reign of Henry VIII, only more radically under his son Edward VI. Cranmer was, in his early days, somewhat conservative, an admirer, if a critical one, of John Fisher. It may have been his visit to Germany in 1532 (where he secretly married) which began the change in his outlook. Then in 1538, as Henry began diplomatic negotiations with Lutheran princes, Cranmer came face-to-face with a Lutheran embassy.

The Exhortation and Litany, the earliest English-language service book of the Church of England, was the first overt manifestation of his changing views. It was thus no mere translation from the Latin: its Protestant character is made clear by the drastic reduction of the place of saints, compressing what had been the major part into three petitions. Published in 1544, it borrowed greatly from Martin Luther's Litany and Myles Coverdale's New Testament and was the only service that might be considered to be "Protestant" to be finished within the lifetime of King Henry VIII.

Prayer Books of Edward VI

It was not until Henry's death in 1547 and the accession of Edward VI that revision could proceed faster. Cranmer finished his work on an English Communion rite in 1548, obeying an order of Convocation of the previous year that Communion was to be given to the people as both bread and wine. The ordinary Roman Rite of the Mass had made no provision for any congregation present to receive Communion. So, Cranmer composed in English an additional rite of congregational preparation and Communion (based on the form of the Sarum rite for Communion of the Sick), to be undertaken immediately following the Communion, in both kinds, of the priest.

Further developed, and fully translated into English, this Communion service was included, one year later, in 1549, in a full prayer book, set out with a daily office, readings for Sundays and Holy Days, the Communion Service, Public Baptism, of Confirmation, of Matrimony, The Visitation of the Sick, At a Burial and the Ordinal.

The Preface to this edition, which contained Cranmer's explanation as to why a new prayer book was necessary, began: "There was never any thing by the wit of man so well devised, or so sure established, which in continuance of time hath not been corrupted." Although the work is commonly attributed to Cranmer, its detailed origins are obscure. A group of bishops and divines met first at Chertsey and then at Windsor in 1548, drawn from both conservatives and reformers, agreed only "the service of the church ought to be in the mother tongue. Cranmer collected the material from many sources; even the opening of Preface was borrowed. He borrowed much from German sources, particularly from work commissioned by Hermann von Wied, Archbishop of Cologne; and also from Osiander (to whom he was related by marriage).

The Church Order of Brandenberg and Nuremberg was partly the work of the latter. Many phrases are characteristic of the German reformer Martin Bucer, or of the Italian Peter Martyr, (who was staying with Cranmer at the time of the finalising of drafts), or of his chaplain, Thomas Becon. However, to Cranmer is 'credited the overall job of editorship and the overarching structure of the book' including the systematic amendment of his materials to remove any idea that human merit contributed to their salvation .

The Communion service of 1549 maintained the format of distinct rites of Consecration and Communion, that had been introduced the previous year; but with the Latin rite of the Mass (chiefly following the familiar structure in the Use of Sarum), translated into English. By outwardly maintaining familiar forms, Cranmer hoped to establish the practice of weekly congregational Communion, and included exhortations to encourage this; and instructions that

Communion should never be received by the priest alone. This represented a radical change from late medieval practice—whereby the primary focus of congregational worship was taken to be attendance at the consecration, and adoration of the elevated Consecrated Host. In late medieval England, congregations only regularly received Communion at Easter; and otherwise individual lay people might expect to receive Communion only when gravely ill, or in the form of a Nuptial Mass on being married.

Introduced on Whitsunday 1549, after considerable debate and revision in Parliament—but there is no evidence that it was ever submitted to either Convocation—it was said to have pleased neither reformers nor their opponents, indeed the Catholic Bishop Gardiner could say of it was that it "was patient of a catholic interpretation". It was widely unpopular in the parishes, especially in places such as Devon and Cornwall. Particularly unpopular was the banning of processions and the sending out of commissioners to enforce the new requirements. There was widespread opposition to the introduction of regular congregational Communion, partly because the extra costs of bread and wine that would fall on the parish; but mainly out of an intense resistance to undertaking in regular worship, a religious practice previously associated with marriage or illness.

The book was, from the outset, intended only as a temporary expedient, as Bucer was assured having met Cranmer for the first time in April 1549: 'concessions...made both as a respect for antiquity and to the infirmity of the present age' as he wrote. It kept the appearance of the Mass but abandoned its theology. AH Couratin in a set of unpublished Oxford

University lectures from 1958 described it as a "bogus Mass". Both Bucer and Peter Martyr wrote detailed proposals for modification; Bucer's *Censura* ran to 28 chapters which influenced Cranmer significantly though he did not follow them slavishly and the new book was duly produced in 1552, making "fully perfect" what was already implicit .

The policy of incremental reform was now unveiled: more Roman Catholic practices were now excised, as doctrines had in 1549 been subtly changed. Thus, in the Eucharist, gone were the words Mass and altar; the 'Lord have mercy' was interleaved into a recitation of the Ten Commandments and the Gloria was removed to the end of the service. The Eucharistic prayer was split in two so that Eucharistic bread and wine were shared immediately after the words of institution (This is my Body..This is my blood...in remembrance of me.); while its final element, the Prayer of Oblation, (with its reference to an offering of a 'Sacrifice of praise and thanksgiving'), was transferred, much changed, to a position after the priest and congregation had received Communion, and was made optional with an alternative prayer of thanksgiving provided.

The Elevation of the Host had been forbidden in 1549; all manual acts were now omitted. The words at the administration of Communion which, in the prayer book of 1549 described the Eucharistic species as 'The body of our Lorde Jesus Christe...', 'The blood of our Lorde Jesus Christe...' were replaced with the words 'Take, eat, in remembrance that Christ died for thee..' etc. The Peace, at which in the early Church the congregation had exchanged a greeting, was removed altogether. Vestments such as the stole, chasuble and cope were no longer to be worn, but only a surplice. It was the final stage of the reformers' work of removing all elements of sacrificial offering from the Latin Mass; so that it should cease to be seen as a ritual at which the priest, on behalf of the faithful offered Christ's body and blood to God; and might rather be seen as a ritual whereby Christ shared his body and blood, according to a different sacramental theology, with the faithful.

Cranmer recognized that the 1549 rite of Communion had been capable of conservative misinterpretation and misuse, in that the consecration rite might still be undertaken even when no congregational Communion followed. Consequently, in 1552 he thoroughly integrated Consecration and Communion into a single rite, with congregational preparation preceding the words of institution—such that it would not be possible to mimic the Mass with the priest communicating alone. He appears nevertheless, to have been resigned to being unable for the present to establish in parishes the weekly practice of receiving Communion; so he restructured the service so as to allow ante-Communion as a distinct rite of worship—following the Communion rite through the readings and offertory, as far as the intercessory "Prayer for the Church Militant".

Diarmaid MacCulloch suggests that Cranmer's own Eucharistic theology in these years approximated most closely to that of Heinrich Bullinger; but that he intended the Prayer Book to be acceptable to the widest range of Reformed Eucharistic belief, including the high sacramental theology of Bucer and John Calvin. At the same time, however, Cranmer intended that constituent parts of the rites gathered into the

Prayer Book should still, so far as possible, be recognizably derived from traditional forms and elements.

In the Baptism service the signing with the cross was moved until after the baptism and the exorcism, the anointing, the putting on of the chrysom robe and the triple immersion were omitted. Most drastic of all was the removal of the Burial service from church: it was to take place at the graveside. In 1549, there had been provision for a Requiem (not so called) and prayers of commendation and committal, the first addressed to the deceased. All that remained was a single reference to the deceased, giving thanks for their delivery from 'the myseryes of this sinneful world'. This new Order for the Burial of the Dead was a drastically stripped-down memorial service designed to undermine definitively the whole complex of traditional beliefs about Purgatory and intercessory prayer.

In other respects, however, both the Baptism and Burial services imply a theology of salvation that accords notably less with Reformed teachings than do the counterpart passages in the Articles of Religion. In the Burial service, the possibility that a deceased person who has died in the faith may nevertheless not be counted amongst God's elect, is not entertained. In the Baptism service the priest explicitly pronounces the baptised infant as being now *regenerate*. In both cases, conformity with strict Reformed Protestant principles would have resulted in a conditional formulation. The continued inconsistency between the Articles of Religion and the Prayer Book remained a point of contention for Puritans; and would in the 19th century come close to tearing the Church of England apart, through the course of the Gorham judgement.

Cranmer's work of simplification and revision was also applied to the Daily Offices, which were to become Morning, and Evening Prayer; and which he hoped would also serve as a daily form of prayer to be used by the Laity, thus replacing both the late medieval lay observation of the Latin Hours of the Virgin, and its English equivalent, the *Primer*. This simplification was anticipated by the work of Cardinal Francis Quiñones, a Spanish Franciscan, in his abortive revision of the Roman Breviary published in 1537.

Cranmer took up Quiñones's principle that everything should be sacrificed to secure continuity in singing the Psalter and reading the Bible. His first draft, produced during Henry's reign, retained the traditional seven distinct Canonical hours of Office prayer; but in his second draft, while he retained the Latin, he consolidated these into two.

The 1549 book then dispensed with the Latin, and with all non-biblical readings; and established a rigorously biblical cycle of readings for Morning and Evening Prayer (set according to the calendar year, rather than the ecclesiastical year) and a Psalter to be read consecutively throughout each month. He provided that the New Testament (other than the Book of Revelation) be read through three times in a year, while the Old Testament, including the Apocrypha would be read through once.

Of the set canticles, only the Te Deum was retained of the non-biblical material. In the 1552 Prayer book, this pattern was retained. Following the publication of the 1552 Prayer Book, a revised English Primer was published in 1553; adapting the Offices and Morning and Evening Prayer, and other prayers, for lay domestic piety.

English Prayer Book in the Reign of Mary

Before the book was in general use, however, Edward VI died. In 1553, Mary, upon her succession to the throne, restored the old religion. The Mass was re-established, altars, roods and statues were re-instated; an attempt was made to restore the Church to its Roman affiliation. Cranmer was punished for his work in the English Reformation by being burned at the stake on 21 March 1556. Nevertheless, the 1552 book was to survive. After Mary's death in 1558, it became the primary source for the Elizabethan Book of Common Prayer, with subtle if significant changes only.

Hundreds of Protestants fled into exile—establishing an English church in Frankfurt am Main. A bitter, and very public, dispute ensued between those, like Edmund Grindal and Richard Cox, who wished to preserve in exile the exact form of worship of the 1552 Prayer Book; and those, like John Knox the pastor of the congregation, who regarded that book as still partially tainted with compromise. Eventually in 1555 the civil authorities expelled Knox and his supporters to Geneva, where they adopted a new Prayer Book *The Form of Prayers,* that derived chiefly from Calvin's French *La Forme des Prières*(Maxwell 1965, p. 5). Consequently, when the accession of Elizabeth I re-asserted the dominance of Protestantism in England, there remained a significant body of Reformed believers who were nevertheless hostile to the Book of Common Prayer. John Knox took *The Form of Prayers* with him to Scotland, where it formed the basis of the Scots *Book of Common Order.*

1559 Prayer Book

Thus, under Elizabeth, a more permanent enforcement

of the Reformed religion was undertaken, and the 1552 book was republished in 1559, scarcely altered.

The alterations, though minor, were however to cast a long shadow. One related to what was worn. Instead of the banning of all vestments save the rochet (for bishops) and the surplice for parish clergy, it permitted 'such ornaments...as were in use...in the second year of K. Edward VI'. This allowed substantial leeway for more traditionalist clergy to retain at least some of the vestments which they felt were appropriate to liturgical celebration. It was to be the basis of claims in the 19th Century that vestments such as chasubles, albs, and stoles were legal. At the Communion, the words from the 1549 book 'the Body of our Lord Jesus Christ' etc. was combined with the words of Edward's second book, 'Take eat in remembrance.' etc. The instruction to the congregation to kneel at the Communion was retained; but the accompanying Black Rubric denying any "real and essential presence" of Christ's flesh and blood, was removed.

The conservative nature of these changes underlines the fact that Protestantism was by no means universally popular – a fact that the queen herself recognized: her revived Act of Supremacy, giving her the ambiguous title of Supreme Governor passed without difficulty, but the Act of Uniformity 1559 giving statutory force to the Prayer Book, passed through Parliament by only three votes. It made constitutional history in being imposed by the laity alone, as all the bishops, except those imprisoned by the Queen and unable to attend, voted against it. Convocation had made its position clear by affirming the traditional doctrine of the Eucharist, the authority of the Pope, and the reservation by divine law to ecclesiastics 'of handling and defining concerning the things belonging to faith, sacraments, and discipline ecclesiastical'.

After the several innovations and reversals, the new forms of worship took time to settle in. Among Cranmer's innovations, retained in the new book was the requirement of weekly communion. In practice, as before the Reformation, many received communion rarely, as little as once a year in some cases; George Herbert estimated it as no more than six times.

However practice was variable: very high attendance at festivals was in most places the order of the day and in some places regular communion was very popular, in other places they stayed away or sent "a servant to be the liturgical representative of their household.". Few parish clergy were initially licensed to preach by the bishops; in the absence of a licensed preacher, Sunday services were required to be accompanied by reading one of the homilies written by Cranmer.

George Herbert was however, not alone in his enthusiasm for preaching which he regarded as one of the prime functions of a parish priest. Music was much simplified; and a radical distinction developed between, on the one hand, parish worship where only the metrical psalms of Sternhold and Hopkins might be sung; and on the other hand, worship in churches with organs and surviving choral foundations, where the music of John Marbeck and others was developed into a rich choral tradition.

The whole act of parish worship might take well over two hours; and accordingly, churches were equipped with pews in which households could sit together (whereas in the medieval church, men and women had worshipped separately). Diarmaid MacCulloch describes the new act of worship as, "a morning marathon of prayer, scripture reading, and praise, consisting of mattins, litany, and ante-communion, preferably as the matrix for a sermon to proclaim the message of scripture anew week by week."

Many ordinary churchgoers—that is those who could afford a copy as it was expensive in terms of most people's incomes—would own a copy of the prayer book. Judith Maltby cites a story of parishioners at Flixton in Suffolk who brought their own prayer books to church in order to shame their Vicar into conforming with it: they eventually ousted him . Between 1549 and 1642, roughly 290 editions of the prayer book were produced. Before the end of the Civil War and the introduction of the 1662 prayer book, something like a half a million prayer books are estimated to have been in circulation.

On the queen's death in 1603, this book, substantially the book of 1552, having been regarded as offensive by the likes of Bishop Stephen Gardiner in the sixteenth century as being a break with the tradition of the Western church, as it was, by the seventeenth century had come to be regarded by some as unduly Catholic. The objections of the English Puritans were; firstly, that it was improper for the lay congregation to take any vocal part in prayer (as in the Litany or Lord's Prayer), other than to say "Amen"; secondly, that no set prayer should exclude the option of an extempore alternative from the Minister; thirdly, that the Minister should have the option to omit part of the set liturgy at his discretion; fourthly, that short

Collects should be replaced by longer prayers and exhortations; and fifthly, that all surviving "Catholic" ceremonial should be removed.

On the accession of James I, following the so-called Millenary Petition, the Hampton Court conference of 1604—the same meeting of bishops and Puritan divines that initiated the Authorized version of the Bible—resisted the pressure for change (save to the catechism). With the defeat of Charles I (1625-1649) in the Civil War the Puritan pressure, exercised through a much-changed Parliament, had increased. Puritan-inspired petitions for the removal of the prayer book and episcopacy 'root and branch' resulted in local disquiet in many places and eventually the production of locally organized counter petitions. The Parliamentary government had its way but it became clear that the division was not between Catholics and Protestants, but between Puritans and those who valued the Elizabethan settlement..

The 1559 book was finally outlawed by Parliament in 1645 to be replaced by the Directory of Public Worship, which was more a set of instructions than a prayer book. How widely the Directory was used is not certain; there is some evidence of its having been purchased, in churchwardens' accounts, but not widely. The Prayer Book certainly was used clandestinely in some places, not least because the Directory made no provision at all for burial services. Following the execution of Charles I in 1649 and the establishment of the Commonwealth under Lord Protector Cromwell, it would not be reinstated until shortly after the restoration of the monarchy to England.

John Evelyn records in his Diary, taking Communion according to the 1559 Prayer Book rite:

> Christmas Day 1657. I went to London with my wife to celebrate Christmas Day... Sermon ended, as [the minister] was giving us the holy sacrament, the chapel was surrounded with soldiers, and all the communicants and assembly surprised and kept prisoners by them, some in the house, others carried away... These wretched miscreants held their muskets against us as we came up to receive the sacred elements, as if they would have shot us at the altar.

Prayer Book in Scotland

In 1557, the Scots Protestant lords had adopted the English Prayer Book of 1552, for reformed worship in Scotland. However, when John Knox returned to Scotland in 1559, he continued to use the *Form of Prayer* he had created for the English exiles in Geneva, and in 1564, this supplanted the *Book of Common Prayer* under the title of the *Book of Common Order.*

Following the accession of King James VI of Scotland to the throne of England, his son King Charles I, with the assistance of Archbishop Laud sought to impose the prayer book on Scotland. The book concerned was not, however, the 1559 book but very much that of 1549,the first book of Edward VI. First used in 1637, it was never accepted, having been violently rejected by the Scots. Following the Wars of the Three Kingdoms (including the English Civil War), the Church of Scotland was re-established on a presbyterian basis but by the Act of Comprehension 1690, the rump of Episcopalians were allowed to hold onto their benefices. For liturgy they looked to Laud's book and in 1724 the first of the 'Wee Bookies' was published, containing, for the sake of economy, the central part of the Communion beginning with the Offertory.

Between then and 1764, when a more formal revised version was published, a number of things happened which were to separate the Scottish liturgy more firmly from either the English books of 1549 or 1559. First, informal changes were made to the order of the various parts of the service and inserting words indicating a sacrificial intent to the Eucharist; secondly, as a result of Bishop Rattray's researches into the liturgies of St. James and St. Clement, published in 1744, the form of the invocation was changed. These changes were incorporated into the 1764 book which was to be the liturgy of the Scottish Episcopal Church but it was to influence the liturgy of the Episcopal Church in the United States. A completely new revision was finished in 1929, and several alternative orders of the communion service and other services have been prepared since then.

1662 Prayer Book

The 1662 prayer book was printed only two years after the restoration of the monarchy, following the Savoy Conference convened by Royal Warrant to review the book of 1559. Attempts by Presbyterians led by Richard Baxter to gain approval for an alternative service book failed. In reply to the Presbyterian Exceptions, some 600 changes were made to the book of 1559, mostly minor; giving the Puritans little of what they wanted, but implementing rather more (though by no means all) of the changes suggested by High Anglicans.

Among them was the reference, in the prayer for the Church Militant, those 'departed this life in thy faith and fear' thus contradicting the statement at the beginning of the prayer that it was for the church 'militant here in earth'. Secondly, an attempt was made to restore the Offertory. This was achieved by the insertion of the words 'and oblations' into the prayer for the Church and the revision of the rubric so as to require the monetary offerings to be brought to the Table (instead of being put in the poor box) and the bread and wine placed upon the Table. Previously it had not been clear when and how bread and wine got onto the altar.

The so-called manual acts, whereby the priest took the bread and the cup during the prayer of consecration, which had been deleted in 1552, were restored; and an "Amen" was inserted after the words of institution and before the Communion, hence separating the elements of Consecration and Communion that Cranmer had tried to knit together. After the communion, the unused but consecrated bread and wine were to be reverently consumed in church rather than being taken away for the Priest's own use. By such subtle means were Cranmer's purposes further confused, leaving it for generations to argue over the precise theology of the rite. One change made that constituted a concession to the Presbyterian Exceptions, was the updating and re-insertion of the so-called Black Rubric, which had been removed in 1559. This now declared that kneeling in order to receive the communion did not imply adoration of the species of the Eucharist nor 'to any Corporal Presence of Christ's natural Flesh and Blood'—which, said the rubric, were in heaven, not here.

Unable to accept the new book 1,760 ministers were deprived of their livings. In effect, the 1662

Prayer Book marked the end of a period of just over 100 years, when a common form of liturgy served for almost all Reformed public worship in England; and the start of the continuing division between Anglicans and Nonconformists. The actual language of the 1662 revision was little changed from that of Cranmer. With two exceptions, some words and phrases which had become archaic were modernized; secondly, the readings for the Epistle and Gospel at the Holy Communion, which had been set out in full since 1549, were now set to the text of the 1611 Authorized Version of the Bible. The Psalter, which had not been printed out in the 1549, 1552 or 1559 Books—was in 1662 provided in Miles Coverdale's translation from the Great Bible of 1538.

It was this edition which was to be the official *Book of Common Prayer*, during the growth of the British Empire, and, as a result, has been a great influence on the prayer books of Anglican churches worldwide, liturgies of other denominations in English, and of the English language as a whole.

Further Attempts at Revision

1662 - 1832

After the 1662 prayer book, development ceased in England until the twentieth century; that it did was, however, a bit of a close run thing. On the death of Charles II his brother, a Roman Catholic, became James II. James wished to achieve toleration for those of his own Roman Catholic faith, whose practices were still banned. This, however, drew the Presbyterians closer to the Church of England in their common desire to resist 'popery'; talk of reconciliation and liturgical compromise was thus in the air. But with the flight of James in 1688 and the arrival of the Calvinist William of Orange the position of the parties changed.

The Presbyterians could achieve toleration of their practices without such a right being given to Roman Catholics and without, therefore, their having to submit to the Church of England, even with a liturgy more acceptable to them. They were now in a much stronger position to demand changes that were ever more radical. John Tillotson, Dean of Canterbury pressed the king to set up a Commission to produce such a revision. The so-called *Liturgy of Comprehension* of 1689, which was the result, conceded two thirds of the Presbyterian demands of 1661; but when it came to Convocation the members, now more fearful of William's perceived agenda, did not even discuss it and its contents were, for a long time, not even accessible. This work, however, did go on to influence the prayer books of many British colonies.

1833 - 1906

By the 19th century other pressures upon the book of 1662 had arisen. Adherents of the Oxford Movement, begun in 1833, raised questions about the relationship of the Church of England to the apostolic church and thus about its forms of worship. Known as Tractarians after their production of *Tracts for the Times* on theological issues, they advanced the case for the Church of England being essentially a part of the 'Western Church', of which the Roman Catholic Church was the chief representative. The illegal use of elements of the Roman rite, the use of candles, vestments and incense, practices known as Ritualism, had become widespread and led to the Public Worship Regulation Act 1874 which established a new system of discipline, intending to bring the 'Romanisers' into conformity. The Act had no effect on illegal practices: five clergy were imprisoned for contempt of court and after the trial of the much loved Bishop Edward King of Lincoln, it became clear that some revision of the liturgy had to be embarked upon.

One branch of the ritualistic movement argued that both 'Romanisers' (by imitating the Church of Rome) and their Evangelical opponents (by imitating Reformed churches) transgressed the Ornaments Rubric of 1559, 'that such Ornaments of the Church, and of the Ministers thereof, at all Times of their Ministration, shall be retained, and be in use, as were in this Church of England, by the Authority of Parliament, in the Second Year of the Reign of King Edward the Sixth'. These adherents of ritualism, among whom were Percy Dearmer and others, claimed that the Ornaments Rubric prescribed the ritual usages of the Sarum Rite with the exception of a few minor things already abolished by the early reformation. Following a Royal Commission report in 1906, work began on a new prayer book, work that was to take twenty years.

1906 - 2000

In 1927, this proposed prayer book was finished. It was decided, during development, that the use of the services therein would be decided on by each given congregation, so as to avoid as much conflict as possible with traditionalists. With these open guidelines the book was granted approval by the Church of England Convocations and Church Assembly in July 1927. Since the Church of England is a state church, a further step; sending the proposed revision to Parliament; was required. A Resolution under the Church of England Assembly (Powers) Act 1919, directing that the Measure should be presented to His Majesty, was passed in the House of Lords by a large majority. However a similar resolution was defeated in the House of Commons on December 15 1927 when the MPs William Joynson-Hicks and Rosslyn Mitchell "reached and inflamed all the latent Protestant prejudices in the House" and argued strongly against it on the grounds that the proposed book was "papistical" and was a restoration of the Roman Mass and implied the doctrine of Transubstantiation.

Early in the year 1928 a second Measure was introduced in the Church Assembly, proposing to authorise the use of the Deposited Book with certain amendments thereto which were set out in a Schedule to Measure. This Measure again was approved by large majorities in both the Convocations and the Church Assembly; but a Resolution directing that it should be presented to His Majesty was defeated in the House of Commons on June 14 1928. In response to this rejection, the bishops issued a unanimous statement, asserting the Church's right to order its forms of worship, and in 1929 the Upper House of the Convocation of Canterbury resolved that bishops might approve the use of the 1928 book, notwithstanding the lack of parliamentary authority. It became common for Prayer Books to print the 1662 and 1928 forms of service in parallel columns, although the legal basis of the revision remained unclear. The 1928 revised forms of Matrimony and Baptism were quite widely adopted, but those of other rites tended not to be; the consequence, in practice, being very wide variation in liturgical practice from parish to parish, with very few churchmen adhering consistently to the strict observation of either the 1662 or the 1928 forms of worship.

The effect of the failure of the 1928 book was salutary: no further attempts were made to change the book, other than those required for the changes to the monarchy. Instead a different process, that of producing an alternative book, led to the publication of Series 1, 2 and 3 in the 1960s, the 1980 Alternative Service Book and subsequently to the 2000 *Common Worship* series of books. Both differ substantially from the *Book of Common Prayer,* though the latter includes in the Order Two form of the Holy Communion a very slight revision of the prayer book service altering only one or two words and allowing the insertion of the Agnus Dei (Lamb of God) before Communion. Order One follows the pattern of modern liturgical scholarship.

2001 -2003

In 2003, a Roman Catholic adaptation of the BCP was published called the *Book of Divine Worship.* It is a compromise of material drawn from the proposed 1928 book, the 1979 ECUSA book, and the Roman Missal. Catholic converts from Anglicanism within the Anglican Use published it primarily for their use.

Prayer Book in the Anglican Communion

With British colonial expansion from the seventeenth century onwards, the Anglican Church was planted across the globe. These churches at first used and then revised the use of the Prayer Book, until they, like their parent, produced prayer books which took into account the developments in liturgical study and practice in the nineteenth and twentieth centuries, which come under the general heading of the Liturgical Movement.

Africa-Asia

India

The Church of South India was the first Episcopal uniting church of our age, consisting as it did, from its foundation in 1947, at the time of Indian independence, of Anglicans, Methodists, Congregationalists, Presbyterians and Reformed Christians. Its liturgy, from the first, combined the free use of Cranmer's language with an adherence to the principles of congregational participation and the centrality of the Eucharist, much in line with the Liturgical Movement. Because it was a minority church of widely differing traditions in a non-Christian culture (except in Kerala, where Christianity has a long history), practice varied wildly but the retention of Cranmerian language, and a sympathy with his theology, in the 2004 revision, is a reminder of both the richness of his language and the breadth of his influence.

The Philippines

As the Philippines is connected to the worldwide Anglican Communion through the Episcopal Church, the main edition of the Book of Common Prayer throughout the Islands is the same as that of the United States. However, with the granting of the full autonomy on 1 May 1990, the Episcopal Church in the Philippines has published its own Book of Common Prayer. This is notable for the inclusion of the prayers for the Misa de Gallo, a popular tradition among Filipinos. Aside from the *American Book of Common*

Prayer and the newly published Philippine Book of Common Prayer, the Chinese community of Saint Stephen's Pro-Cathedral in the Diocese of the Central Philippines uses the English-Chinese *Diglot Book of Common Prayers,* published by the Episcopal Church of Southeast Asia.

Europe

Ireland

William Bedell had undertaken an Irish translation of the Book of Common Prayer in 1606. An Irish translation of the revised prayer book of 1662 was effected by John Richardson (1664-1747) and published in 1712. It has been revised several times, and the present edition has been used since 2004.

Wales

Even after the creation of the Church in Wales 1920, the 1662 book was used until 1966, when trials of new services began. The current book was published in 1984, and is currently under revision.

Oceania

Australia

The Anglican Church of Australia, until 1981 officially known as the *Church of England in Australia and Tasmania,* became self-governing in 1961. Among other things the General Synod agreed that the Book of Common Prayer was to 'be regarded as the authorised standard of worship and doctrine in this Church...'. In 1978 *An Australian Prayer Book* was produced which sought to adhere to this principle, so that where the Liturgical Committee could not agree on a formulation, the words or expressions of the BCP were to be used. The result was conservative revision.

In 1995 a similar process could be observed as elsewhere with the production of *A Prayer Book for Australia* which departed from both the structure and wording of the BCP. The process was accompanied by numerous objections, notably from the deeply conservatively evangelical Diocese of Sydney which noted the loss of BCP wording and of an explicit 'biblical doctrine of substitutionary atonement'. On the other hand, the rest of the Australian church has not proved as difficult as prayer book revisers might have supposed. The Diocese of Sydney has developed its own small prayer book, called Sunday Services, to supplement the existing prayer book and preserve the original theology, which the Sydney diocese asserts has been changed.

North and Central America

Canada

The Anglican Church of Canada developed its first Book of Common Prayer separately from the English version in 1918. The revision of 1962 was much more substantial, bearing a family relationship to that of the abortive 1928 book in England. The language was conservatively modernized, and additional seasonal material was added. As in England, while many prayers were retained the structure of the Communion service was altered: a Prayer of Oblation was added to the Eucharistic prayer after the 'words of institution', thus reflecting the rejection of Cranmer's theology in liturgical developments across the Anglican Communion. More controversially, the Psalter included in the book omitted certain sections, including the entirety of Psalm 58. A French translation, *Le Recueil des Prières de la Communauté Chrétienne,* was published in 1967.

After a period of experimentation with the publication of various supplements, the *Book of Alternative Services* was published in 1985. This book (which owes much to Roman Catholic, Lutheran, Anglican, and other sources) has widely supplanted the 1962 book, though the latter remains authorized. As in other places, there has been a reaction and the Canadian version of the Book of Common Prayer has found supporters.

Indigenous Languages

The Book of Common Prayer has also been translated into these North American indigenous languages: Cowitchan, Cree, Haida, Ntlakyapamuk, Slavey, Eskimo-Aleut, Dakota, Delaware, Mohawk, Ojibwe.

Ojibwa

Joseph Gilfillan was the chief editor of the 1911 Ojibwa edition of the Book of Common Prayer entitled *Iu Wejibuewisi Mamawi Anamiawini Mazinaigun.*

United States of America

The Episcopal Church separated itself from the Church of England in 1789, having been established in the United States in 1607. Its prayer book, published in 1790, had as its sources, the 1662 English book and the 1764 Scottish Liturgy which Bishop Seabury of Connecticut had brought over following his consecration in Aberdeen in 1784, containing elements of each. The preface to the 1789 Book of Common Prayer says "this Church is far from intending to depart from the Church of England in any essential point of doctrine, discipline, or worship...further than local circumstances require." There were some notable differences. For example, in the Communion service after the words of institution there follows a Prayer of Oblation from 1549, but into which were inserted the words 'which we now offer unto thee' with reference to the 'holy gifts' An epiclesis was included, as in the Scottish book, though modified to meet reformist objections. Overall the book was modelled in the English Prayer Book, the Convention having resisted attempts at deletion and revision.

Further revisions occurred in 1892 and 1928, in which minor changes were made, removing, for instance, some of Cranmer's Exhortations and introducing such innovations as prayers for the dead.

In 1979, a more substantial revision was made. There were now two rites for the most common services, the first that kept most of the language of 1928, and the second using only contemporary language (some of it newly composed, and some adapted from the older language). Many changes were made in the rubrics and the shapes of the services, which were generally made for both the traditional and contemporary language versions. However, there was arguably a greater degree of continuity than was the case in England, which may account for the fact that all the books of the series, from 1790 to 1979 retain the same title. The 1979 book owes a good deal to the Liturgical Movement and to the 19th century Catholic revival. Many Anglo-Catholics felt alienated by the contemporary language changes to the 1979 BCP and in 1991 The Church of the Good Shepherd in Rosemont, PA published a book entitled, the Anglican

Service Book which is "a traditional language adaptation of the 1979 Book of Common Prayer together with the Psalter or Psalms of David and Additional Devotions." Books like this are allowed because of a rubric in the 1979 Prayer Book which allows for the translation of the contemporary language into the traditional language of the 1928 Book of Common Prayer.

Even so, the revision caused some controversy and in 2000, the General Convention of the Episcopal Church issued an apology to those "offended or alienated during the time of liturgical transition to the 1979 Book of Common Prayer." Use of the 1928 Book of Common Prayer is currently forbidden in most American parishes, but there is a growing revival of its use, both for doctrinal reasons and the beauty of its language.

The Prayer Book Cross was erected in San Francisco's Golden Gate Park in 1894 as a gift from the Church of England. Created by Ernest Coxhead, it stands on one of the higher points in Golden Gate Park. It is located between John F. Kennedy Drive and Park Presidio Drive, near Cross Over Drive. This 57 ft (17 m) sandstone cross commemorates the first use of the Book of Common Prayer in California by Sir Francis Drake's chaplain on June 24, 1579.

South America

Religious Influence

The *Book of Common Prayer* has had a great influence on a number of other denominations. While theologically different, the language and flow of the service of many other churches owes a great debt to the prayer book. In particular, many Christian prayer books have drawn on the Collects for the Sundays of the Churches Year—mostly translated by Cranmer from a wide range of Christian traditions, but including a number of original compositions—which are widely recognized as masterpieces of compressed liturgical construction.

John Wesley, an Anglican priest whose revivalist preaching led to the creation of Methodism wrote, "I believe there is no Liturgy in the world, either in ancient or modern language, which breathes more of a solid, scriptural, rational piety than the Common Prayer of the Church of England." Many Methodist churches in England and the United States continued to use a slightly revised version of the book for communion services well into the 20th century. In the United Methodist Church, the liturgy for Eucharistic celebrations is almost identical to what is found in the Book of Common Prayer, as are some of the other liturgies and services.

In the 1960s, when Roman Catholicism adopted a vernacular revised mass, many translations of the English prayers followed the form of Cranmer's translation.

Literary Influence

Together with the Authorized version and the works of Shakespeare, the Book of Common Prayer has been one of the three fundamental underpinnings of modern English. As it has been in regular use for centuries, many phrases from its services have passed into the English language, either as deliberate quotations or as unconscious borrowings. They are used in non-liturgical ways. For example, many authors have used quotes from the prayer book as titles for their books.

Some examples of well-known phrases from the Book of Common Prayer are:

1) "Speak now or forever hold your peace" from the marriage liturgy.
2) "Till death us do part", from the marriage liturgy.
3) "Earth to earth, ashes to ashes, dust to dust" from the funeral service.
4) "From all the deceits of the world, the flesh, and the devil" from the litany.
5) "Read, mark, learn, and inwardly digest" from the collect for the second Sunday of Advent.

The phrase "till death us do part" has been changed to "till death do us part" in some more recent prayer books, such as the 1962 Canadian Book of Common Prayer.

References and allusions to Prayer Book services in the works of Shakespeare were tracked down and identified by Richmond Noble. Derision of the Prayer Book or its contents "in any interludes, plays, songs, rhymes, or by other open words" was a criminal offence under the 1559 Act of Uniformity, and consequently Shakespeare avoids too direct reference; but Noble particularly identifies the reading of the Psalter according to the Great Bible version specified in the Prayer Book, as the biblical book generating the largest number of Biblical references in Shakespeare's plays. Noble found a total of 157 allusions to the Psalms in the plays of the First Folio, relating to 62 separate Psalms—all, save one, of which he linked to the version in the Psalter, rather than those in the

Geneva Bible or Bishops' Bible. In addition, there are a small number of direct allusions to liturgical texts in the Prayer Book; e.g. Henry VIII 3:2 where Wolsey states "Vain Pomp and Glory of this World, I hate ye!", a clear reference to the rite of Public Baptism; where the Godparents are asked "Doest thou forsake the vaine pompe and glory of the worlde..?"

More recently, P.D. James used phrases from the *Book of Common Prayer* and made them into bestselling titles—*Devices and Desires* and *The Children of Men*, while Alfonso Cuarón's 2006 film *Children of Men* placed the phrase onto cinema marquees worldwide.

Copyright Status

In most of the world the Book of Common Prayer can be freely reproduced as it is long out of copyright. This is not the case in the United Kingdom itself.

In the United Kingdom, the British Crown holds the rights to the Book of Common Prayer. The rights fall outside the scope of copyright as defined in statute law. Instead, they fall under the purview of the royal prerogative and as such, they are perpetual in subsistence. Publishers are licensed to reproduce the Book of Common Prayer under letters patent. In England, Wales and Northern Ireland the letters patent are held by the Queen's Printer, and in Scotland by the Scottish Bible Board. The office of Queen's Printer has been associated with the right to reproduce the Bible for many years, with the earliest known reference coming in 1577. In England, Wales and Northern Ireland the Queen's Printer is Cambridge University Press. CUP inherited the right of being Queen's Printer when they took over the firm of Eyre & Spottiswoode in the late 20th century. Eyre & Spottiswoode had been

Queen's Printer since 1901. Other letters patent of similar antiquity grant Cambridge University Press and Oxford University Press the right to produce the Book of Common Prayer independently of the Queen's Printer.

The terms of the letters patent prohibit those other than the holders, or those authorized by the holders from printing, publishing or importing the Book of Common Prayer into the United Kingdom. The protection that the Book of Common Prayer, and the Authorized version, enjoy is the last remnant of the time when the Crown held a monopoly over all printing and publishing in the United Kingdom.

This protection should not be confused with Crown copyright, or copyright in works of the United Kingdom's government; that is part of modern UK copyright law. Like other copyrights, Crown copyright is time-limited and potentially enforceable worldwide. The non-copyright Royal Prerogative is perpetual, but applies only to the UK; though many other Royal Prerogatives apply to the other Commonwealth realms, this one does not.

It is common misconception that the Controller of Her Majesty's Stationery Office holds letters patent for being Queen's Printer. The Controller of HMSO holds a separate set of letters patent, which cover the office Queen's Printer of Acts of Parliament. The Scotland Act 1998 defines the position of Queen's Printer for Scotland as being held by the Queen's Printer of Acts of Parliament. The Controller of HMSO holds the position of Government Printer for Northern Ireland.

The Episcopal Church's book is always released into the public domain. Trial use and supplemental liturgies are however copyrighted by Church Publishing, the official publishing arm of the church.

14

Catechism

A catechism is a summary or exposition of doctrine, traditionally used in Christian religious teaching from New Testament times to the present. Catechisms are doctrinal manuals often in the form of questions followed by answers to be memorized, a format that has been used in non-religious or secular contexts as well.

As defined in the Catechism of the Catholic Church, paragraph 5:

> *Catechesis* is an education in the faith of children, young people and adults which includes especially the teaching of Christian doctrine imparted, generally speaking, in an organic and systematic way, with a view to initiating the hearers into the fullness of Christian life.

A *catechist* is one who engages in such religious instruction. Typically, it is a lay minister trained in the art of catechesis. It might also be a pastor or priest, religious teacher, or other individuals in church roles (including a deacon, religious brother or sister, or nun). The primary catechists for children are their parents. A *catechumen* is one who receives catechetical instruction.

Traditional Format

Catechisms have, historically, typically followed a dialogue or question-and-answer format. This format calls upon two parties to participate, a master and a student (traditionally termed a "scholar"), a parent and a child. A modern revision of the famous Westminster Shorter Catechism is an example:

Q. What is the chief end of man?

A. To glorify God and enjoy Him forever!

Q. What rule hath God given to direct us how we may glorify and enjoy him?

A. The word of God as heard by all people directly.

Catholic Catechisms

The *Catechism of the Catholic Church* is the catechism that is in most widespread use among Catholics today. It is the official Catechism of the Church.

For Catholics, all the canonical books of the Bible (including the Deuterocanonical books), the Tradition of the Church and the interpretation of these by the Magisterium (which may be outlined in a catechism, a compendium or a declaration) constitute the complete and best resource for fully attaining to God's revelation to mankind. Catholics believe that Sacred Scripture and Sacred Tradition preserved and interpreted by the Magisterium are both necessary for attaining to the fullest understanding of all of God's revelation.

The term *catechist* is most frequently used in Catholicism, often to describe a *lay catechist* or layperson with catechetical training who engages in such teaching and evangelization. This can be in both parish church and mission contexts.

Roman Catechism

The *Roman Catechism* (also called, the Catechism of the Council of Trent) was first published in 1566 under the authority of the Council of Trent. It was not intended for common use by the laity, but as a general use reference book for priests and bishops.

Catechism of Saint Pius X

The *Catechism of Saint Pius X* is a short catechism with questions and answers regarding the essentials of Catholic faith and doctrine. It was issued by Pope Pius X at the beginning of the twentieth century in Italian. This Pope's intention is that all Catholic faithful could understand easily their faith.

Baltimore Catechism

Various editions of the *Baltimore Catechism* were the de facto standard Catholic school text in America from 1885 to the late 1960s. It was often taught by rote. The most common edition has a series of questions with their answers, which are followed by explanations in more depth. These are often accompanied by Biblical quotes. There is a test at the end of every chapter.

Catechism of Christian Doctrine (or "Penny Catechism")

A question and answer format Catechism that was the standard catechetical text in Great Britain in the twentieth century. Popularly called *Penny Catechism* as the original version only cost one penny. Various editions of the *Penny Catechism* were issued through the century and changes were made to the text.

Dutch Catechism

The hotly debated Dutch Catechism of 1966 was the

first post-Vatican II comprehensive Catholic catechism, and reflects the teachings of the Dutch bishops. It was commissioned and authorized by the Catholic hierarchy of the Netherlands, "to make the message of Jesus Christ sound as new as it is" The Catechism, which sold record number of copies throughout the world, contains controversial views, which were reviewed by a group of Cardinals. They pointed to several errors but decided to "nonetheless leave by far the greatest part of the New Catechism untouched. So too, they support the praiseworthy intention of the authors".

Catechism of the Catholic Church

The current *Catechism of the Catholic Church* is the first complete systematic synthesis of faith issued since the Council of Trent in 1566. It contains articles on the classical topics of the official teaching of the Catholic Church on all matters of faith and morals. Since the official language of the Catholic Church is Latin, official teaching documents distributed in Latin are unlikely to change in perceived meaning over time. The Latin language version of the Catechism, published September 8, 1992, is the *editio typica*—the normative and definitive text. The principal source materials for this work are the Sacred Scriptures, the Church Fathers, the liturgy, and the Magisterium. This Catechism is intended to serve "as a point of reference for the catechisms or compendia that are composed in the various countries." – Extraordinary Synod of Bishops 1985, Final Report II B a, 4.

Fidei depositum is an Apostolic Constitution which states that the Catechism of the Catholic Church is for the laity in its address to all the people of God.

Compendium of the Catechism of the Catholic Church

It originated with a request of Pope John Paul II in February 2003 and was issued by his successor Pope Benedict XVI June 28, 2005. The English version was printed at Libreria Editrice Vaticana in 2006. Unlike the larger catechism, the Compendium is similar in format to the Baltimore Catechism with 598 questions and answers, providing an easier format with only the "essential" contents of the Catechism of the Catholic Church as the title suggests.

United States Catholic Catechism for Adults

The 1992 Vatican catechism had several aims, among them to be an "authentic reference text for teaching Catholic doctrine and particularly for preparing local catechisms". The American bishops responded with the 2006 United States Catholic Catechism for Adults – similar in format to a college text book, targeting adults, contain seven elements that bring more depth to the material than the 'Compendium', providing more flexibility for diverse groups of people to study its contents. Each section or chapter contains the following: Story or lesson of faith, foundation and application, sidebars, relationship to culture, discussion questions, doctrinal statements, and meditation and prayer. The lessons of faith stories are about individuals from the United States and allow the U.S. reader to better relate to these individuals. This version of the Catechism is available on Audio CD-ROM as well.

Enchiridion Symbolorum, Definitionum et Declarationum de rebus Fidei et Morum

The Enchiridion symbolorum, definitionum et

declarationum de rebus fidei et morum also known as Enchiridion or Denzinger, is a compendium of all basic texts of Catholic dogma and morality since the Apostles. Commissioned by Pope Pius IX, it has been in use since 1854, and has been updated periodically. It is a compendium of faith, like a Catechism. By including all relevant teachings throughout history, it is at the same, more than a Catechism. It is a search instrument for theologians, historians and anybody interested in Christian religion. The latest updates of the Enchiridion extend to the teachings of Pope John Paul II.

The Archbishop of Baltimore James Cardinal Gibbons is quoted in earlier versions of the Enchiridion, that every theologian should have always two books at hand, the Holy Bible and this *Enchiridion.*

Reformation Catechisms

The catechism's question-and-answer format, with a view toward the instruction of children, was a form adopted by the various Protestant confessions almost from the beginning of the Reformation.Among the first projects of the Reformation, was the production of catechisms self-consciously modelled after the older traditions of Cyril and Augustine. These catechisms showed special admiration for Chrysostom's view of the family as a "little church", and placed strong responsibility on every father to teach his children, in order to prevent them from coming to Baptism or the Lord's Table ignorant of the doctrine under which they are expected to live as Christians.

Lutheran

Luther's Large Catechism typifies the emphasis which

the Churches of the Augsburg Confession placed on the importance of knowledge and understanding of the articles of the Christian faith. Primarily intended as instruction to teachers, especially to parents, the Catechism consists of a series of exhortations on the importance of each topic of the Catechism. It is meant for those who have the capacity to understand, and is not meant to be memorized but to be repeatedly reviewed so that the Small Catechism could be taught with understanding. For example, the author stipulates in the preface:

Therefore it is the duty of every father of a family to question and examine his children and servants at least once a week and to ascertain what they know of it, or are learning and, if they do not know it, to keep them faithfully at it. The câtechism, Luther wrote, should consist of instruction in the rule of conduct, which always accuses us because we fail to keep it (Ten Commandments), the rule of faith (Apostles' Creed), the rule of prayer (Lord's Prayer), and the sacraments (Baptism, Confession, and Communion).

However, it is not enough for them to comprehend and recite these parts according to the words only, but the young people should also be made to attend the preaching, especially during the time which is devoted to the Catechism, that they may hear it explained and may learn to understand what every part contains, so as to be able to recite it as they have heard it, and, when asked, may give a correct answer, so that the preaching may not be without profit and fruit.

Luther's Small Catechism, in contrast, is written to accommodate the understanding of a small child or an uneducated person. It begins:

The First Commandment

You shall have no other gods.

Q. What does this mean?

A. We should fear, love, and trust God above all things.

Reformed

Calvin's 1545 preface to the Genevan catechism begins with an acknowledgement that the several traditions and cultures which were joined in the Reformed movement, would produce their own form of instruction in each place. While no effort should be expended on preventing this, Calvin argues, he adds:

> We are all directed to one Christ, in whose truth being united together, we may grow up into one body and one spirit, and with the same mouth also proclaim whatever belongs to the sum of faith. Catechists not intent on this end, besides fatally injuring the Church, by sowing the materials of dissension in religion, also introduce an impious profanation of baptism. For where can any longer be the utility of baptism unless this remain as its foundation — that we all agree in one faith?
>
> Wherefore, those who publish Catechisms ought to be the more carefully on their guard, by producing anything rashly, they may not for the present only, but in regard to posterity also, do grievous harm to piety, and inflict a deadly wound on the Church.

The scandal of diverse instruction, is that it produces diverse baptisms and diverse communions, and diverse faith. However, forms may vary without introducing substantial differences, according to the Reformed view of doctrine.

Genevan Catechism

John Calvin produced a catechism while at Geneva, which underwent two major revisions. Calvin's aim in writing the Catechism of 1545, was to set a basic pattern of doctrine, meant to be imitated by other catechists, which would not affirm local distinctions or dwell on controversial issues, but would serve as a pattern for what was expected to be taught by Christian fathers and other teachers of children in the Church. The catechism is organized on the topics of Faith, Law, Prayer and Sacraments.

1. Master: What is the chief end of human life?

   Scholar: To know God by whom men were created.

2. Master: What reason have you for saying so?

   Scholar: Because he created us and placed us in this world to be glorified in us. And it is indeed right that our life, of which himself is the beginning, should be devoted to his glory.

3. Master: What is the highest good of man?

   Scholar: The very same thing.

Heidelberg Catechism

After Protestantism entered into the Palatinate, in 1546 the controversy between Lutherans and Calvinists broke out, and especially while the region was under the elector Otto Heinrich (1556–59), this conflict in Saxony, particularly in Heidelberg, became increasingly bitter and turned violent.

When Frederick III, Elector Palatine, came into power in 1559, he put his authority behind the Calvinistic view on the Lord's Supper, which denied the local presence of the body of Jesus Christ in the elements of the sacrament. He turned Sapienz College into a school of divinity, and in 1562 he placed over it a pupil and friend of Luther's colleague, Philipp Melanchthon, named Zacharias Ursinus. In an attempt to resolve the religious disputes in his domain, Frederick called upon Ursinus and his colleague Caspar Olevianus (preacher to Frederick's court) to produce a Catechism. The two collaborators referred to existing catechetical literature, and especially relied on the catechisms of Calvin and of John Lasco. To prepare the Catechism, they adopted the method of sketching drafts independently, and then bringing together the work to combine their efforts. "The final preparation was the work of both theologians, with the constant co-operation of Frederick III. Ursinus has always been regarded as the principal author, as he was afterwards the chief defender and interpreter of the Catechism; still, it would appear that the nervous German style, the division into three parts (as distinguished from the five parts in the Catechism of Calvin and the previous draft of Ursinus), and the genial warmth and unction of the whole work, are chiefly due to Olevianus.".

The structure of the Heidelberg Catechism is spelled out in the second question, and the three-part structure seen there is based on the belief that the single work of salvation brings forward the three persons of the Trinity in turn, to make God fully and intimately known by his work of salvation, referring back to the Apostles' Creed as an epitome of Christian faith. Assurance of salvation is the unifying theme throughout this catechism: assurance obtained by the work of Christ, applied through the sacraments, and resulting in grateful obedience to the commandments and persistence in prayer.

Lord's Day:

1. Q. What is thy only comfort in life and death?

A. That I with body and soul, both in life and death, am not my own, but belong unto my faithful Saviour Jesus Christ; who, with his precious blood, has fully satisfied for all my sins, and delivered me from all the power of the devil; and so preserves me that without the will of my heavenly Father, not a hair can fall from my head; yea, that all things must be subservient to my salvation, and therefore, by his Holy Spirit, He also assures me of eternal life, and makes me sincerely willing and ready, henceforth, to live unto him.

Q. How many things are necessary for thee to know, that thou, enjoying this comfort, mayest live and die happily?

A. Three; the first, how great my sins and miseries are; the second, how I may be delivered from all my sins and miseries; the third, how I shall express my gratitude to God for such deliverance.

The Heidelberg Catechism is the most widely used of the Catechisms of the Reformed churches.

Westminster Catechisms

Together with the Westminster Confession of Faith, the Westminster Assembly also produced two catechisms, a Larger and a Shorter, which were intended for use in Christian families and in churches. These documents have served as the doctrinal standards, subordinate to the Bible, for Presbyterians and other Reformed churches around the world. The Shorter Catechism shows the Assembly's reliance upon the previous work of Calvin, Lasco, and the theologians of Heidelberg. It is organized in two main sections summarizing what the Scriptures principally teach: the doctrine of God, and the duty required of men. Questions and answers cover the usual elements: Faith, the Ten Commandments, the Sacraments, and Prayer.

Q. What is the chief end of man?

A. Man's chief end is to glorify God, and to enjoy him forever.

Q. What rule hath God given to direct us how we may glorify and enjoy him?

A. The Word of God, which is contained in the Scriptures of the Old and New Testaments, is the only rule to direct us how we may glorify and enjoy him.

Q. What do the scriptures principally teach?

A. The scriptures principally teach, what man is to believe concerning God, and what duty God requires of man.

Other Reformed Catechisms

Oecolampadius composed the *Basel Catechism* in 1526, Leo Juda (1534) followed by Bullinger (1555) published catechisms in Zurich. The French Reformed used Calvin's Genevan Catechism, as well as works published by Louis Cappel (1619), and Charles Drelincourt (1642).

Anglican Catechism

The Anglican Book of Common Prayer includes a brief catechism for the instruction of all persons preparing to be brought before the bishop for Confirmation. The baptized first professes his baptism, and then rehearses the principal elements of the faith into which he has been baptized: Apostles' Creed, Ten Commandments, the Lord's Prayer, and the Sacraments.

Catechist: What is your Name?

Answer : N. or M.

Catechist: Who gave you this Name?

Answer : My Godfathers and Godmothers in my Baptism; wherein I was made a member of Christ, the child of God, and an inheritor of the kingdom of heaven.

Socinian and other Sectarian Catechisms

Besides the manuals of instruction that were published by the Protestants for use in their families and churches, there were other works produced by sectarian groups intended as a compact refutation of "orthodoxy".

For example, Socinians in Poland published the *Rakow Catechism* in 1605, using the question and answer format of a catechism for the orderly presentation of their arguments against the Trinity and the doctrine of Hell, as these were understood by the Reformed churches from which they were forced to separate.

Baptist affiliations of congregations have at times adopted the Reformed catechisms, modified to reflect Baptist convictions, especially concerning the nature of the church and the ordinances of baptism and communion. The Anabaptists have also produced catechisms of their own, to explain and defend their distinctives.

Non-Christian Catechisms

Catechisms represent an obvious, practical method of passing on instruction, and as such examples can be found in many traditions. For example, Asiatic schools of esoteric learning also used a catechetical style of instruction, as this Zodiac catechism shows:

Q. "Where is the animal, O Lanoo? and where the Man?

A. Fused into one, O Master of my Life. The two are one. But both have disappeared and naught remains but the deep fire of my desire.

Judaism does not have a formal catechism. While there have been several attempts to formulate Jewish principles of faith, and some of these have achieved wide acceptance, none can be described as being in the form of a catechism. The most widely recited formulation, Yigdal, is in the form of a hymn based on Maimonides' 13 Articles of Faith.

Secular Catechisms

In the past, catechisms were written to rehearse the basic knowledge of a non-religious subject. Examples include the *Catechism of the History of Newfoundland* (c1856), the *Coal Catechism* (1898), and *A Catechism of the Steam Engine* (1856). The 17th episode of James Joyce's novel *Ulysses,* known as "Ithaca", is written in the form of a catechism. Ted Hughes' poem *Examination at the Womb Door,* from the collection *Crow,* is written in the form of a catechism.

15

Writings of Robert Burns

Robert Burns (25 January 1759 – 21 July 1796) was a Scottish poet and a lyricist. He is widely regarded as the national poet of Scotland, and is celebrated worldwide. He is the best known of the poets who have written in the Scots language, although much of his writing is also in English and a "light" Scots dialect, accessible to an audience beyond Scotland. He also wrote in standard English, and in these pieces, his political or civil commentary is often at its most blunt.

He is regarded as a pioneer of the Romantic movement and after his death became a great source of inspiration to the founders of both liberalism and socialism. A cultural icon in Scotland and among the Scottish Diaspora around the world, celebration of his life and work became almost a national charismatic cult during the 19th and 20th centuries, and his influence has long been strong on Scottish literature. In 2009 he was voted by the Scottish public as being the Greatest Scot, through a vote run by Scottish television channel STV.

As well as making original compositions, Burns also collected folk songs from across Scotland, often revising or adapting them. His poem (and song) *Auld*

Lang Syne is often sung at Hogmanay (the last day of the year), and *Scots Wha Hae* served for a long time as an unofficial national anthem of the country. Other poems and songs of Burns that remain well-known across the world today, include *A Red, Red Rose, A Man's A Man for A' That, To a Louse, To a Mouse, The Battle of Sherramuir, Tam o' Shanter* and *Ae Fond Kiss.*

Alloway

Burns was born two miles (3 km) south of Ayr, in Alloway, South Ayrshire, Scotland, the eldest of the seven children of William Burness (1721-1784) (Robert Burns spelled his surname Burness until 1786), a self-educated tenant farmer from Dunnottar, The Mearns, and Agnes Broun (1732-1820), the daughter of a tenant farmer from Kirkoswald, South Ayrshire.

He was born in a house built by his father (now the Burns Cottage Museum), where he lived until Easter 1766, when he was seven years old. William Burness sold the house and took the tenancy of the 70-acre Mount Oliphant farm, southeast of Alloway. Here Burns grew up in poverty and hardship, and the severe manual labour of the farm left its traces in a premature stoop and a weakened constitution.

He had little regular schooling and got much of his education from his father, who taught his children reading, writing, arithmetic, geography, and history and also wrote for them *A Manual Of Christian Belief.* He was also taught by John Murdoch (1747-1824), who opened an 'adventure school' in Alloway in 1763 and taught Latin, French, and mathematics to both Robert and his brother Gilbert (1760-1827) from 1765 to 1768 until Murdoch left the parish. After a few years of home education, Burns was sent to Dalrymple Parish

School during the summer of 1772 before returning at harvest time to full-time farm labouring until 1773, when he was sent to lodge with Murdoch for three weeks to study grammar, French, and Latin.

By the age of 15, Burns was the principal labourer at Mount Oliphant. During the harvest of 1774, he was assisted by Nelly Kilpatrick (1759-1820), who inspired his first attempt at poetry, *O, Once I Lov'd A Bonnie Lass*. In the summer of 1775, he was sent to finish his education with a tutor at Kirkoswald, where he met Peggy Thomson (b.1762), to whom he wrote two songs, *Now Westlin' Winds* and *I Dream'd I Lay.*

Tarbolton

At Whitsun, 1777, William Burness removed his large family from the unfavourable conditions of Mount Oliphant to the 130-acre farm at Lochlea, near Tarbolton, where they stayed until William Burness' death in 1784. Subsequently, the family became integrated into the community of Tarbolton. To his father's disapproval, Robert joined a country dancing school in 1779 and, with Gilbert, formed the Tarbolton Bachelors' Club the following year. His earliest existing letters date from this time, when he began making romantic overtures to Alison Begbie. In spite of four songs written for her and a suggestion that he was willing to marry her, she rejected him.

In December 1781, Burns moved temporarily to Irvine to learn to become a flax-dresser, but during the New Year celebrations of 1781/1782 the flax shop caught fire and was sufficiently damaged to eventually send him home to Lochlea farm.

He continued to write poems and songs and began a Commonplace Book in 1783, while his father fought a legal dispute with his landlord. The case went to the Court of Session, and Burness was upheld in January 1784, a fortnight before he died.

Mauchline

Robert and Gilbert made an ineffectual struggle to keep on the farm, but after its failure they moved to the farm at Mossgiel, near Mauchline in March, which they maintained with an uphill fight for the next four years. During the summer of 1784, he came to know a group of girls known collectively as The Belles of Mauchline, one of whom was Jean Armour, the daughter of a stonemason from Mauchline.

Robert Burns was initiated into Lodge St David Tarbolton on 4 July 1781, when he was 22. He was passed and raised on 1 October 1781. Later his lodge became dormant and Burns joined Lodge St James Tarbolton Kilwinning number 135. The location of the Temple where he was made a Freemason is unknown, but on 30 June 1784 the meeting place of the lodge became the "Manson Inn" in Tarbolton, and one month later, on 27 July 1784, Burns became *Depute Master*, which he held until 1788, often honoured with supreme command.

Although regularly meeting in Tarbolton, the "Burns Lodge" also removed itself to hold meetings in Mauchline. During 1784 he was heavily involved in Lodge business, attending all nine meetings, passing and raising brethren and generally running the Lodge. Similarly, in 1785 he was equally involved as Depute Master, where he again attended all nine lodge meetings amongst other duties of the Lodge. During 1785 he initiated and passed his brother Gilbert being raised on 1 March 1788. He must have been a very popular and well-respected Depute Master, as the minutes show that there were more lodge meetings well attended during the Burns period than at any other time.

At a meeting of Lodge St. Andrew in Edinburgh in 1787, in the presence of the Grand Master and Grand Lodge of Scotland, Burns was toasted by the Grand Master, Francis Chateris. When he was received into Edinburgh Lodges, his occupation was recorded as a "poet". In early 1787, he was feted by the Edinburgh Masonic fraternity and named the Poet Laureate of the lodge - a title which has since been accepted by Freemasonry in general. The Edinburgh period of Burns's life was fateful, as further editions of the Kilmarnock Edition were sponsored by the Edinburgh Freemasons, ensuring that his name spread around Scotland and subsequently to England and abroad.

During his tour of the South of Scotland, as he was collecting material for The Scots Musical Museum, he visited lodges throughout Ayrshire and became an honorary member of a number of them. On 18 May 1787, he arrived at Eyemouth, Berwickshire, where a meeting was convened of Royal Arch and Burns became a Royal Arch Mason.On his journey home to Ayrshire, he passed through Dumfries.

On 25 July 1787, after being re-elected Depute Master, he presided at a meeting where several well-known Masons were given honorary membership. During his Highland tour, he visited many other lodges. During the period from his election as Depute Master in 1784, Lodge St James had been convened 70 times. Burns was present 33 times and was 25 times the presiding officer. His last meeting at his mother lodge, St James Kilwinning, was on 11 November 1788.

He joined Lodge Dumfries St Andrew Number 179 on 27 December 1788. Out of the six Lodges in Dumfries, he joined the one which was the weakest. The records of this lodge are scant, and we hear no more of him until 30 November 1792, when Burns was elected Senior Warden. From this date until his final meeting in the Lodge on 14 April 1796, it appears that the Lodge met only five times. There are no records of Burns visiting any other Lodges.

On 28 August 1787, Burns visited Stirling and passed through Bridge of Allan on his way to the Roman fort at Braco. In 1793, he wrote his poem "By Allan Stream".

Love Affairs

His casual love affairs did not endear him to the elders of the local kirk and created for him a reputation for dissoluteness amongst his neighbours. His first illegitimate child, Elizabeth Paton Burns (1785-1817), was born to his mother's servant, Elizabeth Paton (1760-circa 1799), while he was embarking on a relationship with Jean Armour who bore him twins in 1786. Although Armour's father initially forbade their marriage, they were eventually married in 1788. Armour bore him nine children in total, but only three survived infancy.

During a rift in his relationship with Jean Armour in 1786, and as his prospects in farming declined, he began an affair with Mary Campbell (1763-1786), to whom he dedicated the poems *The Highland Lassie O, Highland Mary* and *To Mary in Heaven*. Their relationship has been the subject of much conjecture, and it has been suggested that they may have married. They planned to emigrate to Jamaica, where it has been widely claimed Burns would have worked as a bookkeeper on a slave plantation. This is a subject of debate because it is inconsistent with Burns' egalitarian views as typified by his writing of The Slave's Lament. He was dissuaded by an encouraging letter from Thomas Blacklock, and before the plans could be acted upon, Mary Campbell died suddenly of a fever in Greenock, Scotland. That summer, he published the first of his collections of verse, *Poems, Chiefly in the Scottish dialect,* which created a sensation and has been recognised as a significant literary event.

Kilmarnock Edition

At the suggestion of his brother, Robert Burns published his poems in the volume *Poems, Chiefly in the Scottish dialect,* known as the Kilmarnock volume. First proposals were published in April 1786 before the poems were finally published in Kilmarnock in July 1786 and sold for 3 shillings. Brought out by John Wilson, a local printer in Kilmarnock, it contained much of his best writing, including *The Twa Dogs, Address to the Deil, Hallowe'en, The Cotter's Saturday Night, To a Mouse,* and *To a Mountain Daisy,* many of which had been written at Mossgiel farm. The success of the work was immediate, and soon he was known across the country.

Edinburgh

Burns was invited to Edinburgh on 14 December 1786 to oversee the preparation of a revised edition, the first Edinburgh edition, by William Creech, which was finally published on 17 April 1787 (within a week of this event, Burns sold his copyright to Creech for 100 guineas). In Edinburgh, he was received as an equal by the city's brilliant men of letters and was a guest at aristocratic gatherings, where he bore himself with unaffected dignity. Here he encountered, and made a lasting impression on, the 16-year-old Walter Scott, who described him later with great admiration:

> "His person was strong and robust; his manners rustic, not clownish, a sort of dignified plainness and simplicity which received part of its effect perhaps from knowledge of his extraordinary talents. His features are presented in Mr Nasmyth's picture but to me it conveys the idea that they are diminished, as if seen in perspective. I think his countenance was more massive than it looks in any of the portraits... there was a strong expression of shrewdness in all his lineaments; the eye alone, I think, indicated the poetical character and temperament. It was large, and of a dark cast, and literally glowed when he spoke with feeling or interest. I never saw such another eye in a human head, though I have seen the most distinguished men of my time."
>
> — Walter Scott

His stay in the city resulted in some lifelong friendships, among which were those with Lord Glencairn, and Frances Anna Dunlop (1730-1815), who became his occasional sponsor and with whom he corresponded for many years until a rift developed. He embarked on a relationship with the separated Agnes 'Nancy' McLehose (1758-1841), with whom he exchanged passionate letters under pseudonyms. When it became clear that Nancy would not be easily seduced into a physical relationship, Burns moved on to Jenny Clow (1766-1792), Nancy's domestic servant, who bore him a son, Robert Burns Clow in 1788. His relationship with Nancy concluded in 1791 with a final meeting in Edinburgh before she sailed to Jamaica for what transpired to be a short-lived reconciliation with her estranged husband. Before she left, he sent her the manuscript of *Ae Fond Kiss* as a farewell to her.

In Edinburgh, in early 1787, he met James Johnson, a struggling music engraver and music seller with a love of old Scots songs and a determination to preserve them. Burns shared this interest and became an enthusiastic contributor to *The Scots Musical Museum*. The first volume of this was published in 1787 and included three songs by Burns. He contributed 40 songs to volume 2, and would end up responsible for about a third of the 600 songs in the whole collection as well as making a considerable editorial contribution. The final volume was published in 1803.

Ellisland Farm

On his return to Ayrshire on 18 February 1788, he resumed his relationship with Jean Armour and took a lease on the farm of Ellisland near Dumfries on 18 March (settling there on 11 June) but trained as a Gauger, or in English, an exciseman; should farming continue to prove unsuccessful. He was appointed duties in Customs and Excise in 1789 and eventually gave up the farm in 1791. Meanwhile, he was writing at his best, and in November 1790 had produced *Tam O' Shanter*. About this time he was offered and declined an appointment in London on the staff of the *Star* newspaper, and refused to become a candidate for a newly-created Chair of Agriculture in the University of Edinburgh, although influential friends offered to support his claims.

Lyricist

After giving up his farm he removed to Dumfries itself. Burns described the Globe Inn (still running today) on the High Street as his "favourite howff".

It was at this time that, being requested to write lyrics for *The Melodies of Scotland,* he responded by contributing over 100 songs. He made major contributions to George Thomson's *A Select Collection of Original Scottish Airs for the Voice* as well as to James Johnson's *The Scots Musical Museum.* Arguably his claim to immortality chiefly rests on these volumes which placed him in the front rank of lyric poets. Burns described how he had to master singing the tune before he composed the words:

> "My way is: I consider the poetic sentiment, correspondent to my idea of the musical expression, then chuse my theme, begin one stanza, when that is composed - which is generally the most difficult part of the business - I walk out, sit down now and then, look out for objects in nature around me that are in unison or harmony with the cogitations of my fancy and workings of my bosom, humming every now and then the air with the verses I have framed. when I feel my Muse beginning tc jade, I retire to the solitary fireside of my study, and there commit my effusions to paper, swinging, at intervals, on the hind-legs of my elbow chair, by way of calling forth my own critical strictures, as my, pen goes."
>
> —Robert Burns

Burns also worked to collect and preserve Scottish folk songs, sometimes revising, expanding, and adapting them. One of the better known of these collections is *The Merry Muses of Caledonia* (the title is not Burns'), a collection of bawdy lyrics that were popular in the music halls of Scotland as late as the 20th century. Many of Burns' most famous poems are songs with the music based upon older traditional songs. For example, *Auld Lang Syne* is set to the traditional tune *Can Ye Labour Lea, A Red, Red Rose* is set to the tune of *Major Graham* and *The Battle of Sherramuir* is set to the *Cameronian Rant.*

Failing Health and Death

As his health began to give way, Burns began to age prematurely and fell into fits of despondency. The habits of intemperance (alleged mainly by temperance activist James Currie) are said to have aggravated his long-standing possible rheumatic heart condition. His death was probably caused by bacterial endocarditis exacerbated by a streptococcal infection reaching his blood following a dental extraction in winter 1795, and it was no doubt further affected by the three months of famine culminating in the Dumfries Food Riots of March 1796.

On the morning of 21 July 1796, Robert Burns died in Dumfries at the age of 37. The funeral took place on Monday 25 July 1796, also the day that his son Maxwell was born. He was at first buried in the far corner of St. Michael's Churchyard in Dumfries; however, his body was eventually moved in September 1815 to its final resting place, in the same cemetery, the Burns Mausoleum. Jean Armour was laid to rest with him in 1834.

His widow, Jean, had taken steps to secure his movable estate, partly by liquidating two promissory notes amounting to fifteen pounds sterling (about 1,100 pounds at 2009 prices). The family went to the Court of Session in 1798 with a scheme to support his surviving children by publishing a four volume edition of his complete works and a biography written by Dr James Currie. Subscriptions were raised to meet the initial cost of publication, which was in the hands of Thomas Cadell and William Davies in London and William Creech, bookseller in Edinburgh Hogg records that fund-raising for Burns' family was embarrassingly slow, and it took several years to accumulate significant funds through the efforts of John Syme and Alexander Cunningham.

Burns was posthumously given the freedom of the town. Hogg records that Burns was given the freedom of the Burgh of Dumfries on 4 June 1787, years before his death, and was also made an Honorary Burgess of Dumfries.

Literary Style

Burns' poetry drew upon a substantial familiarity and knowledge of Classical, Biblical, and English literature, as well as the Scottish Makar tradition. Burns was skilled in writing not only in the Scots language but also in the Scottish English dialect of the English language. Some of his works, such as *Love and Liberty* are written in both Scots and English for various effects.

His themes included republicanism (he lived during the French Revolutionary period) and Radicalism which he expressed covertly in *Scots Wha Hae*, Scottish patriotism, anticlericalism, class inequalities, gender roles, commentary on the Scottish Kirk of his time, Scottish cultural identity, poverty, sexuality, and the beneficial aspects of popular socialising (carousing, Scotch whisky, folk songs, and so forth).

The strong emotional highs and lows associated with many of Burns' poems have led some, such as Burns biographer Robert Crawford, to suggest that he suffered from manic depression—a hypothesis that has been supported by analysis of various samples of his handwriting. Burns himself referred to suffering from episodes of what he called "blue devilism". However, the National Trust for Scotland has downplayed the suggestion on the grounds that the evidence is not sufficient to support the claim.

Influence

Scotland and England

He is generally classified as a proto-Romantic poet, and he influenced William Wordsworth, Samuel Taylor Coleridge, and Percy Bysshe Shelley greatly. His direct literary influences in the use of Scots in poetry were Allan Ramsay (1686-1758) and Robert Fergusson. The Edinburgh literati worked to sentimentalise Burns during his life and after his death, dismissing his education by calling him a *"heaven-taught ploughman"*. Burns would influence later Scottish writers, especially Hugh MacDiarmid, who fought to dismantle the sentimental cult that had dominated Scottish literature in MacDiarmid's opinion.

America

An example of the Burns literary influence in America is the novelist John Steinbeck, who took the title of his 1937 novel *Of Mice and Men* from a line contained in the second-to-last stanza of "To a Mouse": "The best laid schemes o' mice an' men / Gang aft agley". When asked for the source of his greatest creative inspiration, singer songwriter Bob Dylan selected Burns's 1794 song "A Red, Red Rose", as the lyric that had the biggest effect on his life.

Russia

Burns became the "people's poet" of Russia. In Imperial times, the Russian aristocracy were so out of touch with the peasantry that Burns, translated into

Russian, became a symbol for the ordinary Russian people. In Soviet Russia, Burns was elevated as the archetypal poet of the people. A new translation of Burns, begun in 1924 by Samuil Marshak, proved enormously popular, selling over 600,000 copies. Russia was the first country in the world to honour the man with a commemorative stamp in 1956. The poetry of Burns is taught in Russian schools alongside their own national poets. Burns was a great admirer of the egalitarian ethos behind the French Revolution, and that was an additional reason for the Communist regime to endorse him as a "progressive" artist. However, he has remained popular in Russia after the fall of the Soviet Union as well.

Honours

Landmarks and Organisations

Burns' birthplace in Alloway is now a public museum, as is his house in Dumfries. Significant 19th-century monuments to him stand in Alloway, Edinburgh and Dumfries. An early 20th century replica of his birthplace cottage belonging to the Burns Club Atlanta stands in Atlanta, Georgia. These are part of a large list of Robert Burns memorials and statues around the world.

Organisations include the Robert Burns Fellowship of the University of Otago in New Zealand, and the Burns Club Atlanta in the United States. Towns named after Robert Burns include Burns, New York, and Burns, Oregon.

In the suburb of Summerhill, in Dumfries, the majority of the streets have names with Burns connotations. A BR Standard Class 7 steam locomotive was named after him, along with a later British Rail Class 87 electric locomotive, No.87035.

On 24 September 1996, class 156 diesel unit 156433 was named "The Kilmarnock Edition" by Jimmy Knapp, General Secretary of the RMT union, at Girvan Station to launch the new 'Burns Line' services between Girvan, Ayr and Kilmarnock, supported by Strathclyde Passenger Transport (SPT). In the vestibule behind the cycle racks there was a poster explaining the significance of the naming.

Several streets surrounding the Frederick Law Olmsted, Jr.'s Back Bay Fens in Boston, Massachusetts were designed with Burns connotations. A life size statue was dedicated in Burn's honor within the Back Bay Fens of the West Fenway neighborhood in 1912. It stood until 1972 when it was relocated downtown, sparking protests from the neighborhood, literary fans, and preservationists of Olmsted's vision for the Back Bay Fens.

Stamps and Currency

Russia was the first country in the world to honour Burns with a commemorative stamp, in 1956. The Royal Mail has issued postage stamps commemorating Burns three times. In 1966, two stamps were issued, priced fourpence and 1 shilling and threepence, both carrying Burns' portrait. In 1996, an issue commemorating the bicentenary of his death comprised four stamps, priced 19 p, 25 p, 41 p and 60 p, and included quotes from Burns' poems. On 22 January 2009, two stamps were issued by the Royal Mail to commemorate the 250th anniversary of Burns' birth.

Burns is pictured on the £5 banknote (since 1971) of the Clydesdale Bank, one of the Scottish banks with the right to issue banknotes. On the reverse of the note there is a vignette of a field mouse and a wild rose which refers to Burns' poem "to a mouse". In September 2007, the Bank of Scotland redesigned their banknotes, and Robert Burns' statue is now portrayed on the reverse side of new £5.

In 2009, the Royal Mint issued a commemorative two pound coin featuring a quote from "Auld Lang Syne".

Musical Tributes

In 1996, a musical called *Red Red Rose* won third place at a competition for new musicals in Denmark. The musical was about Burns' life, and he was played by John Barrowman. On 25 January 2008, a musical play about the love affair between Robert Burns and Nancy McLehose entitled "Clarinda", premiered in Edinburgh before touring Scotland.

Burns Suppers

Burns Night, effectively a second national day, is celebrated on 25 January with Burns suppers around the world, and is still more widely observed than the official national day, Saint Andrew's Day. The format of Burns suppers has not changed since Robert's death in 1796. The basic format starts with a general welcome and announcements, followed with the Selkirk Grace. After the grace, comes the piping and cutting of the haggis, where Burns' famous *Address To a Haggis* is read and the haggis is cut open. The event usually allows for people to start eating just after the haggis is presented. This is when the reading called the "immortal memory", an overview of Burns' life and work, is given; the event usually concludes with the singing of *Auld Lang Syne.*

Greatest Scot

In 2009, STV ran a televison series and public vote to decide who should be named as being the Greatest Scot. On St Andrew's day, STV revealed the results of the public vote, and Robert Burns was voted as being officially the Greatest Scot of all time, narrowly beating William Wallace, Scottish Patriot and Independence campaigner, for the title.

Bibliography

Arnott, James Fullarton. *English theatrical literature, 1559-1900: a bibliography; incorporating Robert W. Lawe's 'A bibliogra-phical account of English theatrical literature' published in 1888.* London: Society for Theatre Research, 1970.

Barzun, Jacques. *The modern researcher.* 5th ed. Boston: Houghton Mifflin Co., 1992.

Bennett, H. S. *Chaucer and the fifteenth century.* Oxford: Clarendon Press, 1947.

Bennett, J. A. W. *Middle English literature.* Oxford: Clarendon Press; New York: Oxford University Press, 1986.

Bosworth, Joseph. *An Anglo-Saxon dictionary: based on the manuscript collections of the late Joseph Bosworth.* Oxford: Oxford University Press, [1954].

Brogan, T. V. F. *English versification, 1570-1980: a reference guide with a global appendix.* Baltimore: John Hopkins University Press, 1981.

Brown, Carleton Fairchild. *The index of Middle English verse.* New York: Columbia University, 1943. Reference Z2012 B76 (LC)

Cavanagh, John. *British theatre: a bibliography, 1901 to 1985.* Mottisfont, Romsey, Hampshire: Motley, 1989.

Chapman, Dorothy Hilton. *Index to Black poetry.* Boston, MA: G. K. Hall, 1974.

Contemporary dramatists. London: St. James Press; New York: St. Martin's Press, 1973-

Crosby, Everett Uberto. *Medieval studies: a bibliographical guide.* New York: Garland Pub., 1983.

Davis, Gwenn. *Drama by women to 1900: a bibliography of American and British writers.* London: Mansell, 1992.

Davis, Gwenn. *Poetry by women to 1900: a bibliography of American and British writers.* London; New York: Mansell, 1991.

Dyson, A. E. *The English novel: select bibliographical guides.* London: Oxford University Press, 1974.

Harbage, Alfred. *Annals of English drama, 975-1700: an analytical record of all plays, extant or lost, chronologically arranged and indexed by authors, titles, dramatic companies &c.* 3rd ed. London; New York: Routledge, 1989.

International guide to medieval studies. Darien, CT: American Bibliographic Service 1961-

Ker, N. R. *Catalogue of manuscripts containing Anglo-Saxon.* Oxford: Clarendon Press; New York: Oxford University Press, 1990.

Kuntz, Joseph Marshall. *Poetry explication: a checklist of interpretation since 1925 of British and American poems past and present.* 3rd ed. Boston, MA: G. K. Hall, 1980.

Lancashire, Ian. *Dramatic texts and records of Britain: a chronological topography to 1558.* Toronto; Buffalo: University of Toronto Press, 1984.

Lewis, Robert E. *Index of printed Middle English prose.* New York: Garland, 1985.

Martinez, Nancy C. *Guide to British poetry explication.* Boston, MA:G.K. Hall, 1991-1995. 4 v.

New Princeton encyclopedia of poetry and poetics. Ed. Alex Preminger and T. V. F. Brogan. Princeton, NJ: Princeton University Press, 1993.

Wilmeth, Don B. *American and English popular entertainment: a guide to information sources.* Detroit, MI: Gale Research Co., c1980.

Index